JUMP
AT HOME
GRADE
8

NEW EDITION

ALSO BY JOHN MIGHTON

The Myth of Ability

The End of Ignorance

JUMP MATH SERIES

JUMP at Home Grade 1

JUMP at Home Grade 2

JUMP at Home Grade 3

JUMP at Home Grade 4

JUMP at Home Grade 5

JUMP at Home Grade 6

JUMP at Home Grade 7

JUMP at Home Grade 8

JUMP AT HOME GRADE 8

NEW EDITION

Worksheets for the JUMP Math Program

JOHN MIGHTON

ANANSI

This edition published in 2010 by
House of Anansi Press Inc.
110 Spadina Avenue, Suite 801
Toronto, ON, M5V 2K4
Tel. 416-363-4343
Fax 416-363-1017
www.houseofanansi.com

Distributed in Canada by
HarperCollins Canada Ltd.
1995 Markham Road
Scarborough, ON, M1B 5M8
Toll free tel. 1-800-387-0117

Distributed in the United States by
Publishers Group West
1700 Fourth Street
Berkeley, CA 94710
Toll free tel. 1-800-788-3123

House of Anansi Press is committed to protecting our natural environment. As part of our efforts, the interior of this book is printed on Ancient Forest Friendly paper that contains 100% recycled fibres (40% post-consumer waste and 60% pre-consumer waste) and is processed chlorine-free.

Some of the material in this book has previously been published by JUMP Math.

Every reasonable effort has been made to contact the holders of copyright for materials reproduced in this work. The publishers will gladly receive information that will enable them to rectify any inadvertent errors or omissions in subsequent editions.

20 19 18 17 16   4 5 6 7 8

Library and Archives Canada Cataloguing in Publication

Cataloguing data available from Library and Archives Canada

Library of Congress Control Number: 2010924081

Acknowledgements
Writers: Dr. John Mighton, Dr. Sindi Sabourin, and Dr. Anna Klebanov
Text design: Pam Lostracco
Layout: Laura Brady, Rita Camacho, Nuria Gonzalez, Pam Lostracco, and Ilyana Martinez

This book, like the JUMP program itself, is made possible by the efforts of the volunteers and staff of JUMP Math.

Canada Council for the Arts   **Conseil des Arts du Canada**

ONTARIO ARTS COUNCIL
CONSEIL DES ARTS DE L'ONTARIO
an Ontario government agency
un organisme du gouvernement de l'Ontario

We acknowledge for their financial support of our publishing program the Canada Council for the Arts, the Ontario Arts Council, and the Government of Canada through the Canada Book Fund.

Printed and bound in Canada

Contents

Unit 2: Patterns and Algebra 1

Unit 3: Number Sense 2

Unit 4: Measurement 1

Unit 5: Number Sense 3

Introduction: About JUMP Math

There is a prevalent myth in our society that people are born with mathematical talent, and others simply do not have the ability to succeed. Recent discoveries in cognitive science are challenging this myth of ability. The brain is not hard-wired, but continues to change and develop throughout life. Steady, incremental learning can result in the emergence of new abilities.

The carefully designed mathematics in the JUMP Math program provide the necessary skills and knowledge to give your child the joy of success in mathematics. Through step-by-step learning, students celebrate success with every question, thereby increasing achievement and reducing math anxiety.

John Mighton: Founder of JUMP Math

"Nine years ago I was looking for a way to give something back to my local community. It occurred to me that I should try to help kids who needed help with math. Mathematicians don't always make the best teachers because mathematics has become obvious to them; they can have trouble seeing why their students are having trouble. But because I had struggled with math myself, I wasn't inclined to blame my students if they couldn't move forward."

— John Mighton, *The End of Ignorance*

JUMP Math, a national charity dedicated to improving mathematical literacy, was founded by John Mighton, a math-ematician, bestselling author, and award-winning playwright. The organization grew out of John's work with a core group of volunteers in a "tutoring club"; their goal was to meet the needs of the most challenged students from local schools. Over the next three years John developed the early material — simple handouts for the tutors to use during their one-on-one teaching sessions with individual students. This period was one of experimentation in developing the JUMP Math method. Eventually, John began to work in local inner-city schools, by placing tutors in the classrooms. This led to the next period of innovation: using the JUMP Math method on small groups of students.

Teachers responded enthusiastically to the success they saw in their students and wanted to adapt the method for classroom use. In response, the needs of the teachers for curriculum-based resources were met by the development of workbooks. These started out as a series of three remedial books with limited accompanying teacher materials, released in fall 2003. The effectiveness of these workbooks led quickly to the development of grade-specific, curriculum-based workbooks. The grade-specific books were first released in 2004. Around that time, the power of teacher networks in creating learning communities was beginning to take shape.

Inspired by the work he has done with thousands of students over the past twenty years, John has systematically developed an approach to teaching mathematics that is based on fostering brain plasticity and emergent intelligence, and on the idea that children have more potential in mathematics than is generally believed. Linking new research in cognitive science to his extensive observations of students, John calls for a re-examination of the assumptions that underlie current methods of teaching mathematics.

JUMP Math, as a program and as an organization, developed in response to the needs of the students, teachers, schools, and communities where John and the volunteers were working. Recognizing the potential of all students to succeed in mathematics, and to succeed in school, was the motivation that John needed to dedicate more than ten years of his life developing a mathematics program that achieved his vision.

JUMP Math: An Innovative Approach

In only ten years, JUMP Math has gone from John's kitchen table to a thriving organization reaching more than 50,000 students with high-quality learning resources and training for 2,000 teachers. It continues to work with commu-nity organizations to reach struggling students through homework clubs and after-school programs. Through the gener-ous support of our sponsors, JUMP Math donates resources to classrooms and homework clubs across Canada. The organization has also inspired thousands of community volunteers and teachers to donate their time as tutors, mentors, and trainers.

JUMP Math is unique; it builds on the belief that every child can be successful at mathematics by
- Promoting positive learning environments and building confidence through praise and encouragement;
- Maintaining a balanced approach to mathematics by concurrently addressing conceptual and procedural learning;
- Achieving understanding and mastery by breaking mathematics down into small sequential steps;
- Keeping all students engaged and attentive by "raising the bar" incrementally; and,
- Guiding students strategically to explore and discover the beauty of mathematics.

JUMP Math recognizes the importance of reducing math anxiety. Research in psychology has shown that our brains are extremely fallible: our working memories are poor, we are easily overwhelmed by too much new information, and we require a good deal of practice to consolidate skills and concepts. These mental challenges are compounded when we are anxious. The JUMP approach has been shown to reduce math anxiety significantly.

JUMP Math scaffolds mathematical concepts rigorously and completely. The materials were designed by a team of mathematicians and educators who have a deep understanding of and a love for mathematics. Concepts are introduced in rigorous steps, and prerequisite skills are included in the lesson. Breaking down concepts and skills into steps is often necessary even with the more able students. Math is a subject in which a gifted student can become a struggling student almost overnight, because mathematical knowledge is cumulative.

Consistent with emerging brain research, JUMP Math provides materials and methods that minimize differences between students, allowing teachers, tutors, and parents to more effectively improve student performance in mathematics. Today, parents have access to this unique innovation in mathematics learning with the revised JUMP at Home books.

JUMP Math at Home

JUMP at Home has been developed by mathematicians and educators to complement the mathematics curriculum that your child learns at school. Each grade covers core skills and knowledge to help your child succeed in mathematics. The program focuses on building number sense, pattern recognition, and foundations for algebra.

JUMP at Home is designed to boost every student's confidence, skills, and knowledge. Struggling students will benefit from practice in small steps, while good students will be provided with new ways to understand concepts that will help them enjoy mathematics even more and to exceed their own expectations.

JUMP Math in Schools

JUMP Math also publishes full curriculum-based resources — including student workbooks, teacher guides with daily lesson plans, and blackline masters — that cover all of the Ontario and the Western Canada mathematics curriculum. For more information, please visit the JUMP Math website, www.jumpmath.org, to find out how to order.

Evidence that JUMP Math Works

JUMP Math is a leader in promoting third-party research about its work. A recent study by researchers at the Ontario Institute for Studies in Education (OISE), the University of Toronto, and Simon Fraser University found that in JUMP Math classrooms conceptual understanding improved significantly for weaker students. In Lambeth, England, researchers reported that after using JUMP Math for one year, 69 percent of students who were two years behind were assessed at grade level.

Cognitive scientists from The Hospital for Sick Children in Toronto recently conducted a randomized-controlled study of the effectiveness of the JUMP math program. Studies of such scientific rigour remain relatively rare in mathematics education research in North America. The results showed that students who received JUMP instruction outperformed students who received the methods of instruction their teachers would normally use, on well-established measures of math achievement.

Using JUMP at Home

Helping your child discover the joy of mathematics can be fun and productive. You are not the teacher but the tutor. When having fun with mathematics, remember the JUMP Math T.U.T.O.R. principles:

Take responsibility for learning:

If your child doesn't understand a concept, it can always be clarified further or explained differently. As the adult, you are responsible for helping your child understand. If they don't get it, don't get frustrated — get creative!

Use positive reinforcement:

Children like to be rewarded when they succeed. Praise and encouragement build excitement and foster an appetite for learning. The more confidence a student has, the more likely they are to be engaged.

Take small steps:

In mathematics, it is always possible to make something easier. Always use the JUMP Math worksheets to break down the question into a series of small steps. Practice, practice, practice!

Only indicate correct answers:

Your child's confidence can be shaken by a lack of success. Place checkmarks for correct answers, then revisit questions that your child is having difficulty with. Never use Xs!

Raise the bar:

When your child has mastered a particular concept, challenge them by posing a question that is slightly more difficult. As your child meets these small challenges, you will see their focus and excitement increase.

And remember: if your child is falling behind, teach the number facts! It is a serious mistake to think that students who don't know their number facts can always get by in mathematics using a calculator or other aids. Students can certainly perform operations on a calculator, but they cannot begin to solve problems if they lack a sense of numbers. Students need to be able to see patterns in numbers, and to make estimates and predictions about numbers, in order to have any success in mathematics.

Introductory Unit on Fractions

"In the twenty years that I have been teaching mathematics to children, I have never met an educator who would say that students who lack confidence in their intellectual or academic abilities are likely to do well in school. Our introductory unit has been carefully designed and tested with thousands of students to boost confidence. It has proven to be an extremely effective tool for convincing even the most challenged student that they can do well in mathematics."

— John Mighton

Cognitive scientists have discovered that in order for the brain to be "ready to learn" it cannot be distracted by anxiety. If your child struggles with mathematics or has "math anxiety," be sure to start JUMP Math with the introductory unit on Fractions found on page xxvii.

In recent years, research has shown that students are more apt to do well in subjects when they believe they are capable of doing well. It seems obvious, then, that any math program that aims to harness the potential of every student must start with an exercise that builds the *confidence* of every student. The introductory unit on Fractions was designed for this purpose. It has proven to be an extremely effective tool for convincing even the most challenged students that they can do well in mathematics.

The method used in the introductory unit can be described as *guided discovery*. The individual steps that you will follow in teaching the unit are extremely small, so even the weakest student needn't be left behind. Throughout the unit, students are expected to

- Discover or extend patterns or rules on their own;
- See what changes and what stays the same in sequences of mathematical expressions; and
- Apply what they have learned to new situations.

Students become very excited at making these discoveries and meeting these challenges as they learn the material. For many, it is the first time they have ever been motivated to pay attention to mathematical rules and patterns or to try to extend their knowledge in new cases.

How Does the Introductory Unit Build Confidence?

The introductory unit on Fractions has been specifically designed to build confidence by

- **Requiring that students possess only a few very simple skills.** To achieve a perfect score on the final test in the unit, students need only possess three skills. These skills can be taught to the most challenged students in a very short amount of time. Students must be able to do these three things:
  1. Skip count on their fingers.
  2. Add one-digit numbers.
  3. Subtract one-digit numbers.
- **Eliminating heavy use of language.** Mathematics functions as its own symbolic language. Since the vast majority of children are able to perform the most basic operations (counting and grouping objects into sets) long before they become expert readers, mathematics is the lone subject in which the vast majority of kids are naturally equipped to excel at an early age. By removing language as a barrier, students can realize their full potential in mathematics.
- **Allowing you to continually provide feedback.** Moving on too quickly is both a hindrance to a student's confidence and an impediment to their eventual success. In the introductory unit, the mathematics are broken down into small steps so that you can quickly identify difficulties and help as soon as they arise.
- **Keeping the student engaged through the excitement of small victories.** Children respond more quickly to praise and success than to criticism and threats. If students are encouraged, they feel an incentive to learn. Students enjoy exercising their minds and showing off to a caring adult.

Since the introductory unit is about building confidence, work with your child to ensure that they are successful. Celebrate every correct answer. Take your time. Encourage your child. And, most importantly, have fun!

Work on Mental Math

Included in *JUMP at Home Grade 8* is a Mental Math unit, which will provide you with strategies and techniques for sharpening your child's math brain. Mental math is the foundation for all further study in mathematics. Students who cannot see number patterns often become frustrated and disillusioned with their work. Consistent practice in mental math allows students to become familiar with the way numbers interact, enabling them to make simple calculations quickly and effectively without always having to recall their number facts.

Mental math confronts people at every turn, making the ability to quickly calculate numbers an invaluable asset. Calculating how much change you are owed at a grocery store or deciding how much of a tip to leave at a restaurant are both real-world examples of mental math in action. For this reason, it may be the single most relevant strand of mathematics to everyday life.

How Can a Parent Best Use Math Time?

To keep your child engaged and attentive, consider breaking up your half-hour math time together into thirds:

- **First 10 Minutes:** Use this time to focus on Mental Math. This will sharpen your child's mental number skills, and they will find the remainder of the session much more enjoyable if they are not constantly struggling to remember their number facts.
- **Second 10 Minutes:** Use this time to work on grade-specific material. These worksheets have been designed by mathematicians and educators to fill gaps in learning, strengthen basic skills, and reinforce fundamental concepts.
- **Final 10 Minutes:** Save this portion of the session for math games, cards, or board games.

It is important to remember that mathematics can be fun! Liven up things by playing games and being as active as possible. If the opportunity to visually demonstrate a concept arises, JUMP at it! Have your child sort out change, look around them for geometric objects, or pace out a perimeter.

"Children will never fulfill their extraordinary potential until we remember how it felt to have so much potential ourselves. There was nothing we weren't inspired to look at or hold, or that we weren't determined to find out how to do. Open the door to the world of mathematics so your child can pass through."

— John Mighton

Mental Math Skills: Addition and Subtraction

PARENT:

If your child doesn't know their addition and subtraction facts, teach them to add and subtract using their fingers by the methods taught below. You should also reinforce basic facts using drills, games, and flash cards. There are mental math strategies that make addition and subtraction easier. Some effective strategies are taught in the next section. (Until your child knows all their facts, allow them to add and subtract on their fingers when necessary.)

To **add** $4 + 8$, Grace says the greater number (8) with her fist closed. She counts up from 8, raising one finger at a time. She stops when she has raised the number of fingers equal to the lesser number (4):

8   9   10   11   12

She said "12" when she raised her 4th finger, so: $4 + 8 = 12$

1. Add:
   a) $5 + 2 = $ _____
   b) $3 + 2 = $ _____
   c) $6 + 2 = $ _____
   d) $9 + 2 = $ _____

   e) $2 + 4 = $ _____
   f) $2 + 7 = $ _____
   g) $5 + 3 = $ _____
   h) $6 + 3 = $ _____

   i) $11 + 4 = $ _____
   j) $3 + 9 = $ _____
   k) $7 + 3 = $ _____
   l) $14 + 4 = $ _____

   m) $21 + 5 = $ _____
   n) $32 + 3 = $ _____
   o) $4 + 56 = $ _____
   p) $39 + 4 = $ _____

To **subtract** $9 - 5$, Grace says the lesser number (5) with her fist closed. She counts up from 5 raising one finger at a time. She stops when she says the greater number (9):

5   6   7   8   9

She has raised 4 fingers when she stops, so: $9 - 5 = 4$

2. Subtract:
   a) $7 - 5 = $ _____
   b) $8 - 6 = $ _____
   c) $5 - 3 = $ _____
   d) $5 - 2 = $ _____

   e) $9 - 6 = $ _____
   f) $10 - 5 = $ _____
   g) $11 - 7 = $ _____
   h) $17 - 14 = $ _____

   i) $33 - 31 = $ _____
   j) $27 - 24 = $ _____
   k) $43 - 39 = $ _____
   l) $62 - 58 = $ _____

PARENT:

To prepare for the next section (Mental Math), teach your child to add 1 to any number mentally (by counting forward by 1 in their head) and to subtract 1 from any number (by counting backward by 1)

Mental Math Skills: **Addition and Subtraction** *(continued)*

PARENT: Children who don't know how to add, subtract, or estimate readily are at a great disadvantage in mathematics. Children who have trouble memorizing addition and subtraction facts can still learn to mentally add and subtract numbers in a short time if they are given daily practice in a few basic skills.

SKILL 1 – Adding 2 to an Even Number

This skill has been broken down into a number of sub-skills. After teaching each sub-skill, you should give your child a short diagnostic quiz to verify that they have learned the skill. I have included sample quizzes for Skills 1 to 4.

i) *Naming the next one-digit even number:*

Numbers that have ones digit 0, 2, 4, 6, or 8 are called *even numbers*. Using drills or games, teach your child to say the sequence of one-digit even numbers without hesitation. Ask them to imagine the sequence going on in a circle so that the next number after 8 is 0 (0, 2, 4, 6, 8, 0, 2, 4, 6, 8, . . .). Then play the following game: name a number in the sequence and ask your child to give the next number in the sequence. Don't move on until they have mastered the game.

ii) *Naming the next greatest two-digit even number:*

Case 1 – Numbers that end in 0, 2, 4, or 6
Write an even two-digit number that ends in 0, 2, 4, or 6 on a piece of paper. Ask your child to name the next greatest even number. They should recognize that if a number ends in 0, then the next even number ends in 2; if it ends in 2 then the next even number ends in 4, etc. For instance, the number 54 has ones digit 4, so the next greatest even number will have ones digit 6.

> **QUIZ**
>
> Name the next greatest even number:
>
> a) 52 : _____   b) 64 : _____   c) 36 : _____   d) 22 : _____   e) 80 : _____

Case 2 – Numbers that end in 8
Write the number 58 on a piece of paper. Ask your child to name the next greatest even number. Remind them that even numbers must end in 0, 2, 4, 6, or 8. But 50, 52, 54, and 56 are all less than 58, so the next greatest even number is 60. Your child should see that an even number ending in 8 is always followed by an even number ending in 0 (with a tens digit that is one higher).

> **QUIZ**
>
> Name the next greatest even number:
>
> a) 58 : _____   b) 68 : _____   c) 38 : _____   d) 48 : _____   e) 78 : _____

iii) *Adding 2 to an even number:*

Point out to your child that adding 2 to any even number is equivalent to finding the next even number: e.g., 46 + 2 = 48, 48 + 2 = 50, etc. Knowing this, your child can easily add 2 to any even number.

QUIZ

Add:

a) 26 + 2 ___   b) 82 + 2 ___   c) 40 + 2 ___   d) 58 + 2 ___   e) 34 + 2 ___

SKILL 2 – Subtracting 2 from an Even Number

i) *Finding the preceding one-digit even number:*

Name a one-digit even number and ask your child to give the preceding number in the sequence. For instance, the number that comes before 4 is 2 and the number that comes before 0 is 8. (Remember: the sequence is circular.)

ii) *Finding the preceding two-digit even number:*

Case 1 – Numbers that end in 2, 4, 6, or 8

Write a two-digit number that ends in 2, 4, 6, or 8 on a piece of paper. Ask your child to name the preceding even number. They should recognize that if a number ends in 2, then the preceding even number ends in 0; if it ends in 4, then the preceding even number ends in 2, etc. For instance, the number 78 has ones digit 8, so the preceding even number has ones digit 6.

QUIZ

Name the preceding even number:

a) 48 : _____   b) 26 : _____   c) 34 : _____   d) 62 : _____   e) 78 : _____

Case 2 – Numbers that end in 0

Write the number 80 on a piece of paper and ask your child to name the preceding even number. They should recognize that if an even number ends in 0, then the preceding even number ends in 8 (but the ones digit is one less). So the even number that comes before 80 is 78.

QUIZ

Name the preceding even number:

a) 40 : _____   b) 60 : _____   c) 80 : _____   d) 50 : _____   e) 30 : _____

ii) *Subtracting 2 from an even number:*

Point out to your child that subtracting 2 from any even number is equivalent to finding the preceding even number: e.g., 48 – 2 = 46, 46 – 2 = 44, etc.

QUIZ

Subtract:

a) 58 – 2 = ___   b) 24 – 2 = ___   c) 36 – 2 = ___   d) 42 – 2 = ___   e) 60 – 2 = ___

Mental Math Skills: **Addition and Subtraction** *(continued)*

SKILL 3 – Adding 2 to an Odd Number

i) *Naming the next one-digit odd number:*

Numbers that have ones digit 1, 3, 5, 7, or 9 are called *odd numbers*. Using drills or games, teach your child to say the sequence of one-digit odd numbers without hesitation. Ask them to imagine the sequence going on in a circle so that the next number after 9 is 1 (1, 3, 5, 7, 9, 1, 3, 5, 7, 9, . . .). Then play the following game: name a number in the sequence and ask your child to give the next number in the sequence. Don't move on until they have mastered the game.

ii) *Naming the next greatest two-digit odd number:*

Case 1 – Numbers that end in 1, 3, 5, or 7
Write an odd two-digit number that ends in 1, 3, 5, or 7 on a piece of paper. Ask your child to name the next greatest odd number. They should recognize that if a number ends in 1, then the next odd number ends in 3; if it ends in 3, then the next odd number ends in 5, etc. For instance, the number 35 has ones digit 5, so the next greatest odd number will have ones digit 7.

QUIZ
Name the next greatest odd number:

a) 51 : _____   b) 65 : _____   c) 37 : _____   d) 23 : _____   e) 87 : _____

Case 2 – Numbers that end in 9
Write the number 59 on a piece of paper. Ask your child to name the next greatest odd number. Remind them that odd numbers must end in 1, 3, 5, 7, or 9. But 51, 53, 55, and 57 are all less than 59. The next greatest odd number is 61. Your child should see that an odd number ending in 9 is always followed by an odd number ending in 1 (with a tens digit that is one higher).

QUIZ
Name the next greatest odd number:

a) 59 : _____   b) 69 : _____   c) 39 : _____   d) 49 : _____   e) 79 : _____

iii) *Adding 2 to an odd number:*
Point out to your child that adding 2 to any odd number is equivalent to finding the next odd number: e.g., 47 + 2 = 49, 49 + 2 = 51, etc. Knowing this, your child can easily add 2 to any odd number.

QUIZ
Add:

a) $27 + 2 =$ ___   b) $83 + 2 =$ ___   c) $41 + 2 =$ ___   d) $59 + 2 =$ ___   e) $35 + 2 =$ ___

Mental Math Skills: **Addition and Subtraction** *(continued)*

SKILL 4 – Subtracting 2 from an Odd Number

i) *Finding the preceding one-digit odd number:*

Name a one-digit odd number and ask your child to give the preceding number in the sequence. For instance, the number that comes before 3 is 1, and the number that comes before 1 is 9. (Remember: the sequence is circular.)

ii) *Finding the preceding two-digit odd number:*

Case 1 – Numbers that end in 3, 5, 7, or 9
Write a two-digit number that ends in 3, 5, 7, or 9 on a piece of paper. Ask your child to name the preceding odd number. They should recognize that if a number ends in 3, then the preceding odd number ends in 1; if it ends in 5, then the preceding odd number ends in 3, etc. For instance, the number 79 has ones digit 9, so the preceding odd number has ones digit 7.

> **QUIZ**
> Name the preceding odd number:
> a) 49 : _____   b) 27 : _____   c) 35 : _____   d) 63 : _____   e) 79 : _____

Case 2 – Numbers that end in 1
Write the number 81 on a piece of paper and ask your child to name the preceding odd number. They should recognize that if an odd number ends in 1 then the preceding odd number ends in 9 (but the ones digit is one less). So the odd number that comes before 81 is 79.

> **QUIZ**
> Name the preceding odd number:
> a) 41 : _____   b) 61 : _____   c) 81 : _____   d) 51 : _____   e) 31 : _____

iii) *Subtracting 2 from an odd number:*

Point out to your child that subtracting 2 from any odd number is equivalent to finding the preceding odd number: e.g., 49 − 2 = 47, 47 − 2 = 45, etc.

> **QUIZ**
> Subtract:
> a) 59 − 2 = ___   b) 25 − 2 = ___   c) 37 − 2 = ___   d) 43 − 2 = ___   e) 61 − 2 = ___

SKILLS 5 and 6

Once your child can add and subtract the numbers 1 and 2, then they can easily add and subtract the number 3: Add 3 to a number by first adding 2, then adding 1 (e.g., 35 + 3 = 35 + 2 + 1). Subtract 3 from a number by subtracting 2, then subtracting 1 (e.g., 35 − 3 = 35 − 2 − 1).

Mental Math Skills: **Addition and Subtraction** *(continued)*

PARENT: All of the addition and subtraction tricks you teach your child should be reinforced with drills, flashcards, and tests. Eventually they should memorize their addition and subtraction facts and shouldn't have to rely on the mental math tricks. One of the greatest gifts you can give your child is to teach them their number facts.

SKILLS 7 and 8

Add 4 to a number by adding 2 twice (e.g., $51 + 4 = 51 + 2 + 2$). Subtract 4 from a number by subtracting 2 twice (e.g., $51 - 4 = 51 - 2 - 2$).

SKILLS 9 and 10

Add 5 to a number by adding 4 then 1. Subtract 5 by subtracting 4 then 1.

SKILL 11

Your child can add pairs of identical numbers by doubling (e.g., $6 + 6 = 2 \times 6$). They should either memorize the 2 times table or they should double numbers by counting on their fingers by 2s.

Add a pair of numbers that differ by 1 by rewriting the larger number as 1 plus the smaller number, then use doubling to find the sum: e.g., $6 + 7 = 6 + 6 + 1 = 12 + 1 = 13$; $7 + 8 = 7 + 7 + 1 = 14 + 1 = 15$.

SKILLS 12, 13, and 14

Add a one-digit number to 10 by simply replacing the zero in 10 with the one-digit number: e.g., $10 + 7 = 17$.

Add 10 to any two-digit number by simply increasing the tens digit of the two-digit number by 1: e.g., $53 + 10 = 63$.

Add a pair of two-digit numbers (with no carrying) by adding the ones digits of the numbers and then adding the tens digits: e.g., $23 + 64 = 87$.

SKILLS 15 and 16

To add 9 to a one-digit number, subtract 1 from the number and then add 10: e.g., $9 + 6 = 10 + 5 = 15$; $9 + 7 = 10 + 6 = 16$. (Essentially, your child simply has to subtract 1 from the number and then stick a 1 in front of the result.)

To add 8 to a one-digit number, subtract 2 from the number and add 10: e.g., $8 + 6 = 10 + 4 = 14$; $8 + 7 = 10 + 5 = 15$.

SKILLS 17 and 18

To subtract a pair of multiples of ten, simply subtract the tens digits and add a zero for the ones digit: e.g., $70 - 50 = 20$.

To subtract a pair of two-digit numbers (without carrying or regrouping), subtract the ones digit from the ones digit and the tens digit from the tens digit: e.g., $57 - 34 = 23$.

Mental Math — Further Strategies

Further Mental Math Strategies

1. Your child should be able to explain how to use the strategies of "rounding the subtrahend (i.e., the number you are subtracting) up to the nearest multiple of ten."
   Examples:

   Subtrahend   Subtrahend rounded to the nearest tens

   a) $37 - 19 = 37 - 20 + 1$ ◄──── You must add 1 because 20 is 1 greater than 19.
   b) $64 - 28 = 64 - 30 + 2$ ◄──── You must add 2 because 30 is 2 greater than 28.
   c) $65 - 46 = 65 - 50 + 4$

   Practice Questions:
   a) $27 - 17 = 27 - \underline{\quad} + \underline{\quad}$ d) $84 - 57 = 84 - \underline{\quad} + \underline{\quad}$
   b) $52 - 36 = 52 - \underline{\quad} + \underline{\quad}$ e) $61 - 29 = 61 - \underline{\quad} + \underline{\quad}$
   c) $76 - 49 = 76 - \underline{\quad} + \underline{\quad}$ f) $42 - 18 = 42 - \underline{\quad} + \underline{\quad}$

   PARENT: This strategy works well with numbers that end in 6, 7, 8 or 9.

2. Your child should be able to explain how to subtract by thinking of adding.
   Examples:

   Count by ones from 45 to the nearest tens (50).   Count from 50 until you reach the first number (62).

   a) $62 - 45 = 5 + 12 = 17$ ◄──── The sum of counting up to the nearest ten and the original number is the difference.
   b) $46 - 23 = 3 + 20 = 23$ ⎫
   c) $73 - 17 = 6 + 50 = 56$ ⎭ ◄── What method did we use here?

   Practice Questions:
   a) $88 - 36 = \underline{\quad} + \underline{\quad} = \underline{\quad}$ d) $74 - 28 = \underline{\quad} + \underline{\quad} = \underline{\quad}$
   b) $58 - 21 = \underline{\quad} + \underline{\quad} = \underline{\quad}$ e) $93 - 64 = \underline{\quad} + \underline{\quad} = \underline{\quad}$
   c) $43 - 17 = \underline{\quad} + \underline{\quad} = \underline{\quad}$ f) $82 - 71 = \underline{\quad} + \underline{\quad} = \underline{\quad}$

3. Your child should be able to explain how to "use doubles."

   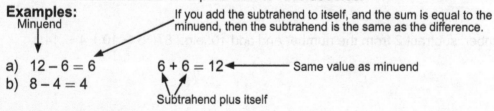

   Examples:
   Minuend

   If you add the subtrahend to itself, and the sum is equal to the minuend, then the subtrahend is the same as the difference.

   a) $12 - 6 = 6$ $6 + 6 = 12$ ◄── Same value as minuend
   b) $8 - 4 = 4$

   Subtrahend plus itself

   Practice Questions:
   a) $6 - 3 = \underline{\quad}$ d) $18 - 9 = \underline{\quad}$
   b) $10 - 5 = \underline{\quad}$ e) $16 - 8 = \underline{\quad}$
   c) $14 - 7 = \underline{\quad}$ f) $20 - 10 = \underline{\quad}$

Mental Math Exercises

PARENT: Teaching the material on these Mental Math worksheets may take several lessons. Your child will need more practice than is provided on these pages. These pages are intended as a test to be given when you are certain your child has learned the materials fully.

- -

PARENT: Teach skills 1, 2, 3 and 4 as outlined on pages xxiv-xxvii before you allow your child to answer Questions 1 through 12:

1. Name the <u>even</u> number that comes <u>after</u> the number. Answer in the blank provided:

   a) 32 _____   b) 46 _____   c) 14 _____   d) 92 _____   e) 56 _____

   f) 30 _____   g) 84 _____   h) 60 _____   i) 72 _____   j) 24 _____

2. Name the <u>even</u> number that comes <u>after</u> the number:

   a) 28 _____   b) 18 _____   c) 78 _____   d) 38 _____   e) 68 _____

3. Add:
   REMEMBER: Adding 2 to an even number is the same as finding the next even number.
   a) $42 + 2 =$ _____   b) $76 + 2 =$ _____   c) $28 + 2 =$ _____   d) $16 + 2 =$ _____

   e) $68 + 2 =$ _____   f) $12 + 2 =$ _____   g) $36 + 2 =$ _____   h) $90 + 2 =$ _____

   i) $70 + 2 =$ _____   j) $24 + 2 =$ _____   k) $66 + 2 =$ _____   l) $52 + 2 =$ _____

4. Name the <u>even</u> number that comes <u>before</u> the number:

   a) **38** _____   b) **42** _____   c) **56** _____   d) **72** _____   e) **98** _____

   f) **48** _____   g) **16** _____   h) **22** _____   i) **66** _____   j) **14** _____

5. Name the <u>even</u> number that comes <u>before</u> the number:

   a) **30** _____   b) **70** _____   c) **60** _____   d) **10** _____   e) **80** _____

6. Subtract:
   REMEMBER: Subtracting 2 from an even number is the same as finding the preceding even number.
   a) $46 - 2 =$ _____   b) $86 - 2 =$ _____   c) $90 - 2 =$ _____   d) $14 - 2 =$ _____

   e) $54 - 2 =$ _____   f) $72 - 2 =$ _____   g) $12 - 2 =$ _____   h) $56 - 2 =$ _____

   i) $32 - 2 =$ _____   j) $40 - 2 =$ _____   k) $60 - 2 =$ _____   l) $26 - 2 =$ _____

7. Name the <u>odd</u> number that comes <u>after</u> the number:

   a) 37 _____   b) 51 _____   c) 63 _____   d) 75 _____   e) 17 _____

   f) 61 _____   g) 43 _____   h) 81 _____   i) 23 _____   j) 95 _____

8. Name the <u>odd</u> number that comes <u>after</u> the number:

   a) 69 _____   b) 29 _____   c) 9 _____   d) 79 _____   e) 59 _____

Mental Math Exercises *(continued)*

9. Add:
    REMEMBER: Adding 2 to an odd number is the same as finding the next odd number.

    a) $25 + 2 = $ _____
    b) $31 + 2 = $ _____
    c) $47 + 2 = $ _____
    d) $33 + 2 = $ _____

    e) $39 + 2 = $ _____
    f) $91 + 2 = $ _____
    g) $5 + 2 = $ _____
    h) $89 + 2 = $ _____

    i) $11 + 2 = $ _____
    j) $65 + 2 = $ _____
    k) $29 + 2 = $ _____
    l) $17 + 2 = $ _____

10. Name the <u>odd</u> number that comes <u>before</u> the number:

    a) **39** _____
    b) **43** _____
    c) **57** _____
    d) **17** _____
    e) **99** _____

    f) **13** _____
    g) **85** _____
    h) **79** _____
    i) **65** _____
    j) **77** _____

11. Name the <u>odd</u> number that comes <u>before</u> the number:

    a) **21** _____
    b) **41** _____
    c) **11** _____
    d) **91** _____
    e) **51** _____

12. Subtract:
    REMEMBER: Subtracting 2 from an odd number is the same as finding the preceding odd number.

    a) $47 - 2 = $ _____
    b) $85 - 2 = $ _____
    c) $91 - 2 = $ _____
    d) $15 - 2 = $ _____

    e) $51 - 2 = $ _____
    f) $73 - 2 = $ _____
    g) $11 - 2 = $ _____
    h) $59 - 2 = $ _____

    i) $31 - 2 = $ _____
    j) $43 - 2 = $ _____
    k) $7 - 2 = $ _____
    l) $25 - 2 = $ _____

PARENT: Teach skills 5 and 6 as outlined on page xvii before you allow your child to answer Questions 13 and 14.

13. Add 3 to the number by adding 2, then adding 1 (e.g., $35 + 3 = 35 + 2 + 1$):

    a) $23 + 3 = $ _____
    b) $36 + 3 = $ _____
    c) $29 + 3 = $ _____
    d) $16 + 3 = $ _____

    e) $67 + 3 = $ _____
    f) $12 + 3 = $ _____
    g) $35 + 3 = $ _____
    h) $90 + 3 = $ _____

    i) $78 + 3 = $ _____
    j) $24 + 3 = $ _____
    k) $6 + 3 = $ _____
    l) $59 + 3 = $ _____

14. Subtract 3 from the number by subtracting 2, then subtracting 1 (e.g., $35 - 3 = 35 - 2 - 1$):

    a) $46 - 3 = $ _____
    b) $87 - 3 = $ _____
    c) $99 - 3 = $ _____
    d) $14 - 3 = $ _____

    e) $8 - 3 = $ _____
    f) $72 - 3 = $ _____
    g) $12 - 3 = $ _____
    h) $57 - 3 = $ _____

    i) $32 - 3 = $ _____
    j) $40 - 3 = $ _____
    k) $60 - 3 = $ _____
    l) $28 - 3 = $ _____

15. Fred has 49 stamps. He gives 2 stamps away. How many stamps does he have left?

16. There are 25 minnows in a tank. Alice adds 3 more to the tank. How many minnows are now in the tank?

Mental Math Exercises *(continued)*

PARENT: Teach skills 7 and 8 as outlined on page xix.

17. Add 4 to the number by adding 2 twice (e.g., $51 + 4 = 51 + 2 + 2$):

a) $42 + 4 =$ _____
b) $76 + 4 =$ _____
c) $27 + 4 =$ _____
d) $17 + 4 =$ _____

e) $68 + 4 =$ _____
f) $11 + 4 =$ _____
g) $35 + 4 =$ _____
h) $8 + 4 =$ _____

i) $72 + 4 =$ _____
j) $23 + 4 =$ _____
k) $60 + 4 =$ _____
l) $59 + 4 =$ _____

18. Subtract 4 from the number by subtracting 2 twice (e.g., $26 - 4 = 26 - 2 - 2$):

a) $46 - 4 =$ _____
b) $86 - 4 =$ _____
c) $91 - 4 =$ _____
d) $15 - 4 =$ _____

e) $53 - 4 =$ _____
f) $9 - 4 =$ _____
g) $13 - 4 =$ _____
h) $57 - 4 =$ _____

i) $40 - 4 =$ _____
j) $88 - 4 =$ _____
k) $69 - 4 =$ _____
l) $31 - 4 =$ _____

PARENT: Teach skills 9 and 10 as outlined on page xix.

19. Add 5 to the number by adding 4, then adding 1 (or add 2 twice, then add 1):

a) $84 + 5 =$ _____
b) $27 + 5 =$ _____
c) $31 + 5 =$ _____
d) $44 + 5 =$ _____

e) $63 + 5 =$ _____
f) $92 + 5 =$ _____
g) $14 + 5 =$ _____
h) $16 + 5 =$ _____

i) $9 + 5 =$ _____
j) $81 + 5 =$ _____
k) $51 + 5 =$ _____
l) $28 + 5 =$ _____

20. Subtract 5 from the number by subtracting 4, then subtracting 1 (or subtract 2 twice, then subtract 1):

a) $48 - 5 =$ _____
b) $86 - 5 =$ _____
c) $55 - 5 =$ _____
d) $69 - 5 =$ _____

e) $30 - 5 =$ _____
f) $13 - 5 =$ _____
g) $92 - 5 =$ _____
h) $77 - 5 =$ _____

i) $45 - 5 =$ _____
j) $24 - 5 =$ _____
k) $91 - 5 =$ _____
l) $8 - 5 =$ _____

PARENT: Teach skill 11 as outlined on page xix.

21. Add:

a) $6 + 6 =$ _____
b) $7 + 7 =$ _____
c) $8 + 8 =$ _____

d) $5 + 5 =$ _____
e) $4 + 4 =$ _____
f) $9 + 9 =$ _____

22. Add by thinking of the larger number as a sum of two smaller numbers. The first one is done for you:

a) $6 + 7 = 6 + 6 + 1$
b) $7 + 8 =$ _____
c) $6 + 8 =$ _____

d) $4 + 5 =$ _____
e) $5 + 7 =$ _____
f) $8 + 9 =$ _____

Mental Math Exercises *(continued)*

PARENT: Teach skills 12, 13, and 14 as outlined on page xix.

23. a) $10 + 3 =$ _____   b) $10 + 7 =$ _____   c) $5 + 10 =$ _____   d) $10 + 1 =$ _____

    e) $9 + 10 =$ _____   f) $10 + 4 =$ _____   g) $10 + 8 =$ _____   h) $10 + 2 =$ _____

24. a) $10 + 20 =$ _____   b) $40 + 10 =$ _____   c) $10 + 80 =$ _____   d) $10 + 50 =$ _____

    e) $30 + 10 =$ _____   f) $10 + 60 =$ _____   g) $10 + 10 =$ _____   h) $70 + 10 =$ _____

25. a) $10 + 25 =$ _____   b) $10 + 67 =$ _____   c) $10 + 31 =$ _____   d) $10 + 82 =$ _____

    e) $10 + 43 =$ _____   f) $10 + 51 =$ _____   g) $10 + 68 =$ _____   h) $10 + 21 =$ _____

    i) $10 + 11 =$ _____   j) $10 + 19 =$ _____   k) $10 + 44 =$ _____   l) $10 + 88 =$ _____

26. a) $20 + 30 =$ _____   b) $40 + 20 =$ _____   c) $30 + 30 =$ _____   d) $50 + 30 =$ _____

    e) $20 + 50 =$ _____   f) $40 + 40 =$ _____   g) $50 + 40 =$ _____   h) $40 + 30 =$ _____

    i) $60 + 30 =$ _____   j) $20 + 60 =$ _____   k) $20 + 70 =$ _____   l) $60 + 40 =$ _____

27. a) $20 + 23 =$ _____   b) $32 + 24 =$ _____   c) $51 + 12 =$ _____   d) $12 + 67 =$ _____

    e) $83 + 14 =$ _____   f) $65 + 24 =$ _____   g) $41 + 43 =$ _____   h) $70 + 27 =$ _____

    i) $31 + 61 =$ _____   j) $54 + 33 =$ _____   k) $28 + 31 =$ _____   l) $42 + 55 =$ _____

PARENT: Teach skills 15 and 16 as outlined on page xix.

28. a) $9 + 3 =$ _____   b) $9 + 7 =$ _____   c) $6 + 9 =$ _____   d) $4 + 9 =$ _____

    e) $9 + 9 =$ _____   f) $5 + 9 =$ _____   g) $9 + 2 =$ _____   h) $9 + 8 =$ _____

29. a) $8 + 2 =$ _____   b) $8 + 6 =$ _____   c) $8 + 7 =$ _____   d) $4 + 8 =$ _____

    e) $5 + 8 =$ _____   f) $8 + 3 =$ _____   g) $9 + 8 =$ _____   h) $8 + 8 =$ _____

PARENT: Teach skills 17 and 18 as outlined on page xix.

30. a) $40 - 10 =$ _____   b) $50 - 10 =$ _____   c) $70 - 10 =$ _____   d) $20 - 10 =$ _____

    e) $40 - 20 =$ _____   f) $60 - 30 =$ _____   g) $40 - 30 =$ _____   h) $60 - 50 =$ _____

31. a) $57 - 34 =$ _____   b) $43 - 12 =$ _____   c) $62 - 21 =$ _____   d) $59 - 36 =$ _____

    e) $87 - 63 =$ _____   f) $95 - 62 =$ _____   g) $35 - 10 =$ _____   h) $17 - 8 =$ _____

Mental Math (Advanced)

<u>Multiples of Ten</u>

NOTE: In the exercises below, you will learn several ways to use multiples of ten in mental addition or subtraction.

> **I** $542 + 214 = 542 + 200 + 10 + 4 = 742 + 10 + 4 = 752 + 4 = 756$
>
> $827 - 314 = 827 - 300 - 10 - 4 = 527 - 10 - 4 = 517 - 4 = 713$
>
>   Sometimes you will need to carry:
>
> $545 + 172 = 545 + 100 + 70 + 2 = 645 + 70 + 2 = 715 + 2 = 717$

1. Warm up:

   a) $536 + 100 =$ b) $816 + 10 =$ c) $124 + 5 =$ d) $540 + 200 =$

   e) $234 + 30 =$ f) $345 + 300 =$ g) $236 - 30 =$ h) $442 - 20 =$

   i) $970 - 70 =$ j) $542 - 400 =$ k) $160 + 50 =$ l) $756 + 40 =$

2. Write the second number in expanded form and add or subtract one digit at a time. The first one is done for you:

   a) $564 + 215 = $ _____ $564 + 200 + 10 + 5$ _____ $= $ ___ 779 ___

   b) $445 + 343 = $ _____ $= $ _____

   c) $234 + 214 = $ _____ $= $ _____

3. Add or subtract mentally (one digit at a time):

   a) $547 + 312 =$ b) $578 - 314 =$ c) $845 - 454 =$

> **II**   If one of the numbers you are adding or subtracting is close to a number that is a multiple of ten, add the multiple of ten and then add or subtract an adjustment factor:
>
> $645 + 99 = 645 + 100 - 1 = 745 - 1 = 744$
>
> $856 + 42 = 856 + 40 + 2 = 896 + 2 = 898$

> **III**   Sometimes in subtraction it helps to think of a multiple of ten as a sum of 1 and a number consisting entirely of 9s (e.g., $100 = 1 + 99$; $1000 = 1 + 999$). You never have to borrow or exchange when you are subtracting from a number consisting entirely of 9s.
>
> $100 - 43 = 1 + 99 - 43 = 1 + 56 = 57 \longleftarrow$ *Do the subtraction, using 99 instead of 100, and then add 1 to your answer*
>
> $1000 - 543 = 1 + 999 - 543 = 1 + 456 = 457$

4. Use the tricks you've just learned:

   a) $845 + 91 =$ b) $456 + 298 =$ c) $100 - 84 =$ d) $1000 - 846 =$

Mental Math Game: Modified Go Fish

PURPOSE:

If children know the pairs of one-digit numbers that add up to particular **target numbers**, they will be able to mentally break sums into easier sums.

EXAMPLE:

As it is easy to add any one-digit number to 10, you can add a sum more readily if you can decompose numbers in the sum into pairs that add to ten. For example:

$$7 + 5 = 7 + 3 + 2 = 10 + 2 = 12$$

These numbers add to 10.

To help children remember pairs of numbers that add up to a given target number, I developed a variation of "Go Fish" that I have found very effective.

THE GAME:

Pick any target number and remove all the cards with value greater than or equal to the target number out of the deck. In what follows, I will assume that the target number is 10, so you would take all the tens and face cards out of the deck (aces count as one).

The dealer gives each player six cards. If a player has any pairs of cards that add to 10, they are allowed to place these pairs on the table before play begins.

Player 1 selects one of the cards in their hand and asks Player 2 for a card that adds to 10 with the chosen card. For instance, if Player 1's chosen card is a 3, they may ask Player 2 for a 7.

If Player 2 has the requested card, Player 1 takes it and lays it down along with the card from their hand. Player 1 may then ask for another card. If Player 2 does not have the requested card, they say, "Go fish," and Player 1 must pick up a card from the top of the deck. (If this card adds to 10 with a card in Player 1's hand, they may lay down the pair right away.) It is then Player 2's turn to ask for a card.

Play ends when one player lays down all of their cards. Players receive 4 points for laying down all of their cards first and 1 point for each pair they have laid down.

PARENT: If your child is having difficulty, I would recommend that you start with pairs of numbers that add to 5. Take all cards with value greater than 4 out of the deck. Each player should be dealt only four cards to start with.

I have worked with several children who have had a great deal of trouble sorting their cards and finding pairs that add to a target number. I have found that the following exercise helps:

Give your child only three cards, two of which add to the target number. Ask them to find the pair that adds to the target number. After your child has mastered this step with three cards, repeat the exercise with four cards, then five cards, and so on.

PARENT: You can also give your child a list of the pairs that add to the target number. As your child gets used to the game, gradually remove pairs from the list so that they learn the pairs by memory.

Fractions

1. Name the following fractions.

a)

b)

c)

d)

e)

f)

g)

h)

i)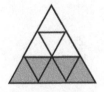

j)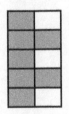

k)

l)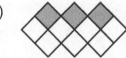

2. Shade the fractions named.

a) $\dfrac{1}{2}$

b) $\dfrac{1}{3}$

c) $\dfrac{3}{4}$

d) $\dfrac{3}{6}$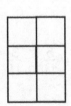

e) $\dfrac{2}{5}$

f) $\dfrac{5}{9}$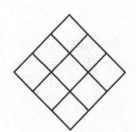

Introduction

Fractions *(continued)*

3. Add.

a) $\frac{1}{3} + \frac{1}{3}$

b) $\frac{2}{7} + \frac{3}{7}$

c) $\frac{2}{11} + \frac{1}{11}$

d) $\frac{2}{5} + \frac{2}{5}$

e) $\frac{2}{11} + \frac{3}{11}$

f) $\frac{3}{8} + \frac{4}{8}$

g) $\frac{3}{17} + \frac{2}{17}$

h) $\frac{1}{21} + \frac{4}{21}$

i) $\frac{4}{9} + \frac{3}{9}$

4. Subtract.

a) $\frac{3}{5} - \frac{1}{5}$

b) $\frac{2}{7} - \frac{1}{7}$

c) $\frac{4}{11} - \frac{2}{11}$

d) $\frac{5}{8} - \frac{2}{8}$

e) $\frac{6}{17} - \frac{2}{17}$

f) $\frac{5}{9} - \frac{1}{9}$

5. **Advanced:** Add or Subtract.

a) $\frac{1}{7} + \frac{1}{7} + \frac{1}{7}$

b) $\frac{1}{7} + \frac{2}{7} + \frac{3}{7}$

c) $\frac{1}{15} + \frac{2}{15} + \frac{5}{15}$

BONUS:

d) $\frac{16}{21} - \frac{5}{21} - \frac{3}{21}$

e) $\frac{7}{9} - \frac{4}{9} + \frac{2}{9}$

f) $\frac{2}{11} + \frac{5}{11} - \frac{3}{11}$

Fractions *(continued)*

6. Write times signs beside the fractions.

Example: $\frac{1}{5} + \frac{1}{3} \longrightarrow \overset{\times}{\times}\ \frac{1}{5} + \frac{1}{3}\ \overset{\times}{\times}$

$\frac{1}{2} + \frac{1}{3}$	$\frac{1}{2} + \frac{1}{5}$	$\frac{1}{3} + \frac{1}{5}$

7. Switch the bottom numbers.

Example: $\frac{1}{5} + \frac{1}{3} \longrightarrow \frac{3}{3} \times \frac{1}{5} + \frac{1}{3} \times \frac{5}{5}$

$\overset{\times}{\times}\ \frac{1}{2} + \frac{1}{3}\ \overset{\times}{\times}$	$\overset{\times}{\times}\ \frac{1}{2} + \frac{1}{5}\ \overset{\times}{\times}$	$\overset{\times}{\times}\ \frac{1}{3} + \frac{1}{5}\ \overset{\times}{\times}$

8. Write times signs and switch the numbers.

Example: $\frac{1}{5} + \frac{1}{3} \longrightarrow \frac{3}{3} \times \frac{1}{5} + \frac{1}{3} \times \frac{5}{5}$

$\frac{1}{2} + \frac{1}{3}$	$\frac{1}{2} + \frac{1}{5}$	$\frac{1}{3} + \frac{1}{5}$
$\frac{2}{3} + \frac{1}{2}$	$\frac{2}{3} + \frac{1}{5}$	$\frac{2}{5} + \frac{1}{3}$

9. Perform the multiplications.

Example: $\frac{1}{5} + \frac{1}{3} \longrightarrow \frac{3}{3} \times \frac{1}{5} + \frac{1}{3} \times \frac{5}{5}$

$$= \frac{3}{15} + \frac{5}{15}$$

$\frac{3}{3} \times \frac{1}{2} + \frac{1}{3} \times \frac{2}{2}$ $= \frac{\ }{\ } + \frac{\ }{\ }$	$\frac{5}{5} \times \frac{1}{2} + \frac{1}{5} \times \frac{2}{2}$ $= \frac{\ }{\ } + \frac{\ }{\ }$	$\frac{5}{5} \times \frac{1}{3} + \frac{1}{5} \times \frac{3}{3}$ $= \frac{\ }{\ } + \frac{\ }{\ }$

Fractions *(continued)*

$\dfrac{2}{2} \times \dfrac{2}{3} + \dfrac{1}{2} \times \dfrac{3}{3}$	$\dfrac{5}{5} \times \dfrac{2}{3} + \dfrac{1}{5} \times \dfrac{3}{3}$	$\dfrac{3}{3} \times \dfrac{2}{5} + \dfrac{1}{3} \times \dfrac{5}{5}$
$= \underline{\ \ } + \underline{\ \ }$	$= \underline{\ \ } + \underline{\ \ }$	$= \underline{\ \ } + \underline{\ \ }$

10. Perform the additions.

Example: $\dfrac{1}{5} + \dfrac{1}{3} \longrightarrow \dfrac{3}{3} \times \dfrac{1}{5} + \dfrac{1}{3} \times \dfrac{5}{5}$

$$= \dfrac{3}{15} + \dfrac{5}{15} = \dfrac{8}{15}$$

$\dfrac{3}{3} \times \dfrac{1}{2} + \dfrac{1}{3} \times \dfrac{2}{2}$	$\dfrac{5}{5} \times \dfrac{1}{2} + \dfrac{1}{5} \times \dfrac{2}{2}$	$\dfrac{5}{5} \times \dfrac{1}{3} + \dfrac{1}{5} \times \dfrac{3}{3}$
$= \dfrac{3}{6} + \dfrac{2}{6} = \underline{\ \ }$	$= \dfrac{5}{10} + \dfrac{2}{10} = \underline{\ \ }$	$= \dfrac{5}{15} + \dfrac{3}{10} = \underline{\ \ }$
$\dfrac{2}{2} \times \dfrac{2}{3} + \dfrac{1}{2} \times \dfrac{3}{3}$	$\dfrac{5}{5} \times \dfrac{2}{3} + \dfrac{1}{5} \times \dfrac{3}{3}$	$\dfrac{3}{3} \times \dfrac{2}{5} + \dfrac{1}{3} \times \dfrac{5}{5}$
$= \dfrac{4}{6} + \dfrac{3}{6} = \underline{\ \ }$	$= \dfrac{10}{15} + \dfrac{3}{15} = \underline{\ \ }$	$= \dfrac{6}{10} + \dfrac{5}{10} = \underline{\ \ }$

11. Perform the multiplications and the additions.

Example: $\dfrac{1}{5} + \dfrac{1}{3} \longrightarrow \dfrac{3}{3} \times \dfrac{1}{5} + \dfrac{1}{3} \times \dfrac{5}{5}$

$$= \dfrac{3}{15} + \dfrac{5}{15} = \dfrac{8}{15}$$

$\dfrac{3}{3} \times \dfrac{1}{2} + \dfrac{1}{3} \times \dfrac{2}{2}$	$\dfrac{5}{5} \times \dfrac{1}{2} + \dfrac{1}{5} \times \dfrac{2}{2}$	$\dfrac{5}{5} \times \dfrac{1}{3} + \dfrac{1}{5} \times \dfrac{3}{3}$
$= \underline{\ \ } + \underline{\ \ } = \underline{\ \ }$	$= \underline{\ \ } + \underline{\ \ } = \underline{\ \ }$	$= \underline{\ \ } + \underline{\ \ } = \underline{\ \ }$
$\dfrac{2}{2} \times \dfrac{2}{3} + \dfrac{1}{2} \times \dfrac{3}{3}$	$\dfrac{5}{5} \times \dfrac{2}{3} + \dfrac{1}{5} \times \dfrac{3}{3}$	$\dfrac{3}{3} \times \dfrac{2}{5} + \dfrac{1}{3} \times \dfrac{5}{5}$
$= \underline{\ \ } + \underline{\ \ } = \underline{\ \ }$	$= \underline{\ \ } + \underline{\ \ } = \underline{\ \ }$	$= \underline{\ \ } + \underline{\ \ } = \underline{\ \ }$

Fractions *(continued)*

12. Add.

a) $\dfrac{1}{2} + \dfrac{1}{3}$

b) $\dfrac{1}{3} + \dfrac{1}{5}$

c) $\dfrac{1}{2} + \dfrac{1}{5}$

13. **Advanced:** Add or Subtract.

a) $\dfrac{2}{5} + \dfrac{1}{3}$

b) $\dfrac{3}{5} + \dfrac{1}{2}$

c) $\dfrac{2}{3} + \dfrac{1}{2}$

d) $\dfrac{1}{5} + \dfrac{2}{3}$

d) $\dfrac{4}{5} + \dfrac{1}{2}$

f) $\dfrac{2}{3} + \dfrac{2}{5}$

BONUS:

a) $\dfrac{1}{2} - \dfrac{1}{3}$

b) $\dfrac{2}{3} - \dfrac{1}{2}$

c) $\dfrac{3}{5} + \dfrac{1}{2}$

Fractions *(continued)*

14. Write how many times the lesser denominator goes into the greater denominator.

Example: $\dfrac{1}{2} + \dfrac{1}{10} \longrightarrow \dfrac{5}{5} \times \dfrac{1}{2} + \dfrac{1}{10}$

$\dfrac{1}{2} + \dfrac{1}{10}$	$\dfrac{1}{5} + \dfrac{1}{10}$	$\dfrac{1}{2} + \dfrac{1}{8}$
$\dfrac{1}{3} + \dfrac{1}{6}$	$\dfrac{1}{5} + \dfrac{1}{20}$	$\dfrac{1}{2} + \dfrac{1}{6}$
$\dfrac{2}{5} + \dfrac{1}{25}$	$\dfrac{3}{5} + \dfrac{1}{15}$	$\dfrac{1}{2} + \dfrac{7}{8}$

15. Change the fraction with the lesser denominator and keep the other fraction the same.

Example: $\dfrac{1}{2} + \dfrac{1}{10} \longrightarrow \dfrac{5}{5} \times \dfrac{1}{2} + \dfrac{1}{10}$

$$= \dfrac{5}{10} + \dfrac{1}{10}$$

$\dfrac{1}{2} + \dfrac{1}{10}$	$\dfrac{1}{5} + \dfrac{1}{10}$	$\dfrac{1}{2} + \dfrac{1}{8}$
$\dfrac{1}{3} + \dfrac{1}{6}$	$\dfrac{1}{5} + \dfrac{1}{20}$	$\dfrac{1}{2} + \dfrac{1}{6}$
$\dfrac{2}{5} + \dfrac{1}{25}$	$\dfrac{3}{5} + \dfrac{1}{15}$	$\dfrac{1}{2} + \dfrac{7}{8}$

Fractions *(continued)*

16. Add. (Remember to change only one denominator.)

a) $\dfrac{1}{2} + \dfrac{1}{10}$

b) $\dfrac{1}{5} + \dfrac{1}{10}$

c) $\dfrac{1}{2} + \dfrac{1}{8}$

d) $\dfrac{1}{3} + \dfrac{1}{6}$

e) $\dfrac{1}{5} + \dfrac{1}{20}$

f) $\dfrac{1}{2} + \dfrac{1}{6}$

17. **Advanced:** Add or Subtract.

a) $\dfrac{2}{3} + \dfrac{1}{15}$

b) $\dfrac{2}{5} + \dfrac{1}{10}$

c) $\dfrac{3}{5} + \dfrac{2}{15}$

d) $\dfrac{2}{3} + \dfrac{1}{12}$

e) $\dfrac{1}{4} + \dfrac{3}{8}$

f) $\dfrac{1}{4} + \dfrac{3}{12}$

g) $\dfrac{3}{4} + \dfrac{1}{2}$

h) $\dfrac{4}{25} + \dfrac{1}{5}$

i) $\dfrac{3}{15} + \dfrac{4}{5}$

BONUS:

j) $\dfrac{7}{20} - \dfrac{1}{5}$

k) $\dfrac{3}{8} - \dfrac{1}{4}$

l) $\dfrac{1}{2} - \dfrac{3}{10}$

Fractions (continued)

18. Write **yes** beside the number in bold if you say the number when counting by 2s.
    If you don't, write **no**.

    a) **6** _____   b) **3** _____   c) **9** _____   d) **8** _____

    e) **10** _____   f) **4** _____   g) **5** _____   h) **7** _____

19. Write **yes** beside the given number if you say the number when counting by 3s.
    If you don't, write **no**.

    a) **9** _____   b) **4** _____   c) **12** _____   d) **13** _____

    e) **6** _____   f) **5** _____   g) **8** _____   h) **14** _____

20. Write **yes** beside the given number if you say the number when counting by 5s.
    If you don't, write **no**.

    a) **10** _____   b) **12** _____   c) **15** _____   d) **8** _____

    e) **20** _____   f) **9** _____   g) **14** _____   h) **11** _____

21. Circle the smaller denominator. The first one has been done for you.

    a) $\dfrac{1}{②} + \dfrac{1}{3}$ b) $\dfrac{1}{3} + \dfrac{1}{5}$ c) $\dfrac{2}{6} + \dfrac{1}{2}$

    d) $\dfrac{1}{4} + \dfrac{1}{8}$ e) $\dfrac{3}{5} + \dfrac{1}{2}$ f) $\dfrac{1}{2} + \dfrac{1}{8}$

22. Count by the lesser denominator, and write **yes** if you say the greater denominator.
    Write **no** if you don't. The first one has been done for you.

    a) ___no___   b) _____   c) _____

    $\dfrac{1}{②} + \dfrac{1}{3}$ $\dfrac{1}{③} + \dfrac{1}{5}$ $\dfrac{2}{6} + \dfrac{1}{②}$

    d) _____   e) _____   f) _____

    $\dfrac{1}{4} + \dfrac{1}{8}$ $\dfrac{3}{5} + \dfrac{1}{2}$ $\dfrac{1}{2} + \dfrac{1}{8}$

    g) _____   h) _____   i) _____

    $\dfrac{1}{2} + \dfrac{1}{8}$ $\dfrac{3}{15} + \dfrac{1}{3}$ $\dfrac{1}{5} + \dfrac{1}{9}$

Fractions *(continued)*

23. Count by the lesser denominator until you reach the greater denominator. Write the number of fingers you have raised beside the times signs.

a) ___yes___

$$\begin{array}{l}\times \\ \times\end{array} \frac{1}{2} + \frac{1}{6}$$

b) ___yes___

$$\begin{array}{l}\times \\ \times\end{array} \frac{1}{5} + \frac{1}{10}$$

c) ___yes___

$$\begin{array}{l}\times \\ \times\end{array} \frac{1}{3} + \frac{1}{9}$$

24. Complete the first step of addition by multiplying each fraction by the opposite denominator.

a) ___no___

$$\begin{array}{l}\times \\ \times\end{array} \frac{1}{2} + \frac{1}{6} \begin{array}{l}\times \\ \times\end{array}$$

b) ___no___

$$\begin{array}{l}\times \\ \times\end{array} \frac{1}{5} + \frac{1}{10} \begin{array}{l}\times \\ \times\end{array}$$

c) ___no___

$$\begin{array}{l}\times \\ \times\end{array} \frac{1}{3} + \frac{1}{9} \begin{array}{l}\times \\ \times\end{array}$$

25. Write **yes** or **no** above the following fractions. If you wrote **yes**, then complete the first step of addition as in Question 23 above. If you wrote **no**, complete the first step as in Question 24.

a) _____

$$\frac{1}{3} + \frac{1}{5}$$

b) _____

$$\frac{3}{5} + \frac{1}{10}$$

c) _____

$$\frac{1}{2} + \frac{1}{4}$$

d) _____

$$\frac{1}{3} + \frac{1}{4}$$

BONUS:

e) _____

$$\frac{3}{15} + \frac{1}{5}$$

f) _____

$$\frac{1}{10} + \frac{1}{5}$$

26. Add or Subtract. Change *one* denominator or change *both*. (For each question you have to decide what to do. Start by writing **yes** or **no** above the fraction.)

a) _____

$$\frac{1}{4} + \frac{1}{5}$$

b) _____

$$\frac{2}{3} + \frac{1}{5}$$

c) _____

$$\frac{2}{5} + \frac{1}{20}$$

BONUS:

d) _____

$$\frac{3}{20} + \frac{4}{5}$$

e) _____

$$\frac{2}{15} + \frac{3}{5}$$

f) _____

$$\frac{1}{16} + \frac{1}{4}$$

Fractions *(continued)*

27. **Advanced:** Add or Subtract. (Change *one* denominator or change *both*.)

a) $\dfrac{1}{3} + \dfrac{1}{9}$

b) $\dfrac{2}{3} + \dfrac{1}{5}$

c) $\dfrac{1}{5} + \dfrac{1}{20}$

d) $\dfrac{1}{2} + \dfrac{1}{3}$

e) $\dfrac{1}{4} + \dfrac{1}{5}$

f) $\dfrac{1}{4} + \dfrac{5}{16}$

g) $\dfrac{1}{2} - \dfrac{1}{10}$

h) $\dfrac{3}{4} - \dfrac{1}{3}$

i) $\dfrac{7}{20} - \dfrac{1}{4}$

28. If the denominators are the same, write **same**. Otherwise change *one* denominator or change *both*. Then complete all the questions.

a) $\dfrac{1}{3} + \dfrac{1}{12}$

b) $\dfrac{1}{4} + \dfrac{3}{5}$

c) $\dfrac{1}{7} + \dfrac{1}{7}$

d) $\dfrac{2}{3} + \dfrac{1}{2}$

e) $\dfrac{10}{11} - \dfrac{6}{11}$

f) $\dfrac{4}{5} - \dfrac{3}{20}$

Fractions *(continued)*

29. Write times signs and numbers where necessary.

Example: $\dfrac{1}{2} + \dfrac{1}{3} + \dfrac{1}{6} \longrightarrow \dfrac{3}{3} \times \dfrac{1}{2} + \dfrac{2}{2} \times \dfrac{1}{3} + \dfrac{1}{6}$

$\dfrac{1}{2} + \dfrac{1}{3} + \dfrac{1}{6}$	$\dfrac{1}{3} + \dfrac{1}{5} + \dfrac{1}{15}$
$\dfrac{1}{2} + \dfrac{1}{4} + \dfrac{3}{8}$	$\dfrac{1}{4} + \dfrac{1}{5} + \dfrac{1}{20}$
$\dfrac{2}{3} + \dfrac{1}{4} + \dfrac{1}{12}$	$\dfrac{1}{5} + \dfrac{3}{10} + \dfrac{2}{20}$

30. Write times signs and numbers, and carry out multiplication as needed.

Example: $\dfrac{1}{2} + \dfrac{1}{3} + \dfrac{1}{6} \longrightarrow \dfrac{3}{3} \times \dfrac{1}{2} + \dfrac{2}{2} \times \dfrac{1}{3} + \dfrac{1}{6}$

$$= \dfrac{3}{6} + \dfrac{2}{6} + \dfrac{1}{6}$$

$\dfrac{1}{2} + \dfrac{1}{3} + \dfrac{1}{6}$	$\dfrac{1}{3} + \dfrac{1}{6} + \dfrac{1}{15}$
$\dfrac{1}{2} + \dfrac{1}{4} + \dfrac{3}{8}$	$\dfrac{1}{4} + \dfrac{1}{5} + \dfrac{1}{20}$
$\dfrac{2}{3} + \dfrac{1}{4} + \dfrac{1}{12}$	$\dfrac{1}{5} + \dfrac{3}{10} + \dfrac{2}{20}$

Fractions *(continued)*

31. Solve completely.

a) $\dfrac{1}{2} + \dfrac{1}{3} + \dfrac{3}{6}$

b) $\dfrac{1}{3} + \dfrac{1}{5} + \dfrac{1}{15}$

c) $\dfrac{1}{2} + \dfrac{1}{4} + \dfrac{3}{8}$

d) $\dfrac{1}{4} + \dfrac{1}{5} + \dfrac{5}{20}$

e) $\dfrac{2}{3} + \dfrac{1}{4} + \dfrac{1}{12}$

f) $\dfrac{1}{5} + \dfrac{3}{10} + \dfrac{2}{20}$

BONUS:

g) $\dfrac{17}{20} - \dfrac{1}{4} - \dfrac{1}{5}$

h) $\dfrac{3}{4} - \dfrac{1}{8} - \dfrac{1}{2}$

i) $\dfrac{1}{2} - \dfrac{1}{6} + \dfrac{1}{3}$

j) $\dfrac{2}{3} + \dfrac{1}{4} - \dfrac{5}{12}$

Binary Code

<u>Step 1</u> – Warm-up

a) Review single digit addition (Basic Number Sense)

　　i.e.,　　$8 + 2 =$

　　　　　$8 + 4 + 2 =$

　　Write down a few questions. Check your child's work.

b) Review Place Value (2 7 3)

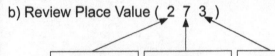

| Hundreds | Tens | Ones |

　　Write down a few questions. Check your child's work.

<u>Step 2</u> – Binary Code Introduction

Talk about the fact that we represent numbers using numerical symbols (i.e., 2 = two).
However, computers do it differently. They use a SECRET electricity CODE!!

electricity = 1; no electricity = 0

You're going to teach them how to CRACK THE CODE!!

<u>Step 3</u> – Binary Code Exercises

Set up the following chart:

	Eights	Fours	Twos	Ones
a)				
b)				
c)				

Explain to your child that if you put a "1" in a column, it means that the number contains the value at the heading of the column.

For example:

	Eights	Fours	Twos	Ones	
a)	0	0	0	1	$1 = 1$
b)	0	0	1	1	$2 + 1 = 3$
c)	0	0	1	0	$2 = 2$

Explanation:

a) There are 0 eights, 0 fours, 0 twos, 1 one. Therefore, the code 0001 = 1

b) There are 0 eights, 0 fours, 1 two, 1 one. Therefore, the code 0011 = 2 + 1 = 3

c) There are 0 eights, 0 fours, 1 two, 0 ones. Therefore, the code 0010 = 2

Write down several questions. Check your child's work.

Binary Code (continued)

NOTE TO PARENT:

All numbers can be coded in this manner by adding columns to the left of the chart as follows:

32s	16s	8s	4s	2s	1s
1	0	1	0	1	1

$32 + 8 + 2 + 1 = 43$

JUMP Binary Code Game (A.K.A. MIND-READING TRICK!!):

Here are the boxes you need for the final part of the game.

Copy the following charts.

Have your child pick a number between 1 and 15. They should NOT reveal this number to you.

Then, have your child tell you which charts contain their number.

If a chart contains the number, then think of it as a "1." If it doesn't, think of it as a "0."

D			
8	9	10	11
12	13	14	15

C			
4	5	6	7
12	13	14	15

B			
2	3	6	7
10	11	14	15

A			
1	3	5	7
9	11	13	15

Chart A represents 1s.

Chart B represents 2s.

Chart C represents 4s.

Chart D represents 8s.

Example:

They choose "14."

14 is in Chart D = 1

14 is in Chart C = 1

14 is in Chart B = 1

14 is NOT in Chart A = 0

Therefore, the code is 1110, or $8 + 4 + 2 = 14!!$

Always/Sometimes/Never True (Numbers)

A If you multiply a 3-digit number by a one-digit number, the answer will be a three-digit number.	**B** If you subtract a three-digit number from 999, you will not have to regroup.	**C** The product of two numbers is greater than the sum.
D If you divide a number by itself, the answer will be 1.	**E** The product of 0 and a number is 0.	**F** Mixed fractions are larger than improper fractions.
G The product of 2 even numbers is an even number.	**H** The product of 2 odd numbers is an odd number.	**I** A number that ends with an even number is divisible by 4.
J When you round to the nearest thousands place, only the thousands digit changes.	**K** When you divide, the remainder is less than the number you are dividing by.	**L** The sum of the digits of a multiple of 3 is divisible by 3.
M The multiples of 5 are divisible by 2.	**N** Improper fractions are greater than 1.	**O** If you have two fractions, the one with the smaller denominator is the larger fraction.

1. Choose a statement from the chart above and say whether it is **always** true, **sometimes** true, or **never** true. Give reasons for your answer.

   What statement did you choose? Statement Letter _____

   This statement is…

   Always True   **Sometimes True**   **Never True**

   Explain: _____

   _____

   _____

2. Choose a statement that is sometimes true, and reword it so that it is always true.

   What statement did you choose? Statement Letter _____

   Your reworded statement: _____

   _____

3. Repeat the exercise with another statement.

Pattern Puzzles

1. One of the most famous sequences in mathematics is the **Fibonacci sequence**.

   a) In the circles, write the amount added between the terms of the Fibonacci sequence. Then use the pattern in the steps to continue the sequence.

   1 , 1 , 2 , 3 , 5 , 8 , 13 , 21 , ____ , ____

   b) Complete the table by writing whether each number in the sequence is even (E) or odd (O).

Number	1	1	2	3	5	8	13	21		
Even or Odd	O	O	E	O						

   c) Describe the odd-even pattern in the Fibonacci sequence.

   d) Is the 38th term in the Fibonacci sequence even or odd? Explain.

   e) Add the first four odd Fibonacci numbers. Then add the first two even Fibonacci numbers. What do you notice?

   f) Add the first six odd Fibonacci numbers. Then add the first three even Fibonacci numbers. What do you notice?

2. Describe any patterns you see in the chart:

   HINT: Look at the rows, columns and diagonals.

1	2	3	4	5	6
12	11	10	9	8	7
13	14	15	16	17	18
24	23	22	21	20	19
25	26	27	28	29	30
36	35	34	33	32	31

3.
$$2 = 1 \times 2$$
$$2 + 4 = 2 \times 3$$
$$2 + 4 + 6 = 3 \times 4$$
$$2 + 4 + 6 + 8 = 4 \times 5$$

   a) Describe any patterns you see in the sums shown.

   b) Using the patterns you found in part a), find the sum of the first ten even numbers.

2-Dimensional Patterns

PARENT: For this worksheet, your child will need the hundreds charts on page xliv.

1. Shade the numbers along any column of a hundreds chart.
Write a rule for the pattern you see.
Look at any other column. How do you explain what you see?

2. This picture shows part of a hundreds chart:
Fill in the missing numbers using the pattern you found in Question 1.

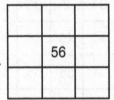

3. Shade a 2 × 2 square as shown.
Then add the pair of numbers on the "left to right" diagonal:
Then add the pair on the "right to left" diagonal.
Try this again with different 2 × 2 squares.
What do you observe?

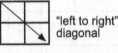

"left to right" diagonal

4. 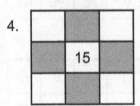 Shade a 4-point square around any number on the chart (as shown).
Add the pair of shaded numbers above and below the middle number.
Add the pair of shaded numbers to the right and left of the middle number.
Try this with several different 4-point squares.
Can you explain what you notice?

5. Shade a 3 × 3 square as shown at left.

   a) Take the average of the two numbers above and below
   the centre square.
   What do you notice?

   b) Add the six numbers that lie in the columns shown:
   Repeat this with several 3 × 3 squares.
   What relation does the sum have to the number in the centre box?

BONUS:

6. a) Using a calculator, find the sums of the
   first 3 columns:
   b) Why are the sums equal?
   c) Describe any patterns you see in the
   hundreds chart.

1	2	3	4	5	6	7	8	9	10
11	12	13	14	15	16	17	18	19	20
21	22	23	24	25	26	27	28	29	30
31	32	33	34	35	36	37	38	39	40
41	42	43	44	45	46	47	48	49	50
51	52	53	54	55	56	57	58	59	60
61	62	63	64	65	66	67	68	69	70
71	72	73	74	75	76	77	78	79	80
81	82	83	84	85	86	87	88	89	90
91	92	93	94	95	96	97	98	99	100

Hundreds Charts

1	2	3	4	5	6	7	8	9	10
11	12	13	14	15	16	17	18	19	20
21	22	23	24	25	26	27	28	29	30
31	32	33	34	35	36	37	38	39	40
41	42	43	44	45	46	47	48	49	50
51	52	53	54	55	56	57	58	59	60
61	62	63	64	65	66	67	68	69	70
71	72	73	74	75	76	77	78	79	80
81	82	83	84	85	86	87	88	89	90
91	92	93	94	95	96	97	98	99	100

1	2	3	4	5	6	7	8	9	10
11	12	13	14	15	16	17	18	19	20
21	22	23	24	25	26	27	28	29	30
31	32	33	34	35	36	37	38	39	40
41	42	43	44	45	46	47	48	49	50
51	52	53	54	55	56	57	58	59	60
61	62	63	64	65	66	67	68	69	70
71	72	73	74	75	76	77	78	79	80
81	82	83	84	85	86	87	88	89	90
91	92	93	94	95	96	97	98	99	100

1	2	3	4	5	6	7	8	9	10
11	12	13	14	15	16	17	18	19	20
21	22	23	24	25	26	27	28	29	30
31	32	33	34	35	36	37	38	39	40
41	42	43	44	45	46	47	48	49	50
51	52	53	54	55	56	57	58	59	60
61	62	63	64	65	66	67	68	69	70
71	72	73	74	75	76	77	78	79	80
81	82	83	84	85	86	87	88	89	90
91	92	93	94	95	96	97	98	99	100

1	2	3	4	5	6	7	8	9	10
11	12	13	14	15	16	17	18	19	20
21	22	23	24	25	26	27	28	29	30
31	32	33	34	35	36	37	38	39	40
41	42	43	44	45	46	47	48	49	50
51	52	53	54	55	56	57	58	59	60
61	62	63	64	65	66	67	68	69	70
71	72	73	74	75	76	77	78	79	80
81	82	83	84	85	86	87	88	89	90
91	92	93	94	95	96	97	98	99	100

Sudoku

1. Each row, column or box should contain the numbers 1, 2, 3, and 4. Find the missing number in each set.

a)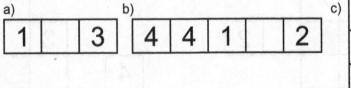

b)

c)

d)

e)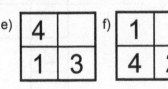

f)

2. Circle the pairs of sets that are missing the SAME number.

a)

b)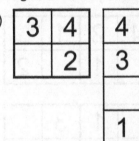

c)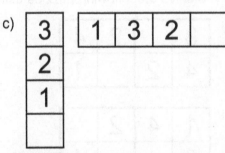

3. Find the number that should be in each shaded square below. **REMEMBER: In sudoku puzzles a number can appear only once in each row, column, or box.**

a)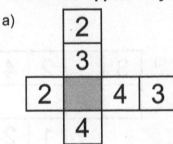

b)

c)

d)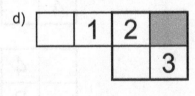

e)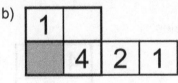

f)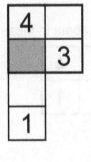

4. Fill in the shaded number. Remember that each row, column, and box must have the numbers 1, 2, 3, and 4.

a)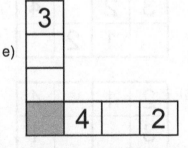

b)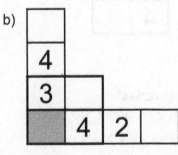

c)

Sudoku (continued)

d)

1		▨	3
	2		

e)

	1		
4		▨	2
4			

f)

			1
	3		
4			▨

BONUS: Can you find the numbers for other empty squares (besides the shaded ones)?

5. Try to solve the following puzzles using the skills you've learned.

a)

3		2	4
4	2		1

b)

4	2	1	
	1		2

c)

2			4
4	1	2	

d)

1	4	2	
3			4

e)

	1	3	
4		2	

f)

3			1
		2	4

6. Find the missing numbers in these puzzles.

a)

1		3	4
4	3		1
	1		
2	4		

b)

		4	
		3	1
3	2		4
	1	2	

c)

3		2	4
	2		
		1	2
		4	

d)

2	3		
1	2	4	
	4	2	

e)

2	1		4
3			1
		3	
4			

e)

			4
			2
4		2	
3			1

Now go back and solve the mini Sudoku puzzles!

In the sudoku pattern blocks, the numbers 1, 2, 3, and 4 are used.

Each number must appear in each row, column, and 2 × 2 box.

Sudoku *(continued)*

When solving Sudoku problems:

1. Start with a row or square that has more than one number.

2. Look along rows, columns, and in the 2 × 2 boxes to solve.

3. Only put in numbers when you are sure the number belongs there (use a pencil with an eraser in case you make a mistake).

Example:

1			
	2		
			3
	4		

1	3	2	4
4	2	3	1
2	1	4	3
3	4	1	2

Here's how you can find the numbers in the shaded second column:
The 2 and 4 are given, so we have to decide where to place 1 and 3.
There is already a 3 in the third row of the puzzle, so we must place a 3 in the first row of the shaded column and a 1 in the third row.

Continue in this way by placing the numbers 1, 2, 3, and 4 throughout the Sudoku. Before you try the problems below, try the Sudoku warm-up on the following Worksheet.

1.

a)
1			4
4	3	2	
	4	1	3
3		4	

b)
	2	1	
1	4		3
4		3	2
	3	4	

c)
1			4
	4	1	
	2	3	
3			2

d)
	4	2	
2			4
4			1
	3	4	

2.

a)
2		1	
	3		
		4	

b)
1			
		2	
4		3	

c)
	4		3
1			
	2		

d)
		4	
3			
	2		2

No unauthorized copying
Games, Activities, and Puzzles

Sudoku *(continued)*

Try these Sudoku Challenges with numbers from 1 to 6. The same rules and strategies apply!

BONUS:

3.

1	4			3	5
	6	4	5		1
	2	3		6	
4	1	6	2		3
		5		1	2
2	5		3	4	6

4.

5	4		2	1	
	1		5		6
3	6	4		5	
6			4		
		2	3		1
	2			3	

5.

4				3	
6		4		5	2
			6		
5					1
1			5	2	3
		2			

6.

	2				
4		1			2
	6		5	1	
	4				3
				6	
	3	5			1

No unauthorized copying

Sudoku *(continued)*

Try these Sudoku puzzles in the original format 9 × 9.

You must fill in the numbers from 1 through 9 in each row, column, and box. Good luck!

BONUS:

4		2		1	8	3		9
	7	1	4				6	
		6		7	3	2		
	3			6			9	5
6	2		8	4	5		1	3
8					7	6		
	9				4		8	
1		8		3	6		5	7
5		7			1	4		2

SUPER BONUS:

5		3		6			7	8
		2		8			6	
		4	7		3	9		
	7			1			3	4
1				4	5		2	
4		9				1		
	2		4		6	8		7
8			3	9			5	1
9					1		4	

For more Sudoku puzzles, check the puzzle section of your local newspaper!

Games, Activities, and Puzzles

Sudoku *(continued)*

The following special situation is useful to look for. Suppose you have a complete line (row or column) within a given box and you have a number which

a) is in another box either on the same level as the original box, or above it or below it (not diagonally);

b) is a different number from the three numbers in the completed line; and

c) is not in the same row or column as the threesome.

For example, in the sample partial grid below, we can see that the number 9 satisfies the above criteria.

As such, you can pencil in the small number 9s in the same row (different box) as the threesome, and again in the third row of the box with the threesome. This means that 9 might go in any of these places. It cannot go anywhere else in those boxes. Can you see why?

Hint: there must be a 9 in the middle row. Can it be in the first box? In the third box?

If there is more information, you might be able to narrow down the position of the number 9 to a single cell. For example, if there were already the numbers 3 and 7 in the middle box:

Or, the numbers 2 and 6 in the right-most box:

Sudoku *(continued)*

Or, the number 3 in the middle box and a 9 in the right-most cell in the box below:

9								
			3	9		5	1	8
						9	9	9
					9			

Now you have a new strategy to add to your other ones. Hopefully, this will help make solving sudokus even more fun. Try to solve the following sudoku and use the new strategy when you can.

HINT: find the numbers in the dotted cells first, then the ones in the lighter highlighted cells, using the strategy, then try to fill in the rest of the puzzle:

	4			1				6
5	9	7					4	
2			5	8				
	8			5		9		
4			7	6	3			1
		2					7	
3	7			4	9		8	2
			6			3	1	5
1	6			2				

Models of Fractions

1. Give your child a ruler and ask them to solve the following puzzles:

   a) Draw a line 1 cm long. If the line represents $\frac{1}{4}$ show what a whole line what look like.

   b) Line: 1 cm long. The line represents $\frac{1}{6}$. Show the whole.

   c) Line: 2 cm long. The line represents $\frac{1}{3}$. Show the whole.

   d) Line: 3 cm long. The line represents $\frac{1}{4}$. Show the whole.

   e) Line: $1\frac{1}{2}$ cm long. The line represents $\frac{1}{2}$. Show the whole.

   f) Line: $1\frac{1}{2}$ cm long. The line represents $\frac{1}{4}$. Show the whole.

   g) Line: 3 cm long. The line represents $\frac{1}{4}$. Show $\frac{1}{2}$.

   h) Line: 2 cm long. The line represents $\frac{1}{8}$. Show $\frac{1}{4}$.

2. Give your child counters to make a model of the following problem:
   Postcards come in packs of 4. How many packs would you need to buy to send 15 postcards?
   Write a mixed and improper fraction for the number of packs you would use.

   Your child could use a counter of a particular colour to represent the postcards they have used and a counter of a different colour to represent the postcards left over. After they have made their model, they could fill in the following chart:

Number of postcards	15
Number of packs of 4 postcards (improper fraction)	$\frac{15}{4}$
Number of packs of 4 postcards (mixed fraction)	$3\frac{3}{4}$

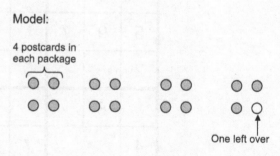

Model:

4 postcards in each package

One left over

   Here is another sample problem your child could try:

   Juice cans come in boxes of 6. How many boxes would you bring if you needed 20 cans? What fraction of the boxes would you use?

3. Give your child blocks of 2 colours and have them make models of fractions of whole numbers using the method described at the top of the worksheet. Here are some fractions they might try:

   a) $\frac{3}{4}$ of 15   b) $\frac{3}{4}$ of 16   c) $\frac{3}{5}$ of 20   d) $\frac{2}{7}$ of 21

Models of Fractions *(continued)*

4. Ask your child to draw 4 boxes of equal length on grid paper and shade 1 box:

Point out to them that $\frac{1}{4}$ of the area of the boxes is shaded. Now ask them to draw the same set of boxes, but in each box to draw a line dividing the box into 2 parts:

Now $\frac{2}{8}$ of the area is shaded. Repeat the exercise, dividing the boxes into 3 equal parts, (roughly: the sketch doesn't have to be perfectly accurate), then 4 parts, then five parts:

$\frac{3}{12}$ of the area is shaded.

$\frac{4}{16}$ of the area is shaded.

$\frac{5}{20}$ of the area is shaded.

Point out to your child that, while the appearance of the fraction changes, the same amount of area is represented:

$\frac{1}{4}$, $\frac{2}{8}$, $\frac{3}{12}$, $\frac{4}{16}$, and $\frac{5}{20}$ all represent the same amount: they are equivalent fractions.

Ask your child how each of the denominators in the fractions above can be generated from the initial fraction of $\frac{1}{4}$:

Answer:
Each denominator is a multiple of the denominator 4 in the original fraction:

$$8 = 2 \times 4 \qquad 12 = 3 \times 4 \qquad 16 = 4 \times 4 \qquad 20 = 5 \times 4$$

Then ask them how each fraction could be generated from the original fraction.

Answer:
Multiplying the numerator and denominator of the original fraction by the same number:

$$\frac{1 \times 2}{4 \times 2} = \frac{2}{8} \qquad \frac{1 \times 3}{4 \times 3} = \frac{3}{12} \qquad \frac{1 \times 4}{4 \times 4} = \frac{4}{16} \qquad \frac{1 \times 5}{4 \times 5} = \frac{5}{20}$$

Models of Fractions (continued)

Point out that multiplying the top and bottom of the original fraction by any given number, say 5, corresponds to cutting each box into that number of pieces:

$\dfrac{1}{4}$ $\begin{matrix}\times 5 \\ \times 5\end{matrix}$ ◄——— There are 5 pieces in each box.
◄——— There are 4 × 5 pieces altogether.

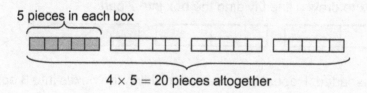

5 pieces in each box

4 × 5 = 20 pieces altogether

The fractions $\dfrac{1}{4}$, $\dfrac{2}{8}$, $\dfrac{3}{12}$, $\dfrac{4}{16}$ ... form a **family of equivalent fractions**. Notice that no whole number greater than 1 will divide into both the numerator and denominator of $\dfrac{1}{4}$: $\dfrac{1}{4}$ is said to be reduced to lowest terms. By multiplying the top and bottom of a reduced fraction by various whole numbers, you can generate an entire fraction family. For instance, $\dfrac{2}{5}$ generates this family:

$$\dfrac{2 \times 2}{5 \times 2} = \dfrac{4}{10} \qquad \dfrac{2 \times 3}{5 \times 3} = \dfrac{6}{15} \qquad \dfrac{2 \times 4}{5 \times 4} = \dfrac{8}{20}$$

Models of Decimals

Children often make mistakes in comparing decimals where one of the decimals is expressed in tenths and the other in hundredths. (For instance, they will say that .17 is greater than .2.) The following activity will help your child understand the relation between tenths and hundredths.

Give your child a set of play-money dimes and pennies. Explain that a dime is a tenth of a dollar (which is why it is written as $0.10), and a penny is a hundredth of a dollar (which is why it is written as $0.01).

Ask your child to make models of the amounts in the left-hand column of the chart below and to write as many names for the amounts as they can think of in the right-hand columns (sample answers are provided in italics):

Amount	Amount in Pennies	Decimal Names (in words)	Decimal Names (in numbers)
2 dimes	*20 pennies*	*2 tenths (of a dollar)* *20 hundredths*	*.2* *.20*
3 pennies	*3 pennies*	*3 hundredths*	*.03*
4 dimes and 3 pennies	*43 pennies*	*4 tenths and 3 hundredths* *43 hundredths*	*.43* *.43*

You should also write various amounts of money on a sheet of paper and have your child make models of the amounts (e.g., make models of .3 dollars, .27 dollars, .07 dollars, etc.). Also challenge them to make models of amounts that have 2 different decimal representations (e.g., 2 dimes can be written as .2 dollars or .20 dollars).

When you feel your child is able to translate between money and decimal notation, ask them to say whether they would rather have .2 dollars or .17 dollars. In their answer, they should say exactly how many pennies each amount represents (e.g., they must articulate that .2 represents 20 pennies and so it is actually the larger amount).

Amount (in dollars)	Amount (in pennies)
.2	
.15	

For extra practice, ask your child to fill in the right-hand column of the chart and then circle the greater amount. (Create several charts of this sort for them.)

Magic Trick

In the magic trick below, the magician can always predict the result of a sequence of operations performed on any chosen number. Try the trick with your child, then encourage them to figure out how it works using a block to stand in for the mystery number (give lots of hints).

The Trick	The Algebra	
Pick any number.	□	Use a square block to represent the mystery number.
Add 4.	□ ○○○○	Use 4 circles to represent the 4 ones that were added.
Multiply by 2.	□ ○○○○ □ ○○○○	Create 2 sets of blocks to show the doubling.
Subtract 2.	□ ○○○ □ ○○○	Take away 2 circles to show the subtraction.
Divide by 2.	□ ○○○	Remove one set of blocks to show the division.
Subtract the mystery number.	○○○	Remove the square.

The answer is 3!

No matter what number you choose, after performing the operations in the magic trick, you will always get the number 3. The model above shows why the trick works.

Encourage your child to make up their own trick of the same type.

Models for Algebra

Give your child two containers to represent the two balance scales in the problems that follow. Your child will place blocks into each container according to the picture (e.g., circle = red block, triangle = blue block). Your child must solve the problem by isolating the block that represents the solution (for instance, in the first **EXAMPLE** they must isolate the triangle). Your child can add or remove blocks from the containers, but they must follow two rules. Start with the first rule:

RULE 1: You may add or remove one or more blocks from one container as long as you add or remove the same number of blocks from the other container. (This mirrors the algebraic rule that whatever you add or subtract from one side of an equation you must add or subtract from the other side.)

EXAMPLE:

If 2 blocks are taken from the left side of the scale,
then 2 blocks must be taken from the right side as well.

Let your students practice with problems such as:

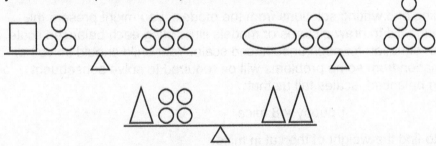

Ask your child to write an equation that represents each scale. What did they do to solve the problem? Ask them to write down the solution. In the **EXAMPLE** above, the equation and the solution will look like:

$\triangle + 2 = 5$ remove (subtract) two from both sides: $\triangle = 5 - 2 = 3$

Present the second rule:

RULE 2: If all the blocks in one container are of a particular type, and all blocks in the other container are of a particular type, and if you can group the blocks in each container equally (and into exactly the same number of sets), you may remove all but one of the sets of blocks from each container.

EXAMPLE:

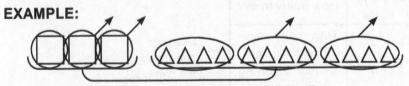

The blocks are placed into 3 equal sets on either side.
So 2 sets can be removed from each side.

In the picture above, the blocks are grouped into three equal sets of squares (1 square in each set) and three equal sets of triangles (4 triangles in each set). Each square must weigh the same as 4 triangles. So you can remove all but one group of squares and triangles without unbalancing the scale.

Models for Algebra *(continued)*

This rule mirrors the algebraic rule that you may divide both sides of an equation by the same number. The equation and the solution for the example above would be written as:

$$3 \times \square = 12, \text{ divide both sides by 3, so } \square = 12 \div 3 = 4.$$

Let your child practice with problems such as:

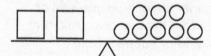 

Encourage your child to replace the symbols in the equations with letters.

Your child should write the equations and solutions for each problem. Now let your child try more complicated problems that require the use of both rules, such as:

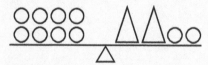 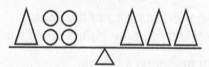

When your child is comfortable finding and writing solutions from the models, you might present the sample problems below and ask your child to draw pictures or models illustrating each balanced scale. Next, ask them to write and solve an equation for each unbalanced scale. Your child should solve the problems in sequence, since information from some problems will be required to solve subsequent problems. For example, the first two balanced scales tell us that:

> 1 puppy = 1 cat + 3 mice   1 puppy = 8 mice

This information will be necessary to find the weight of the cat in mice.

SAMPLE PROBLEMS:

The scales on the left are balanced perfectly. Can you balance the scales on the right?

Balanced Scales		Unbalanced Scales	
A puppy and 2 mice	A cat and 5 mice	A puppy	How many cats and mice?
A puppy and 2 mice	10 mice	A puppy	How many mice?
A dog	5 puppies	A cat	How many mice?
Two cows	5 dogs	A dog and a mouse	How many mice?
		A cow	How many cats? Find a second solution involving dogs, puppies and mice.

Use your solution to the previous problems. ←

Give your child several puzzles of the form: $36 + 2\square = 61$. Which digit is missing? Encourage your child to use a systematic search or to solve the equations by subtraction. (**NOTE:** The square here represents the missing digit, not a number as it did earlier.)

UNIT 1

Number Sense 1

NS8-1 Factors and Multiples

> The **multiples** of a number are the numbers you say when counting by that number.
>
> 15 is a **multiple** of both 3 and 5
>
> $3 \times 5 = 15$
>
> 3 and 5 are both **factors** of 15
>
> 0 is a **multiple** of both 0 and 4
>
> $0 \times 4 = 0$
>
> 0 and 4 are both **factors** of 0

1. List the first few multiples of these numbers.

   a) 3: _0_ , _3_ , _6_ , ____ , ____ , ____ , ____

   b) 4: ____ , ____ , ____ , ____ , ____ , ____ , ____

   c) 5: ____ , ____ , ____ , ____ , ____ , ____ , ____

2. Look at the lists you made in Question 1.

   a) Is 12 a multiple of 4? _____ How do you know? _____

   b) Is 17 a multiple of 5? _____ How do you know? _____

   c) Is 0 a multiple of 3? _____ Of 4? _____ Of 5? _____

3. a) Write 0 as a multiple of 17: $0 = 17 \times$ _____

   b) Which whole numbers is 0 a multiple of? Explain. _____

   _____

4. Rewrite each statement in a way that means the same thing but uses the word "factor."

   a) 20 is a multiple of 5.   _____

   b) 9 is a multiple of 1.   _____

   c) 0 is a multiple of 8.   _____

   d) 8 is a multiple of 8.   _____

   e) 11 is not a multiple of 4.   _____

   f) Every number is a multiple of 1.   _____

   g) Every number is a multiple of itself.   _____

   h) 0 is a multiple of any number.   _____

5. Rewrite each statement in a way that means the same thing but uses the word "multiple."

   a) 5 is a factor of 15.   b) 2 is a factor of 18.
   c) 3 is a factor of 0.   d) Every number is a factor of 0.
   e) 1 is a factor of 7.   f) 1 is a factor of every number.
   g) 6 is a factor of 6.   h) Any number is a factor of itself.

NS8-1 Factors and Multiples (continued)

6. Alana wants to find all pairs of numbers that multiply to give 10.

She lists each number from 1 to 10 in a chart. She looks for a second number that multiplies with the first to give 10.

a) Why didn't Alana list any number greater than 10 in the first column of her table?

b) Why didn't Alana list 0 in the first column of her table?

1st	2nd
1	10
2	5
3	
4	
5	2
6	
7	
8	
9	
10	1

7. Use Alana's method to find all pairs of numbers that multiply to give the number in bold.

a) **6**

1st	2nd
1	
2	
3	
4	
5	
6	

b) **8**

1st	2nd
1	
2	
3	
4	
5	
6	
7	
8	

c) **9**

1st	2nd
1	
2	
3	
4	
5	
6	
7	
8	
9	

8. Cross out the pairs that are repeated in Question 7.

9. Connor makes a chart to list all the factors of 20. He doesn't want to write and check all the numbers from 1 to 20. He starts his list as follows:

a) Connor knows that $5 \times 4 = 20$. He thinks that if $6 \times \blacksquare = 20$, then $\blacksquare$ must be less than 4. Explain his thinking.

b) Explain why Connor's list is complete.

1st	2nd
1	20
2	10
3	
4	5
5	4

10. Connor used this chart to help him identify pairs that multiply to 36. Why did he know that his search was complete as soon as he found a pair with both numbers the same?

1st	2nd
1	36
2	18
3	12
4	9
5	
6	6

11. Find all pairs of numbers that multiply to 120.

NS8-2 LCMs and GCFs

1. Mark the multiples of each number on the number lines.

2. 0 is a multiple of every number. Not counting 0, find the first 2 common multiples of:

a) 2 and 5 ____, ____   b) 2 and 3 ____, ____   c) 3 and 4 ____, ____   d) 2 and 4 ____, ____

> The **lowest common multiple (LCM)** of two or more numbers is the smallest number (not 0) that is a multiple of the numbers.

3. Look at your answers to Question 2. What is the LCM of:

a) 2 and 5 ____   b) 2 and 3 ____   c) 3 and 4 ____   d) 2 and 4 ____

4. Find the lowest common multiple of each pair of numbers.

a) 3 and 5   b) 6 and 10   c) 9 and 12   d) 2 and 6

3: 3, 6, 9, 12, *15*, 18   **6:**   **9:**   **2:**

5: 5, 10, *15*, 20   **10:**   **12:**   **6:**

LCM = _15_   LCM = ____   LCM = ____   LCM = ____

e) 2 and 10   f) 2 and 9   g) 3 and 15   h) 4 and 8   i) 8 and 8

j) 5 and 15   k) 5 and 10   l) 3 and 10   m) 6 and 15   n) 6 and 8

5. a) How can you find the second common multiple of two numbers from the first?

b) The first common multiple of 18 and 42 is 126. What is the second common multiple? _____

6. Find all the factors of each number by dividing the number by the whole numbers in increasing order—divide by 1, 2, 3, 4, 5, and so on. How do you know when you can stop dividing?

a) 33   b) 55   c) 65   d) 66   e) 90

1, 3, 11, 33

NS8-2 LCMs and GCFs *(continued)*

> The greatest number that is a factor of two or more numbers is called the **greatest common factor (GCF)** of the numbers.

7. Use your answers to Question 6. Find the greatest common factor of:

a) 33 and 55   b) 33 and 66   c) 33 and 90   d) 65 and 66

e) 33 and 65   f) 55 and 65   g) 33, 55 and 65   h) 55, 65 and 90

> Two numbers are called **consecutive** if one number is the next number after the other.
>
> Example: 13 and 14 are consecutive because 14 is the next number after 13.

INVESTIGATION 1 ▶ What is the GCF of two consecutive numbers?

A. Find the factors of each number and then the GCF of each pair.

a) 14 and 15   b) 24 and 25   c) 27 and 28   d) 44 and 45

    14: 1, 2, 7, 14   **24**:   **27**:   **44**:

    15: 1, 3, 5, 15   **25**:   **28**:   **45**:

    GCF: __1__   GCF: ____   GCF: ____   GCF: ____

B. Make a conjecture about the GCF of any two consecutive numbers.

_____

C. Test your conjecture on two consecutive numbers of your choice: ____ and ____ GCF: ____

> 9 and 15 are multiples of 3.   So 15 + 9 and 15 − 9 are multiples of 3, too!
>
>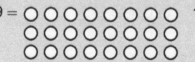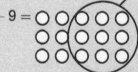

8. a) Rewrite the conclusion in the box using the word factor instead of multiple:

    3 is a factor of both 9 and 15, so 3 is a factor of both _____ *and* _____

    b) Draw pictures to show that any factor of both 8 and 20 is also a factor of both 20 + 8 and 20 − 8.

    c) Explain why any common factor of 99 and 100 must divide the sum 99 + 100.

    d) Explain why any common factor of 99 and 100 must divide the difference 100 − 99.

    e) Without finding the factors of 99 and 100, explain why their GCF is 1.

NS8-2 **LCMs and GCFs** (continued)

INVESTIGATION 2 ▶ How are the GCF, the LCM, and the product of two numbers related?

A. Complete the chart. Include three more values of your choice for *a* and *b*.

a	*b*	*a* × *b*	GCF	LCM	GCF × LCM
3	4				
2	5				
4	6				
10	15				
5	10				
3	5				
4	5				
6	9				
12	15				

B. Which two columns are the same in every row?

_____ and _____

C. Write an expression for the LCM in terms of *a* × *b* and GCF.

LCM = _____

D. When the LCM is the same as the product, what is the GCF? _____

E. Choose two more pairs of numbers *a* and *b* where *a* is a factor of *b*, and complete the chart.

a	*b*	*a* × *b*	GCF	LCM	GCF × LCM
2	6				

Which columns are equal? GCF = _____, LCM = _____ and GCF × LCM = _____ × _____

NS8-3 Prime Numbers

> A **prime** number has **exactly two** distinct factors: itself and 1.
>
> A **composite** number has **more than two** distinct factors: itself, at least one number other than itself, and 1.

1. How many distinct factors does the number 1 have? _____ Is 1 a prime number? _____

2. List all prime numbers less than 10: _____

3. List all composite numbers between 10 and 20: _____

4. What is the greatest prime number less than 30? _____

5. Circle the prime numbers in each list.

   a) 5   4   2   8   9   1   b) 6   2   3   4   7   10

   c) 11   25   14   13   17   20   d) 27   15   12   18   29   33

6. List all the factors of each number.

   a) 25: _____ 1, 5, 25 _____   b) 8: _____

   c) 12: _____   d) 16: _____

   e) 9: _____   f) 18: _____

   g) 50: _____   h) 45: _____

   i) 60: _____   j) 42: _____

7. Put a check mark in front of the numbers that are composite numbers.

   _____ 30   _____ 31   _____ 32   _____ 33   _____ 34   _____ 35   _____ 36   _____ 37

8. Write a number between 0 and 20 that has...

   a) two factors _____   b) four factors _____   c) five factors _____

9. The prime numbers 3 and 5 differ by 2. Find three other pairs of prime numbers less than 20 that differ by 2:

10. Write three consecutive numbers which are also all composite numbers:

NS8-3 Prime Numbers (continued)

11. Eratosthenes was a Greek scholar who was born over 2 000 years ago in what is now Libya. He developed a method to systematically identify prime numbers. It is called **Eratosthenes' Sieve**.

Follow these directions to use Eratosthenes' Sieve:

a) Shade the number 1 (it is not prime).

b) Circle 2, 3, 5, and 7—all the primes less than 10.

c) Shade all the remaining multiples of 2.

d) Shade all the remaining multiples of 3.

e) Shade all the remaining multiples of 5.

f) Shade all the remaining multiples of 7.

g) Circle the next uncircled number (11).

Note that all multiples of 11 less than 100 (11 × 2, 11 × 3, …, 11 × 9) are **already shaded** because they have a factor less than 10.

1	2	3	4	5	6	7	8	9	10
11	12	13	14	15	16	17	18	19	20
21	22	23	24	25	26	27	28	29	30
31	32	33	34	35	36	37	38	39	40
41	42	43	44	45	46	47	48	49	50
51	52	53	54	55	56	57	58	59	60
61	62	63	64	65	66	67	68	69	70
71	72	73	74	75	76	77	78	79	80
81	82	83	84	85	86	87	88	89	90
91	92	93	94	95	96	97	98	99	100

h) Circle the next uncircled number. How do you know all multiples of that number less than 100 are already shaded?

_____

_____

i) Now circle all the remaining numbers.

You've just used Eratosthenes' Sieve to circle all the prime numbers from 1 to 100!

12. How many prime numbers are there between 30 and 50? _____

13. Solve these riddles.

a) I am a prime number less than 100. If you add 10 or 20 to me, the result is prime. What number am I?

b) I am a prime number less than 100. My digits add to 13. What number am I?

c) I am a prime number less than 100. My tens digit is one more than my ones digit. What number am I?

d) I am a prime number between 20 and 70. If you reverse my digits, the result is a larger prime number. What number am I?

NS8-4 Prime Factorizations

Any **composite** number can be written as a product of prime numbers. This product is called the **prime factorization** of the original number.

10 × 2 **is not** a prime factorization of 20 because the number 10 is composite

5 × 2 × 2 **is** a prime factorization of 20

You can find a prime factorization for a number by using a **factor tree**.

Here is how you can make a factor tree for the number 20:

Step 1: Find any pair of numbers (not including 1) that multiply to give 20.

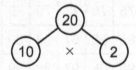

Step 2: Repeat Step 1 for the numbers on the "branches" of the tree.

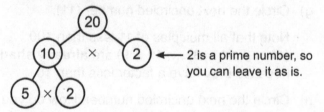

2 is a prime number, so you can leave it as is.

1. Complete the factor trees.

    a)
    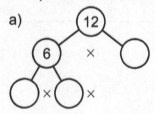

    b)
    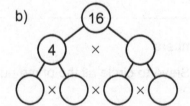

    c)
    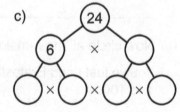

2. Write a prime factorization for each number.

    a) 20 = 10 × 2 = 2 × 5 × 2   b) 18 =   c) 8 =   d) 14 =

3. Use a factor tree to find a prime factorization for each number.

    a) 30   b) 36   c) 27   d) 28   e) 75

4. Here are some **branching patterns** for factor trees:

    Can you find a factor tree for the number 24 that has a different branching pattern from the tree in Question 1 c)?

NS8-5 Prime Factorizations and GCFs

INVESTIGATION ▶ How does the prime factorization of a number compare to the prime factorization of its factors?

A. Write the prime factorization of 72 and all its factors:

Factors of 72	Prime Factorization
1	———
2	2
3	3
4	2 × 2
6	
8	
9	
12	
18	
24	
36	
72	

B. How many 2s are in the prime factorization of 72? _____

Does any factor of 72 have more 2s in its prime factorization than 72 does? _____

C. How many 3s are in the prime factorization of 72? _____

Does any factor of 72 have more 3s in its prime factorization than 72 does? _____

D. Finish the sentences below by writing **at least** or **at most**.

Any factor of 72 must have _____ as many 2s in its prime factorization as 72 does.

Any factor of 72 must have _____ as many 3s in its prime factorization as 72 does.

E. Does 72 have a 5 in its prime factorization?

Does any factor of 72 have a 5 in its prime factorization? Explain why this is so.

---

1. The prime factorization of 180 is 2 × 2 × 3 × 3 × 5. Without doing any calculations, circle the products that show factors of 180:

2 × 3 × 5   2 × 3 × 7   2 × 3 × 3 × 5   3 × 3 × 3   5 × 5

How did you decide which products to circle?

NS8-5 Prime Factorizations and GCFs *(continued)*

2. a) Find the prime factorizations of 84 and 96. Do the rough work in your notebook.

$84 = \underline{\quad 2 \quad} \times \underline{\quad 2 \quad} \times \underline{\quad 3 \quad} \times \underline{\quad 7 \quad}$

$96 = \underline{\qquad} \times \underline{\qquad} \times \underline{\qquad} \times \underline{\qquad} \times \underline{\qquad} \times \underline{\qquad}$

b) Any factor of 84 must have in its prime factorization **at most**:

$\underline{\quad two \quad}$ 2s, $\underline{\quad one \quad}$ 3s, $\underline{\quad one \quad}$ 7s

c) Any factor of 96 must have in its prime factorization **at most**:

$\underline{\qquad\qquad}$ 2s, $\underline{\qquad\qquad}$ 3s

d) Can a common factor of 84 and 96 have any 7s in its prime factorization? $\underline{\qquad\qquad}$

How do you know? $\underline{\qquad\qquad\qquad\qquad\qquad\qquad\qquad\qquad\qquad\qquad}$

e) Any common factor of 84 and 96 must have in its prime factorization **at most**:

$\underline{\qquad\qquad}$ 2s, $\underline{\qquad\qquad}$ 3s

f) The prime factorization of the **greatest common factor (GCF)** of 84 and 96 is:

$\underline{\qquad} \times \underline{\qquad} \times \underline{\qquad}$ So the GCF of 84 and 96 is $\underline{\qquad}$.

3. The prime factorization of each number is given. Match up as many pairs of common prime factors as you can. Then find the prime factorization of the GCF and calculate the GCF.

a) $36 = 2 \times 2 \times 3 \times 3$

$24 = 2 \times 2 \times 2 \times 3$

$GCF = \underline{\quad 2 \quad} \times \underline{\quad 2 \quad} \times \underline{\quad 3 \quad} = \underline{\quad 12 \quad}$

b) $60 = 2 \times 2 \times 3 \times 5$

$50 = 2 \times 5 \times 5$

$GCF = \underline{\qquad} \times \underline{\qquad} = \underline{\qquad}$

c) $42 = 2 \times 3 \times 7$

$72 = 2 \times 2 \times 2 \times 3 \times 3$

$GCF = \underline{\qquad} \times \underline{\qquad} = \underline{\qquad}$

d) $90 = 2 \times 3 \times 3 \times 5$

$140 = 2 \times 2 \times 5 \times 7$

$GCF = \underline{\qquad} \times \underline{\qquad} = \underline{\qquad}$

4. Write a prime factorization for each number, then find the GCF of each pair.

a) 24 and 32   **b)** 24 and 30   **c)** 16 and 40   **d)** 27 and 39   **e)** 70 and 56

5. Find the GCF of the numbers.

a) 24, 30, 54   **b)** 84, 210, 300   **c)** 45, 72, 120

NS8-6 Prime Factorizations and LCMs

INVESTIGATION ▶ How does the prime factorization of a number compare to the prime factorization of its multiples?

A. Write the prime factorizations of the first ten multiples of 90 (don't include zero).

Multiples of 90	Prime factorizations
1 × 90	2 × 3 × 3 × 5
2 × 90	**2** × 2 × 3 × 3 × 5
3 × 90	**3** × 2 × 3 × 3 × 5
4 × 90	**2** × **2** × 2 × 3 × 3 × 5
5 × 90	
6 × 90	
7 × 90	
8 × 90	
9 × 90	
10 × 90	

B. How many 2s are in the prime factorization of 90? _____

Does any multiple of 90 have fewer 2s in its prime factorization than 90 does? _____

C. How many 3s are in the prime factorization of 90? _____

Does any multiple of 90 have fewer 3s in its prime factorization than 90 does? _____

D. How many 5s are in the prime factorization of 90? _____

Does any multiple of 90 have fewer 5s in its prime factorization than 90 does? _____

E. Finish the sentences below by writing **at least** or **at most**.

Any multiple of 90 must have _____ as many 2s in its prime factorization as 90 does.

Any multiple of 90 must have _____ as many 3s in its prime factorization as 90 does.

Any multiple of 90 must have _____ as many 5s in its prime factorization as 90 does.

F. Does 90 have a 7 in its prime factorization? _____

Does any multiple of 90 have a 7 in its prime factorization? _____

1. The prime factorization of 60 is 2 × 2 × 3 × 5.

Without doing any calculations, circle the products that show multiples of 60:

2 × 2 × 3 × 3 × 5   2 × 3 × 5 × 7 × 7   2 × 2 × 5 × 5 × 5   2 × 2 × 2 × 2 × 3 × 5 × 11

How did you decide which products to circle?

NS8-6 Prime Factorizations and LCMs *(continued)*

2. a) Find the prime factorizations of 90 and 168. Do the rough work in your notebook.

   90 = ___2___ × ___3___ × ___3___ × ___5___

   168 = _____ × _____ × _____ × _____ × _____

   b) Any multiple of 90 must have in its prime factorization **at least**:

   ___one___ 2s, ___two___ 3s, ___one___ 5s

   c) Any multiple of 168 must have in its prime factorization **at least**:

   _____ 2s, _____ 3s, _____ 7s

   d) Any common multiple of 90 and 168 must have in its prime factorization **at least**:

   _____ 2s, _____ 3s, _____ 5s, and _____ 7s.

   e) The **lowest common multiple (LCM)** of 90 and 168 must be:

   _____ × _____ × _____ × _____ × _____ × _____ × _____ = _____

3. a) Find the prime factorizations of 100 and 126.

   100 = _____ × _____ × _____ × _____

   126 = _____ × _____ × _____ × _____

   b) Any multiple of 100 must have in its prime factorization **at least**:

   _____ 2s, and _____ 5s

   c) Any multiple of 126 must have in its prime factorization **at least**:

   _____ 2s, _____ 3s, and _____ 7s

   d) Any common multiple of 100 and 126 must have in its prime factorization **at least**:

   _____ 2s, _____ 3s, _____ 5s, and _____ 7s.

   e) The **lowest common multiple (LCM)** of 100 and 126 must be:

   _____ × _____ × _____ × _____ × _____ × _____ × _____ = _____

4. The prime factorization of each number is given. Find the prime factorization of the LCM. Then calculate the LCM.

   a) 90 = 2 × 3 × 3 × 5 and 140 = 2 × 2 × 5 × 7

   So LCM = _____ × _____ × _____ × _____ × _____ × _____ = _____

   b) 120 = 2 × 2 × 2 × 3 × 5 and 180 = 2 × 2 × 3 × 3 × 5

   So LCM = _____ × _____ × _____ × _____ × _____ × _____ = _____

5. Find the prime factorizations of each number. Then find the prime factorization of the LCM and calculate the LCM.

   a) 35 and 84   b) 15 and 21   c) 50 and 60   d) 42 and 72   e) 24 and 48

NS8-7 Order of Operations

Addition and subtraction are done from left to right. If there are brackets, do the operations in brackets first. Example: $7 - 3 + 2 = 4 + 2 = 6$ but $7 - (3 + 2) = 7 - 5 = 2$

1. a) Calculate each expression using the correct order of operations.

$(12 + 9) - 2 - 1$ $\qquad$ $12 + (9 - 2) - 1$ $\qquad$ $12 + 9 - (2 - 1)$

$(12 + 9 - 2) - 1$ $\qquad$ $12 + (9 - 2 - 1)$ $\qquad$ $(12 + 9) - (2 - 1)$

   b) How many different answers did you get in part a)? _____

2. a) Add brackets in different ways to get as many different answers as you can.

   i) $12 + 9 + 2 + 1$ $\qquad$ ii) $12 - 9 + 2 - 1$ $\qquad$ iii) $12 - 9 - 2 - 1$

   b) How many different answers did you get in part a)? i) _____ ii) _____ iii) _____

   c) Check all that apply. The order of operations affects the answer when the expression consists of…

   ☐ addition only $\qquad$ ☐ subtraction only $\qquad$ ☐ addition and subtraction

Multiplication and division are done from left to right. If there are brackets, do the operations in brackets first. Example: $15 \div 5 \times 3 = 3 \times 3 = 9$ but $15 \div (5 \times 3) = 15 \div 15 = 1$

3. Evaluate each expression.

   a) $4 \times 3 \div 6 \times 7$ $\qquad$ b) $6 \times 4 \div 2 \div 3$ $\qquad$ c) $30 \div 5 \div (2 \times 3)$ $\qquad$ d) $16 \times 2 \div (4 \times 2)$

4. a) Add brackets in different ways to get as many different answers as you can.

   i) $2 \times 3 \times 2 \times 5$ $\qquad$ ii) $64 \div 8 \div 4 \div 2$ $\qquad$ iii) $90 \div 5 \times 6 \div 3$

   b) Which expressions in part a) give the same answer, no matter where you place the brackets?

5. Do the operation in brackets first.

   a) $18 + (6 \times 3)$ $\qquad$ b) $(18 + 6) \times 3$ $\qquad$ c) $(18 + 6) \div 3$ $\qquad$ d) $18 + (6 \div 3)$
   $= 18 + 18 = 36$

   e) $18 - (6 \times 3)$ $\qquad$ f) $(18 - 6) \times 3$ $\qquad$ g) $(18 - 6) \div 3$ $\qquad$ h) $18 - (6 \div 3)$

6. Check all that apply. The order of operations affects the answer when the expression combines…

   ☐ addition and multiplication $\qquad\qquad$ ☐ addition and division

   ☐ subtraction and multiplication $\qquad\qquad$ ☐ subtraction and division

   ☐ addition and subtraction $\qquad\qquad$ ☐ multiplication and division

NS8-7 Order of Operations (continued)

Mathematicians have ordered the operations to avoid writing brackets all the time. The order is:

1. Operations in brackets.

2. Multiplication and division, from left to right.

3. Addition and subtraction, from left to right

Example: $3 \times 5 + 3 \times 6 = (3 \times 5) + (3 \times 6)$ but $3 \times (5 + 3) \times 6$
$\qquad\qquad\qquad\qquad = 15 + 18 \qquad\qquad\qquad\qquad\qquad\qquad = 3 \times 8 \times 6$
$\qquad\qquad\qquad\qquad = 33 \qquad\qquad\qquad\qquad\qquad\qquad\quad\ = 144$

Notice that the brackets in the first expression are not necessary.

7. Evaluate each expression. Use the correct order of operations.

a) $4 \times 2 - 7$ 　　　 b) $3 + 6 \div 3$ 　　　 c) $9 - 2 \times 4$ 　　　 d) $70 \div 7 + 4$

e) $9 + 9 \div 3 - 5$ 　　 f) $3 \times 7 - 6 \div 2$ 　　 g) $(9 - 5) \times 3$ 　　 h) $(17 - 9) \div 4$

8. Translate the instructions into mathematical expressions.

a) Add 8 and 3. Then subtract 4. Then multiply by 3. $\qquad\underline{\quad (8 + 3 - 4) \times 3 \quad}$

b) Subtract 6 from 9. Then multiply by 2. Then add 4. $\underline{\qquad\qquad\qquad\qquad}$

c) Multiply 6 and 5. Then subtract from 32. Then add 5. $\underline{\qquad\qquad\qquad\qquad}$

9. Write the expressions in words.

a) $(6 + 2) \times 3$ 　　 $\underline{Add \qquad and \qquad . \text{ Then multiply by} \qquad .}$

b) $(24 - 2 \times 6) \div 4$ 　 $\underline{Multiply \qquad and \qquad . \text{ Then subtract from} \qquad . \text{ Then}}$

c) $4 \times (3 - 1 + 5)$ 　 $\underline{\qquad\qquad\qquad\qquad\qquad\qquad\qquad}$

d) $(3 + 2 \times 6) \div 5$ 　 $\underline{\qquad\qquad\qquad\qquad\qquad\qquad\qquad}$

10. Calculate the expression in the box in your notebook. Which expression without brackets gives the same answer?

a) $\boxed{8 - (5 + 2)}$ $=$ $8 - 5 - 2$ or $8 - 5 + 2$ 　　 b) $\boxed{7 - (3 - 2)}$ $=$ $7 - 3 - 2$ or $7 - 3 + 2$

c) $\boxed{7 + (5 - 2)}$ $=$ $7 + 5 - 2$ or $7 + 5 + 2$ 　　 d) $\boxed{6 + (2 + 4)}$ $=$ $6 + 2 + 4$ or $6 + 2 - 4$

11. a) Add brackets in different ways to get as many different answers as you can.

　　 i) $3 + 1 \times 7 - 2$ 　　　　 ii) $16 - 4 \times 2 + 8$ 　　　　 iii) $16 \div 4 \times 2 + 8$

b) How many different answers did you get in part a)? i) _____ ii) _____ iii) _____

12. How would you write the expressions below without brackets? Justify your answer.

a) $5 \times 8 \div (4 \div 2)$ 　　　　 b) $5 \times 8 \div (4 \times 2)$ 　　　　 c) $5 \times 8 \times (4 \div 2)$

NS8-8 Fractions

Fractions name equal parts of a whole.

This pie is cut into 4 equal parts, and 3 of the parts are shaded.

So $\frac{3}{4}$ of the pie is shaded.

$\frac{3}{4}$

The **numerator** tells you how many parts are counted.

The **denominator** tells you how many equal parts are in a whole.

1. Name the following fractions.

a)

b)

c)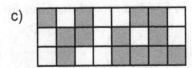

2. Draw lines to divide each figure into equal parts. Then say what fraction of each figure is shaded.

a)

b)

c)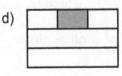

d)

3. Divide each line into the given parts, as done in part a).

a) Thirds

b) Halves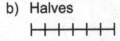

c) Thirds

d) Quarters

e) Fifths

Fractions can name parts of a set. In this set, $\frac{3}{5}$ of the figures are pentagons, $\frac{1}{5}$ are squares, and $\frac{1}{5}$ are circles:

4. Fill in the blanks for this set:

a) $\frac{4}{10}$ of the figures are _____.

b) $\frac{3}{10}$ of the figures are _____.

c) _____ of the figures are squares.

d) _____ of the figures are triangles.

5.

	Whole Numbers from 2 to 9	Whole Numbers from 10 to 16
Prime Numbers	2, 3,	
Composite Numbers		

a) Fill in the chart.

b) What fraction of the whole numbers from 2 to 9 are composite?

c) What fraction of the whole numbers from 2 to 16 are prime?

NS8-9 Mixed Numbers

Mattias and his friends ate the amount of pie shown.

They ate two and three quarter pies altogether (or $2\frac{3}{4}$ pies).

$2\frac{3}{4}$ is called a **mixed number** because it is a mixture of a whole number and a fraction.

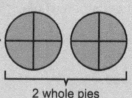

2 whole pies   and $\frac{3}{4}$ of another pie

1. Follow the example to find the **mixed number** for each picture.

a)

___2___ whole pies and ___$\frac{1}{3}$___

of another pie = __$2\frac{1}{3}$__ pies

b)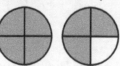

____ whole pie and ____

of another pie = ____ pies

c)

____ whole pies and ____

of another pie = ____ pies

2. Write each fraction as a **mixed number**.

a)

b)

c)

d)

3. Shade the area given by the mixed number. Note: There may be more figures than you need.

a) $2\frac{2}{3}$

b) $3\frac{5}{6}$

c) $1\frac{3}{4}$

d) $2\frac{4}{5}$

4. Sketch:

a) $2\frac{1}{3}$ pies   b) $3\frac{3}{4}$ squares   c) $1\frac{3}{5}$ pies   d) $2\frac{5}{6}$ rectangles   e) $3\frac{7}{8}$ circles

5. Order from smallest to largest: $4\frac{2}{3}$, $4\frac{1}{4}$, $3\frac{3}{4}$.

6. Which is closer to 5: $5\frac{3}{4}$ or $4\frac{2}{3}$? Explain.

NS8-10 Improper Fractions

Huan-Yue and her friends ate **9** quarter-sized pieces of pizza:

Altogether, they ate $\frac{9}{4}$ pizzas.

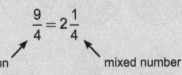

$$\frac{9}{4} = 2\frac{1}{4}$$

improper fraction · · · · · mixed number

When the numerator of a fraction is larger than the denominator, the fraction represents
more than a whole. Such fractions are called **improper fractions**.

1. Write these fractions as **improper fractions**.

   a)

   b)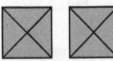

   c)

   d)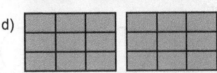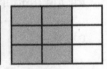

   e)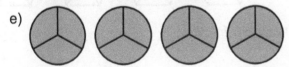

   f)

2. Shade one piece at a time until you have shaded the amount given by the
   improper fraction.

   a) $\frac{13}{4}$

   b) $\frac{5}{2}$

   c) $\frac{8}{3}$

   d) $\frac{15}{5}$

3. Sketch:

   a) $\frac{7}{3}$ pies

   b) $\frac{13}{4}$ squares

   c) $\frac{9}{2}$ parallelograms

   d) $\frac{11}{6}$ rectangles

   e) $\frac{17}{8}$ circles

4. Order from smallest to largest: $\frac{7}{4}, \frac{9}{4}, \frac{9}{3}, \frac{10}{3}$.

5. Which fractions are improper fractions? How do you know?

   a) $\frac{5}{7}$

   b) $\frac{13}{11}$

   c) $1\frac{9}{8}$

   d) $\frac{8}{3}$

NS8-11 Mixed and Improper Fractions

1. Write these fractions as **mixed numbers** and as **improper fractions**.

a)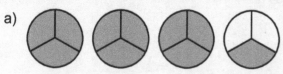

b)

c)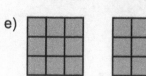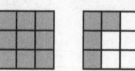

d)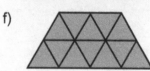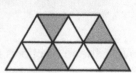

e)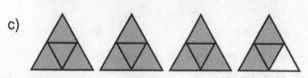

f)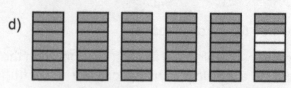

2. Shade the amount of pie given by the mixed fraction. Then write an improper fraction for the amount.

a) $4\frac{1}{2}$

b) $3\frac{3}{5}$

Improper fraction: _____

Improper fraction: _____

3. Shade the amount of area given by the improper fraction. Then write a mixed number for the amount.

a) $\frac{11}{3}$

b) $\frac{11}{4}$

Mixed number: _____

Mixed number: _____

c) $\frac{17}{6}$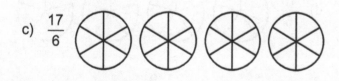

d) $\frac{21}{8}$

Mixed number: _____

Mixed number: _____

4. Draw a picture to find out which fraction is greater.

a) $3\frac{1}{2}$, $2\frac{2}{3}$, $\frac{5}{3}$
b) $1\frac{4}{5}$, $2\frac{1}{4}$, $\frac{11}{5}$
c) $\frac{13}{4}$, $\frac{7}{2}$, $2\frac{2}{3}$
d) $\frac{15}{8}$, $\frac{13}{5}$, $\frac{7}{3}$

5. How could you use division to find out how many whole pies are in $\frac{24}{7}$ of a pie? Explain.

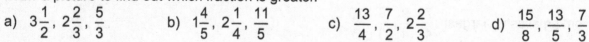

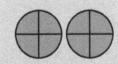

There are 4 quarter pieces in 1 pie.   There are 8 (2 × 4) quarters in 2 pies.   There are 12 (3 × 4) quarters in 3 pies.

12 pieces (3 × 4)   1 extra piece

How many quarter pieces are in $3\frac{1}{4}$ pies? $3\frac{1}{4}$ So there are 13 quarter pieces altogether.

1. Find the number of **halves** in each amount.

   a) 1 pie = _____ halves

   b) 3 pies = _____ halves

   c) 5 pies = _____ halves

   d) $2\frac{1}{2}$ pies = _____ halves

   e) $4\frac{1}{2}$ pies = _____ halves

   f) $6\frac{1}{2}$ pies = _____

2. Find the number of **thirds** in each amount.

   a) 1 pie = _____ thirds

   b) 2 pies = _____ thirds

   c) 3 pies = _____ thirds

   d) $1\frac{1}{3}$ pies = _____ thirds

   e) $3\frac{2}{3}$ pies = _____

   f) $5\frac{1}{3}$ pies = _____

3. A box holds 4 cans, so each can is a **fourth**. Find the number of cans in each amount.

   a) 2 boxes hold _____ cans

   b) $2\frac{1}{2}$ boxes hold _____ cans

   c) $4\frac{3}{4}$ boxes hold _____ cans

4. If a bag holds 16 peas, then…

   a) $1\frac{1}{16}$ bags hold _____ peas

   b) $2\frac{1}{2}$ bags hold _____ peas

   c) $3\frac{1}{4}$ bags hold _____ peas

5. Write the mixed numbers as improper fractions.

   a) $2\frac{2}{3} = \frac{}{3}$

   b) $3\frac{1}{2} = \frac{}{2}$

   c) $5\frac{4}{5} =$

   d) $4\frac{3}{4} =$

   e) $5\frac{2}{7} =$

6. Envelopes come in packs of 8. Alice used $3\frac{7}{8}$ packs. How many envelopes did she use? _____

7. Maia and her friends ate $2\frac{3}{4}$ pizzas. How many quarter-sized pieces did they eat? _____

BONUS ▶

8. How many quarters are there in $7\frac{1}{2}$ dollars? _____

9. Cindy needs $4\frac{2}{3}$ cups of flour.

   a) How many scoops of cup A would she need? _____

   b) How many scoops of cup B would she need? _____

A   B

$\frac{1}{3}$ cup $\frac{1}{6}$ cup

NS8-13 More Mixed Numbers and Improper Fractions

How many whole pies are there in $\frac{13}{4}$ pies?

There are 13 pieces altogether, and each pie has 4 pieces. So you can find the number of whole pies by dividing 13 by 4: **13 ÷ 4 = 3 remainder 1**

There are 3 whole pies and 1 quarter left over: $\frac{13}{4} = 3\frac{1}{4}$

1. Find the number of whole pies in each amount by dividing.

   a) $\frac{4}{2}$ pies = _____ whole pies   b) $\frac{15}{3}$ pies = _____ whole pies   c) $\frac{16}{4}$ pies = _____ whole pies

   d) $\frac{21}{7}$ pies = _____ whole pies   e) $\frac{25}{5}$ pies = _____ whole pies   f) $\frac{30}{6}$ pies = _____ whole pies

2. Find the number of whole pies and the number of pieces remaining by dividing.

   a) $\frac{5}{2}$ pies = ___2___ whole pies and ___1___ half pie = ___$2\frac{1}{2}$___ pies

   b) $\frac{11}{2}$ pies = _____ whole pies and _____ half pie = _____ pies

   c) $\frac{13}{3}$ pies = _____ whole pies and _____ third = _____ pies

   d) $\frac{17}{4}$ pies = _____ whole pies and _____ fourth = _____ pies

3. Write the following improper fractions as mixed numbers.

   a) $\frac{5}{2}$ b) $\frac{14}{3}$ c) $\frac{17}{6}$ d) $\frac{21}{4}$ e) $\frac{29}{5}$ f) $\frac{31}{7}$ g) $\frac{70}{9}$ h) $\frac{61}{8}$

4. Write a mixed number and improper fraction for the total number of litres:

5. Write a mixed number and improper fraction for the length of the rope:

1 m

6. Order from smallest to largest: $\frac{7}{3}, \frac{9}{4}, \frac{5}{2}$.

7. Between which two whole numbers is $\frac{21}{8}$?

8. How much greater than a whole is each fraction?

   a) $\frac{11}{7}$ b) $\frac{8}{5}$ c) $\frac{5}{3}$ d) $\frac{19}{10}$

9. Which fractions are greater than 3 but less than 4?

   a) $\frac{17}{4}$ b) $\frac{5}{3}$ c) $\frac{16}{5}$ d) $\frac{5}{2}$ e) $\frac{11}{6}$

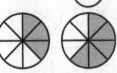

NS8-14 Comparing Fractions — Introduction

1. Shade the given amount in each pie. Then circle the greater fraction in each pair.

   a) $\frac{3}{8}$ $\boxed{\frac{5}{8}}$

   b) $\frac{7}{9}$ $\frac{5}{9}$

   c) $\frac{9}{10}$ $\frac{8}{10}$

2. Two fractions have the same denominators (bottoms) but different numerators (tops)?

   How can you tell which fraction is greater?

   _____

   _____

3. Shade the given amount in each pie. Then circle the greater fraction in each pair.

   a) $\frac{1}{3}$ $\frac{1}{4}$

   b) $\frac{1}{10}$ $\frac{1}{2}$

   c) $\frac{3}{5}$ $\frac{3}{10}$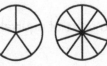

4. Two fractions have the same numerators (tops) but different denominators (bottoms).

   How can you tell which fraction is greater?

   _____

   _____

5. Write the fractions in order from least to greatest.

   a) $\frac{1}{8}, \frac{1}{3}, \frac{1}{15}$

   b) $\frac{2}{9}, \frac{2}{6}, \frac{2}{8}, \frac{2}{12}$

   c) $\frac{4}{5}, \frac{1}{5}, \frac{3}{5}$

   ___ ___ ___   ___ ___ ___   ___ ___ ___

   d) $\frac{9}{10}, \frac{2}{10}, \frac{1}{10}, \frac{5}{10}$

   e) $\frac{5}{8}, \frac{7}{8}, \frac{5}{9}$

   f) $\frac{4}{7}, \frac{3}{7}, \frac{4}{5}$

   ___ ___ ___   ___ ___ ___   ___ ___ ___

   BONUS ▶ $\frac{15}{19}$ $\frac{9}{23}$ $\frac{11}{21}$ $\frac{11}{19}$ $\frac{6}{23}$ $\frac{9}{22}$ $\frac{15}{17}$ $\frac{9}{21}$

6. Which fraction is greater? How do you know?

   a) $\frac{7}{5}$ or $\frac{9}{5}$

   b) $4\frac{1}{4}$ or $4\frac{3}{4}$

NS8-15 Equivalent Fractions

1. Compare the fractions by shading to see which is more. Write > (more than), < (less than), or = (equal).

a)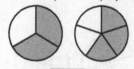

$\frac{2}{3}$ > $\frac{3}{5}$

b)

$\frac{2}{3}$ ☐ $\frac{4}{6}$

c)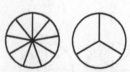

$\frac{5}{9}$ ☐ $\frac{2}{3}$

d)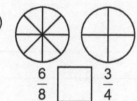

$\frac{6}{8}$ ☐ $\frac{3}{4}$

e)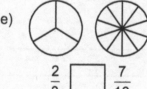

$\frac{2}{3}$ ☐ $\frac{7}{10}$

f)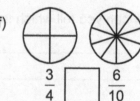

$\frac{3}{4}$ ☐ $\frac{6}{10}$

> Two fractions are said to be **equivalent** if they represent the same amount.

2. List two pairs of equivalent fractions from Question 1. _____ = _____ and _____ = _____

3. Group the squares to make an equivalent fraction. How many of the equal larger groups are shaded?

a)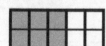

$\frac{6}{10} = \frac{3}{5}$

b)

$\frac{4}{6} = \frac{}{3}$

c)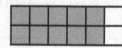

$\frac{10}{12} = \frac{}{6}$

4. Write three equivalent fractions for the amount shaded here: ___ ___ ___

5. a) Draw lines to cut the pies into:

4 equal pieces   6 equal pieces   8 equal pieces

b) Then fill in the numerators of the equivalent fractions: $\frac{1}{2} = \frac{}{4} = \frac{}{6} = \frac{}{8}$

6. Make an equivalent fraction by cutting each piece into the same number of parts.

a) $\frac{1}{2} = \frac{3}{6}$

b) $\frac{2}{3} = \frac{4}{}$

c) $\frac{2}{3} = \frac{}{9}$

d) $\frac{2}{5} = \frac{}{15}$

NS8-16 Comparing Fractions Using Equivalent Fractions

When you multiply the numerator and denominator of a fraction by the same number, you create an **equivalent fraction**.

$$\frac{1}{2} = \frac{1 \times 5}{2 \times 5} = \frac{5}{10}$$

You are cutting each piece into 5 parts

1. Write six equivalent fractions by skip counting to find the numerators.

a) $\dfrac{2}{3} = \dfrac{}{6} = \dfrac{}{9} = \dfrac{}{12} = \dfrac{}{15} = \dfrac{}{18} = \dfrac{}{21}$

b) $\dfrac{3}{5} = \dfrac{}{10} = \dfrac{}{15} = \dfrac{}{20} = \dfrac{}{25} = \dfrac{}{30} = \dfrac{}{35}$

2. Find two fractions with the same denominators from the lists in Question 1. _____ and _____

Which fraction is greater: $\dfrac{2}{3}$ or $\dfrac{3}{5}$? _____

How do you know? _____

3. Create an equivalent fraction with denominator 36 by multiplying the numerator and denominator by the same number:

a) $\dfrac{1}{2} \dfrac{\times 18}{\times 18} = \dfrac{18}{36}$ b) $\dfrac{4}{9} = \dfrac{}{36}$ c) $\dfrac{5}{6} = \dfrac{}{36}$ d) $\dfrac{11}{18} = \dfrac{}{36}$

e) $\dfrac{2}{3} = \dfrac{}{36}$ f) $\dfrac{3}{4} = \dfrac{}{36}$ g) $\dfrac{1}{6} = \dfrac{}{36}$ h) $\dfrac{5}{12} = \dfrac{}{36}$

4. Write the fractions from Question 3 in order from smallest to largest.

5. a) Write several fractions equivalent to $\dfrac{1}{2}$.

$\dfrac{1}{2} = \dfrac{}{4} = \dfrac{}{6} = \dfrac{}{8} = \dfrac{}{10} = \dfrac{}{12} = \dfrac{}{14} = \dfrac{}{16} = \dfrac{}{18} = \dfrac{}{20}$

b) How much more than a half is each fraction below?

$\dfrac{3}{4}$ is _____ more than $\dfrac{1}{2}$ $\dfrac{4}{6}$ is _____ more than $\dfrac{1}{2}$ $\dfrac{5}{8}$ is _____ more than $\dfrac{1}{2}$

$\dfrac{6}{10}$ is _____ more than $\dfrac{1}{2}$ $\dfrac{7}{12}$ is _____ more than $\dfrac{1}{2}$ $\dfrac{8}{14}$ is _____ more than $\dfrac{1}{2}$

c) Write all the fractions from part b) in order from smallest to largest.

NS8-17 Adding and Subtracting Fractions — Introduction

1. Imagine moving the shaded pieces from pies A and B into pie plate C.
   Show how much of pie C would be filled, then write a fraction for pie C.

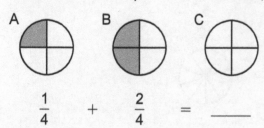

$$\frac{1}{4} \quad + \quad \frac{2}{4} \quad = \quad \underline{}$$

2. Imagine pouring the liquid from cups A and B into cup C.

   Shade the amount of liquid that would be in C. Then complete the addition statements.

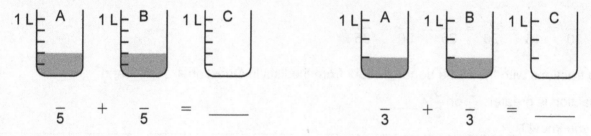

$$\frac{}{5} \quad + \quad \frac{}{5} \quad = \quad \underline{} \qquad\qquad \frac{}{3} \quad + \quad \frac{}{3} \quad = \quad \underline{}$$

3. Add.

   a) $\frac{3}{5} + \frac{1}{5} =$ b) $\frac{1}{4} + \frac{2}{4} =$ c) $\frac{2}{7} + \frac{4}{7} =$ d) $\frac{5}{8} + \frac{2}{8} =$

   e) $\frac{3}{11} + \frac{6}{11} =$ f) $\frac{10}{17} + \frac{6}{17} =$ g) $\frac{15}{24} + \frac{4}{24} =$ h) $\frac{18}{57} + \frac{13}{57} =$

4. Show how much pie would be left if you took away the amount shown.
   Then complete the fraction statement.

   a)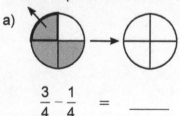

   $$\frac{3}{4} - \frac{1}{4} \quad = \quad \underline{}$$

   b)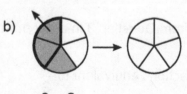

   $$\frac{3}{5} - \frac{2}{5} \quad = \quad \underline{}$$

5. Subtract.

   a) $\frac{2}{3} - \frac{1}{3} =$ b) $\frac{3}{5} - \frac{2}{5} =$ c) $\frac{6}{7} - \frac{3}{7} =$ d) $\frac{5}{8} - \frac{2}{8} =$

   e) $\frac{10}{12} - \frac{3}{12} =$ f) $\frac{6}{19} - \frac{4}{19} =$ g) $\frac{9}{28} - \frac{3}{28} =$ h) $\frac{17}{57} - \frac{12}{57} =$

6. Calculate.

   a) $\frac{2}{7} + \frac{1}{7} + \frac{3}{7} =$ b) $\frac{4}{11} + \frac{5}{11} - \frac{2}{11} =$ c) $\frac{10}{18} - \frac{7}{18} + \frac{5}{18} =$

NS8-18 Adding and Subtracting Fractions

To add fractions with different denominators:

Step 1: Find the LCM of the denominators.

Step 2: Create equivalent fractions with that denominator.

$$\frac{1}{3} + \frac{2}{5}$$

Multiples of 3: 0, 3, 6, 9, 12, **15**, 18

Multiples of 5: 0, 5, 10, **15**, 20, 25, 30

LCM (3, 5) = 15

$$\frac{1}{3} + \frac{2}{5} = \frac{5 \times 1}{5 \times 3} + \frac{2 \times 3}{5 \times 3}$$

$$= \frac{5}{15} + \frac{6}{15}$$

$$= \frac{11}{15}$$

The LCM of the denominators is called the **lowest common denominator (LCD)** of the fractions.

1. Find the LCD of each pair of fractions. Then show what numbers you would multiply the numerator and denominator of each fraction by in order to add.

a) LCD = ___6___

$$\frac{3 \times 1}{3 \times 2} + \frac{2 \times 2}{3 \times 2}$$

b) LCD = _____

$$\frac{3}{4} + \frac{1}{8}$$

c) LCD = _____

$$\frac{1}{30} + \frac{1}{6}$$

d) LCD = _____

$$\frac{3}{4} + \frac{2}{3}$$

e) LCD = _____

$$\frac{3}{7} + \frac{1}{3}$$

f) LCD = _____

$$\frac{3}{4} + \frac{1}{6}$$

g) LCD = _____

$$\frac{4}{5} + \frac{1}{10}$$

h) LCD = _____

$$\frac{1}{8} + \frac{5}{7}$$

2. Add or subtract the fractions by changing them to equivalent fractions with denominator equal to the LCD of the fractions.

a) $\frac{2}{5} + \frac{1}{4}$

b) $\frac{4}{15} + \frac{2}{3}$

c) $\frac{2}{3} - \frac{1}{8}$

d) $\frac{2}{3} - \frac{1}{12}$

=

=

=

=

=

=

=

=

e) $\frac{3}{4} + \frac{1}{8}$

f) $\frac{1}{6} + \frac{13}{24}$

g) $\frac{11}{28} - \frac{2}{7}$

h) $\frac{4}{7} + \frac{1}{8}$

i) $\frac{4}{9} - \frac{1}{6}$

3. Add or subtract.

a) $\frac{5}{6} + \frac{1}{12}$

b) $\frac{19}{25} - \frac{3}{5}$

c) $\frac{5}{7} - \frac{1}{4}$

d) $\frac{4}{9} + \frac{2}{5}$

e) $\frac{5}{8} - \frac{7}{12}$

f) $\frac{2}{3} + \frac{1}{4} + \frac{1}{2}$

g) $\frac{3}{15} + \frac{2}{3} + \frac{1}{5}$

h) $\frac{11}{15} + \frac{2}{3} - \frac{1}{5}$

i) $\frac{3}{5} + \frac{17}{30} - \frac{5}{6}$

A fraction is reduced to **lowest terms** when the greatest common factor of its numerator and denominator is the number 1.

$\frac{6}{8}$ **is not** in lowest terms because the GCF of 6 and 8 is 2.

       Factors of 6: 1, **2**, 3, 6
       Factors of 8: 1, **2**, 4, 8

$\frac{3}{4}$ **is** in lowest terms because the GCF of 3 and 4 is 1.

       Factors of 3: **1**, 3
       Factors of 4: **1**, 2, 4

4. Find the GCF of the numerator and denominator. Is the fraction in lowest terms? Write yes or no.

a) $\frac{2}{6}$ b) $\frac{3}{5}$ c) $\frac{4}{5}$ d) $\frac{5}{10}$ e) $\frac{8}{10}$

  GCF = __2__   GCF = _____   GCF = _____   GCF = _____   GCF = _____

    __*no*__   _____   _____   _____   _____

f) $\frac{7}{10}$ g) $\frac{15}{16}$ h) $\frac{14}{12}$ i) $\frac{9}{5}$ j) $\frac{5}{9}$

To reduce a fraction to lowest terms:

Step 1: Find the GCF of the numerator and denominator

Step 2: Divide both the numerator and denominator by the GCF.

5. Reduce the fractions below by dividing the numerator and the denominator by their GCF.

a) $\frac{2 \div 2}{10 \div 2} = \frac{1}{5}$ b) $\frac{2 \div}{6 \div} =$ ___   c) $\frac{2 \div}{8 \div} =$ ___   d) $\frac{2 \div}{12 \div} =$ ___

e) $\frac{6}{9} =$ ___   f) $\frac{3}{15} =$ ___   g) $\frac{4}{12} =$ ___   h) $\frac{20}{25} =$ ___

6. Add or subtract, then reduce your answer to lowest terms.

a) $\frac{5 \times 1}{5 \times 6} + \frac{1 \times 3}{10 \times 3}$ b) $\frac{13}{15} - \frac{2}{5}$ c) $\frac{5}{6} + \frac{7}{10}$ d) $\frac{22}{28} - \frac{2}{7}$

   $= \frac{5}{30} + \frac{3}{30}$

   $= \frac{8}{30} = \frac{4}{15}$

e) $\frac{1}{10} + \frac{1}{2} + \frac{1}{5}$ f) $\frac{5}{8} + \frac{1}{5} + \frac{1}{20}$ g) $\frac{1}{7} + \frac{4}{5} - \frac{8}{35}$ h) $\frac{5}{7} - \frac{8}{21} + \frac{2}{3}$

NS8-19 Adding and Subtracting Mixed Numbers

1. Add or subtract.

a) $2\frac{1}{5}$ + $3\frac{2}{5}$ = _____

b) $4\frac{3}{5} - 3\frac{1}{5} =$

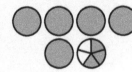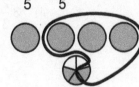

c) $2\frac{1}{5} + 2\frac{2}{5} =$

d) $3\frac{3}{7} + 2\frac{1}{7} =$

e) $5\frac{7}{8} - 3\frac{2}{8} =$

f) $7\frac{9}{15} - 4\frac{2}{15} =$

2. Add or subtract by changing the fractions to equivalent fractions.

a) $2\frac{1}{2} + 1\frac{1}{3}$

$= 2 + 1 + \frac{1}{2} + \frac{1}{3}$

$= 3 + \frac{}{6} + \frac{}{6}$

$= 3\frac{}{6}$

b) $3\frac{3}{4} - 1\frac{1}{3}$

$= 3 - 1 + \frac{3}{4} - \frac{1}{3}$

$= 2 + \frac{}{12} - \frac{}{12}$

$= 2\frac{}{12}$

c) $5\frac{2}{3} - 2\frac{3}{5}$

d) $2\frac{2}{7} + 4\frac{1}{2}$

e) $4\frac{2}{5} - 1\frac{1}{6}$

f) $2\frac{3}{8} + 4\frac{1}{3}$

3. $1\frac{1}{2} + 2\frac{2}{3} = 3\frac{7}{6}$. How can you simplify this answer?

4. $\frac{4}{5}$ is greater than $\frac{1}{3}$. How can you subtract $4\frac{1}{3} - 2\frac{4}{5}$?

5. a) Change the improper fractions to mixed numbers.

i) $\frac{7}{6} = 1\frac{1}{6}$

ii) $\frac{11}{5} =$

iii) $\frac{13}{7} =$

iv) $\frac{11}{4} =$

b) Rewrite each mixed number to make the improper fraction a proper fraction.

i) $3\frac{7}{6} = 3 + \frac{7}{6}$

$= 3 + 1\frac{1}{6}$

$= 4\frac{1}{6}$

ii) $2\frac{4}{3} =$

$=$

$=$

iii) $4\frac{8}{5} =$

$=$

$=$

c) Add by changing the fractions to equivalent fractions. Simplify your answer as in part b).

i) $2\dfrac{2}{5}+\dfrac{2}{3}$

$= 2 + \dfrac{2}{5} + \dfrac{2}{3}$

$= 2 + \dfrac{}{15} + \dfrac{}{15}$

$= 2\dfrac{}{15} = 3\dfrac{}{15}$

ii) $3\dfrac{2}{3}+\dfrac{5}{6}$

iii) $4\dfrac{3}{4}+2\dfrac{3}{5}$

6. a) Rewrite each mixed number by regrouping 1 whole as a fraction.

Example: $4\dfrac{1}{3} = 3 + 1\dfrac{1}{3} = 3\dfrac{4}{3}$

i) $5\dfrac{3}{4}$ ii) $5\dfrac{1}{2}$ iii) $1\dfrac{1}{6}$ iv) $2\dfrac{3}{4}$ v) $3\dfrac{2}{5}$ vi) $4\dfrac{5}{7}$

b) Subtract by rewriting the first mixed number as in part a):

i) $3\dfrac{1}{5} - 1\dfrac{3}{4} = 2\dfrac{6}{5} - 1\dfrac{3}{4}$

$= 2\dfrac{24}{20} - 1\dfrac{15}{20} = 1\dfrac{9}{20}$

ii) $4\dfrac{1}{3} - 2\dfrac{3}{5}$

7. Add or subtract by first changing the mixed numbers to improper fractions.

a) $3\dfrac{1}{3}+5\dfrac{3}{4}$

$= \dfrac{10}{3} + \dfrac{23}{4}$

$= \dfrac{40}{12} + \dfrac{69}{12}$

$= \dfrac{109}{12} = 9\dfrac{1}{12}$

b) $1\dfrac{1}{5} - \dfrac{2}{3}$

c) $4\dfrac{2}{3}+2\dfrac{4}{5}$

d) $5\dfrac{1}{8} - 3\dfrac{1}{3}$

8. Sonjay cycled $6\dfrac{7}{8}$ km in the first hour, $5\dfrac{1}{2}$ km the second hour, and $4\dfrac{3}{4}$ km the third hour. How many kilometres did he cycle in the three hours?

9. A cafeteria sold $2\dfrac{5}{8}$ cheese pizzas, $4\dfrac{1}{3}$ vegetable pizzas, and $3\dfrac{1}{4}$ deluxe pizzas at lunchtime. How many pizzas did they sell altogether?

10. Gerome bought $5\dfrac{3}{4}$ metres of cloth. He used $3\dfrac{4}{5}$ to make a banner. How many metres of cloth were left over?

NS8-20 Fractions of Whole Numbers

Dan has 6 cookies. He wants to give $\frac{2}{3}$ of his cookies to his friends. To do so, he shares the cookies equally onto 3 plates:

There are 3 equal groups, so each group is $\frac{1}{3}$ of 6.

There are 2 cookies in each group, so $\frac{1}{3}$ of 6 is 2.

There are 4 cookies in two groups, so $\frac{2}{3}$ of 6 is 4.

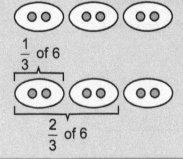

$\frac{1}{3}$ of 6

$\frac{2}{3}$ of 6

1. Write a fraction for the amount of dots shown.

a)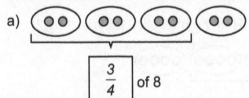

$\frac{3}{4}$ of 8

b)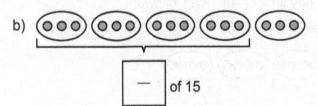

$\boxed{}$ of 15

2. Fill in the missing numbers.

a)

$\boxed{\frac{1}{3}}$ of 9 = _____

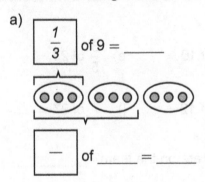

$\boxed{-}$ of _____ = _____

b)

$\boxed{-}$ of 8 = _____

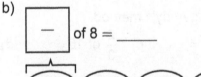

$\boxed{-}$ of _____ = _____

c)

$\boxed{-}$ of 12 = _____

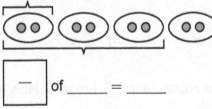

$\boxed{-}$ of _____ = _____

d)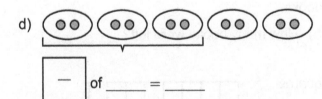

$\boxed{-}$ of _____ = _____

e)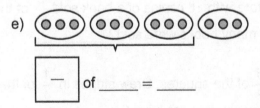

$\boxed{-}$ of _____ = _____

3. Draw a circle to show the given amount.

a) $\frac{2}{3}$ of 6

b) $\frac{3}{4}$ of 8

4. Draw the correct number of dots in each circle, then draw a larger circle to show the given amount.

a) $\frac{2}{3}$ of 12

b) $\frac{1}{3}$ of 15

NS8-20 Fractions of Whole Numbers *(continued)*

5. Find the fraction of the whole amount by sharing the cookies equally.

   Hint: Draw the correct number of plates, place the cookies one at a time, then circle the correct amount.

   a) Find $\frac{2}{3}$ of 9 cookies.

   b) Find $\frac{3}{5}$ of 10 cookies.

   $\frac{2}{3}$ of 9 is _____

   $\frac{3}{5}$ of 10 is _____

Andy finds $\frac{2}{3}$ of 12 as follows:

Step 1: He finds $\frac{1}{3}$ of 12 by dividing 12 by 3:

Step 2: Then he multiplies the result by 2:

12 ÷ 3 = 4 (4 is $\frac{1}{3}$ of 12)

4 × 2 = 8 (8 is $\frac{2}{3}$ of 12)

---

6. Find the following amounts using Andy's method.

   a) $\frac{2}{3}$ of 9 =

   b) $\frac{3}{4}$ of 8 =

   c) $\frac{2}{3}$ of 15 =

   d) $\frac{2}{5}$ of 10 =

   e) $\frac{3}{5}$ of 25 =

   f) $\frac{3}{7}$ of 21 =

   g) $\frac{5}{7}$ of 28 =

   h) $\frac{3}{8}$ of 24 =

   i) $\frac{3}{4}$ of 12 =

   j) $\frac{1}{3}$ of 27 =

7. There are 24 students on a soccer team. $\frac{3}{8}$ are girls. How many girls are on the team? _____

8. A bookstore with 18 copies of a book sold $\frac{5}{6}$ of the books.

   a) How many books were sold? _____

   b) How many books were left? _____

9. Shade $\frac{5}{8}$ of the squares. Draw stripes in $\frac{1}{4}$ of the squares.
   How many squares are blank? _____

   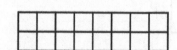

10. Una has a collection of 28 insects: $\frac{1}{4}$ are butterflies, $\frac{2}{7}$ are moths, and the rest are beetles.
    How many insects are beetles? _____

11. Eldon started practising piano at 7:45. He played scales for $\frac{1}{6}$ of an hour,
    popular songs for $\frac{2}{5}$ of an hour, and his solo for $\frac{1}{4}$ of an hour.
    At what time did he stop playing? _____

NS8-21 Multiplying Fractions by Whole Numbers

> **REMINDER** ▶ Multiplication is a short form for addition.
>
> $3 \times 4 = 4 + 4 + 4$ $\qquad\qquad$ $5 \times 7 = 7 + 7 + 7 + 7 + 7$ $\qquad\qquad$ $2 \times 9 = 9 + 9$

1. Write each product as a sum.

   a) $3 \times \dfrac{1}{4} = \dfrac{1}{4} + \dfrac{1}{4} + \dfrac{1}{4}$ $\qquad$ b) $2 \times \dfrac{3}{7} =$ $\qquad$ c) $4 \times \dfrac{5}{11} =$

2. Write each sum as a product.

   a) $\dfrac{1}{2} + \dfrac{1}{2} + \dfrac{1}{2} =$ $\qquad$ b) $\dfrac{5}{9} + \dfrac{5}{9} =$ $\qquad$ c) $\dfrac{3}{4} + \dfrac{3}{4} + \dfrac{3}{4} + \dfrac{3}{4} + \dfrac{3}{4} =$

> **REMINDER** ▶ To add fractions with the same denominator, add the numerators.

3. Find the products by first writing each product as a sum.

   a) $4 \times \dfrac{3}{5} = \dfrac{3}{5} + \dfrac{3}{5} + \dfrac{3}{5} + \dfrac{3}{5}$ $\qquad$ b) $2 \times \dfrac{3}{4} =$ $\qquad$ c) $2 \times \dfrac{4}{7} =$

   $\qquad = \dfrac{12}{5} = 2\dfrac{2}{5}$

   d) $5 \times \dfrac{4}{11} =$ $\qquad\qquad\qquad\qquad$ e) $6 \times \dfrac{3}{7} =$

> To multiply a fraction with a whole number, multiply the numerator by the whole number and leave the denominator the same.
>
> Example: $\dfrac{2}{9} + \dfrac{2}{9} + \dfrac{2}{9} = \dfrac{2+2+2}{9}$ so $3 \times \dfrac{2}{9} = \dfrac{3 \times 2}{9}$

4. Multiply the fractions with the whole number. Write your answer as a mixed number.

   a) $4 \times \dfrac{3}{7} = \dfrac{4 \times 3}{7} = \dfrac{12}{7} = 1\dfrac{5}{7}$ $\qquad$ b) $5 \times \dfrac{2}{3} = \dfrac{}{3} = \dfrac{}{3} = \dfrac{}{3}$

   c) $3 \times \dfrac{4}{5} = \dfrac{}{5} = \dfrac{}{5} = \dfrac{}{5}$

5. Find the products. Simplify your answer. (Show your work in your notebook.)

   a) $3 \times \dfrac{4}{6} = \dfrac{12}{6} = 2$ $\qquad$ b) $8 \times \dfrac{3}{4} =$ $\qquad$ c) $5 \times \dfrac{4}{10} =$ $\qquad$ d) $3 \times \dfrac{6}{9} =$ $\qquad$ e) $12 \times \dfrac{2}{8} =$

6. Find the products.

   a) $4 \times \dfrac{5}{4} = \dfrac{20}{4} = 5$ $\qquad$ b) $3 \times \dfrac{2}{3} =$ $\qquad$ c) $7 \times \dfrac{9}{7} =$ $\qquad$ d) $8 \times \dfrac{5}{8} =$ $\qquad$ e) $a \times \dfrac{b}{a} =$

NS8-21 Multiplying Fractions by Whole Numbers *(continued)*

In mathematics, the word "of" can mean multiply.

Examples: "2 groups of 3" means 2×3

"6 groups of $\frac{1}{2}$" means $6 \times \frac{1}{2} = \frac{1}{2} + \frac{1}{2} + \frac{1}{2} + \frac{1}{2} + \frac{1}{2} + \frac{1}{2}$

"$\frac{1}{2}$ of 6" means $\frac{1}{2} \times 6$ Reminder: $\frac{a}{b}$ of c is $a \times c \div b$

7. Calculate each product by finding the fraction of the whole number.

a) $\frac{1}{3}$ of 6 = _____ so $\frac{1}{3} \times 6$ = _____   b) $\frac{3}{5}$ of 10 = _____ so $\frac{3}{5} \times 10$ = _____

c) $\frac{2}{3}$ of 6 = _____ so $\frac{2}{3} \times 6$ = _____   d) $\frac{3}{4}$ of 20 = _____ so $\frac{3}{4} \times 20$ = _____

When multiplying whole numbers, the order we multiply in does not affect the answer.

Examples: $2 \times 3 = 3 \times 2 = 6$ $4 \times 5 = 5 \times 4 = 20$

INVESTIGATION 1 ▶ When multiplying a fraction and a whole number, does the order we multiply in affect the answer?

A. Calculate the products in both orders.

i) $8 \times \frac{1}{4} = \frac{1}{4} + \frac{1}{4} + \frac{1}{4} + \frac{1}{4} + \frac{1}{4} + \frac{1}{4} + \frac{1}{4} + \frac{1}{4} =$ _____   ii) $6 \times \frac{2}{3} = \frac{2}{3} + \frac{2}{3} + \frac{2}{3} + \frac{2}{3} + \frac{2}{3} + \frac{2}{3} =$ _____

$\frac{1}{4} \times 8 = \frac{1}{4}$ of 8 = _____ $\frac{2}{3} \times 6 = \frac{2}{3}$ of 6 = _____

iii) $10 \times \frac{3}{5}$ and $\frac{3}{5} \times 10$ iv) $12 \times \frac{5}{6}$ and $\frac{5}{6} \times 12$

B. Does changing the order we multiply in affect the answer? _____

INVESTIGATION 2 ▶ The fractions $\frac{1}{3}$ and $\frac{2}{6}$ are equivalent. Does multiplying by $\frac{2}{6}$ result in the same answer as multiplying by $\frac{1}{3}$?

A. Multiply these numbers by both $\frac{1}{3}$ and $\frac{2}{6}$. Reduce your answer to lowest terms.

i) $4 \times \frac{1}{3} =$ _____ $4 \times \frac{2}{6} =$ _____ = _____   ii) $11 \times \frac{1}{3} =$ _____ $11 \times \frac{2}{6} =$ _____ = _____

B. Does multiplying by $\frac{2}{6}$ result in the same answer as multiplying by $\frac{1}{3}$? _____

NS8-22 Multiplying Fractions by Fractions

Here is $\frac{1}{3}$ of a rectangle. 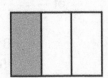	Here is $\frac{1}{4}$ of $\frac{1}{3}$ of the rectangle. 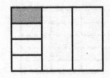	How much is $\frac{1}{4}$ of $\frac{1}{3}$? Extend the lines to find out. 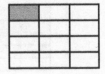 $\quad \frac{1}{4}$ of $\frac{1}{3} = \frac{1}{12}$

1. Extend the horizontal lines in each picture, then write a fraction statement for each figure using the word "of."

   a)   b)   c)   d)    e)

   $\frac{1}{2}$ of $\frac{1}{4} = \frac{1}{8}$ $\frac{1}{3}$ of $\frac{1}{5} =$ $\frac{1}{5}$ of $\frac{1}{2} =$

2. Rewrite the fraction statements from Question 1 using the multiplication sign instead of the word "of."

   a) $\frac{1}{2} \times \frac{1}{4} = \frac{1}{8}$ b)   c)   d)   e)

3. Write a multiplication statement for each figure.

   a)   b)   c)   d)   e)

   $\frac{1}{3} \times \frac{1}{4} = \frac{1}{12}$ _____   _____   _____   _____

4. Write a formula for multiplying fractions that both have numerator 1.

   $\frac{1}{a} \times \frac{1}{b} =$ _____

5. Multiply.

   a) $\frac{1}{2} \times \frac{1}{5} =$ b) $\frac{1}{2} \times \frac{1}{7} =$ c) $\frac{1}{3} \times \frac{1}{6} =$ d) $\frac{1}{5} \times \frac{1}{7} =$

   e) $\frac{1}{5} \times \frac{1}{2} =$ f) $\frac{1}{7} \times \frac{1}{2} =$ g) $\frac{1}{6} \times \frac{1}{3} =$ h) $\frac{1}{7} \times \frac{1}{5} =$

6. Look at your answers to Question 5. Does the order you multiply in affect the answer? _____

NS8-22 Multiplying Fractions by Fractions (continued)

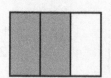 Here is $\frac{2}{3}$ of a rectangle.

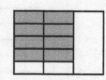 Here is $\frac{4}{5}$ of $\frac{2}{3}$.

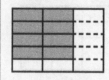 How much is $\frac{4}{5}$ of $\frac{2}{3}$? Extend the lines to find out.

$\frac{4}{5}$ of $\frac{2}{3} = \frac{8}{15}$

Notice:

$\frac{4}{5}$ of $\frac{2}{3} = \frac{4 \times 2}{5 \times 3}$

$= \frac{8}{15}$

7. Write a fraction statement for each figure. Use multiplication instead of the word "of."

a)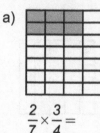

$\frac{2}{7} \times \frac{3}{4} =$

b)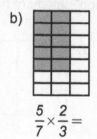

$\frac{5}{7} \times \frac{2}{3} =$

c)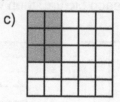

d)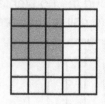

8. Find the following amounts by multiplying the numerators and denominators of the fractions.

a) $\frac{2}{3} \times \frac{4}{7} = \frac{8}{21}$

b) $\frac{1}{2} \times \frac{3}{5} =$

c) $\frac{3}{4} \times \frac{5}{7} =$

d) $\frac{2}{5} \times \frac{3}{8} =$

9. Write a formula for multiplying fractions by fractions.

$\frac{a}{b} \times \frac{c}{d} = \underline{\hspace{5cm}}$

10. Multiply the following fractions. (Reduce your answers to lowest terms.)

a) $\frac{2}{3} \times \frac{3}{5} =$

b) $\frac{3}{4} \times \frac{5}{7} =$

c) $\frac{1}{3} \times \frac{4}{5} =$

d) $\frac{4}{6} \times \frac{8}{7} =$

e) $\frac{3}{7} \times \frac{8}{9} =$

11. Multiply the following fractions. (Reduce your answers to lowest terms.) What do you notice?

a) $\frac{3}{5} \times \frac{5}{3}$

b) $\frac{2}{7} \times \frac{7}{2}$

c) $\frac{3}{2} \times \frac{2}{3}$

d) $\frac{4}{5} \times \frac{5}{4}$

e) $\frac{7}{9} \times \frac{9}{7}$

12. a) Circle the fractions that are more than $\frac{2}{3}$.

$\frac{5}{7}$ $\frac{5}{8}$ $\frac{3}{5}$ $\frac{7}{10}$

b) Without calculating the products, circle the products that are greater than 1 $(= \frac{2}{3} \times \frac{3}{2})$.

$\frac{5}{7} \times \frac{3}{2}$ $\frac{5}{8} \times \frac{3}{2}$ $\frac{3}{5} \times \frac{3}{2}$ $\frac{7}{10} \times \frac{3}{2}$

c) Verify your answers to part b) by calculating the products.

NS8-23 Dividing Fractions by Whole Numbers

1. In each picture, one half of the bar is shaded. What is the size of the smaller cross-shaded piece?

   Hint: How many cross-shaded pieces fit into the whole bar?

   a)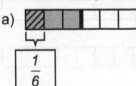

   $\dfrac{1}{6}$

   b)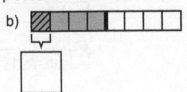

   c)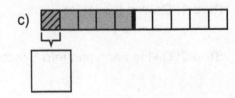

2. What is the size of the smaller cross-shaded piece?

   Hint: Cut the entire bar into smaller pieces if necessary, as in a).

   $\dfrac{1}{12}$

   a) 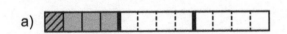 $\dfrac{1}{12}$

   b)

   c)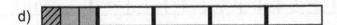

   d)

3. What fraction of the bar is cross-shaded?

   a)

   b)

   c)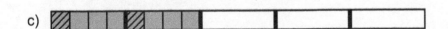

4. a) Explain how the picture in Question 2 a) shows that $\dfrac{1}{3} \div 4 = \dfrac{1}{12}$.

   b) Write division statements for the other pictures in Question 2.

To divide a fraction by a whole number, use a picture. Example: $\frac{2}{3} \div 5$

Step 1: Draw a model for $\frac{2}{3}$.

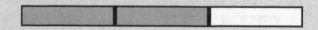

Step 2: Divide each part into 5 parts.

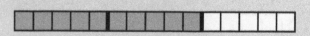

Step 3: Cross-shade 1 of every 5 shaded parts.

Step 4: Name the fraction shown by cross-shading. $\frac{2}{3} \div 5 = \frac{2}{15}$

5. Use the picture to find each quotient.

a) $\frac{3}{5} \div 5 =$ _____

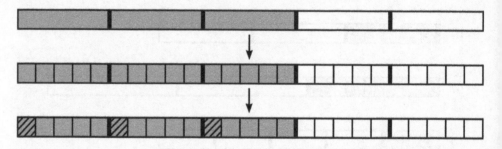

b) $\frac{2}{3} \div 4 =$ _____

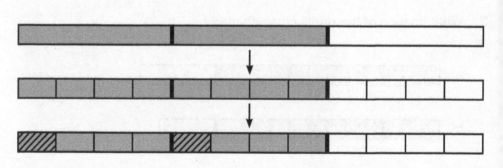

6. Draw a picture to find each quotient.

a) $\frac{4}{5} \div 2$
b) $\frac{1}{4} \div 3$
c) $\frac{3}{4} \div 2$
d) $\frac{2}{3} \div 3$
e) $\frac{2}{3} \div 2$
f) $\frac{4}{5} \div 3$

7. Look at your answers to Question 6. Finish writing the formula.

$$\frac{a}{b} \div c = \frac{a}{\rule{2cm}{0.4pt}}$$

8. Use your formula from Question 7 to find each quotient.

a) $\frac{2}{3} \div 5 = \frac{2}{3 \times 5} = \frac{2}{15}$
b) $\frac{3}{4} \div 4 =$ _____
c) $\frac{3}{5} \div 4 =$ _____

NS8-24 Dividing Whole Numbers by Fractions

Lina divides a string 6 m long into pieces 2 m long:

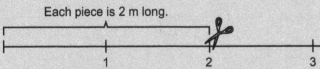

Each piece is 2 m long.

3 pieces of length 2 fit into 6, so **6 ÷ 2 = 3**

James divides a string 3 m long into pieces $\frac{1}{2}$ m long:

Each piece is $\frac{1}{2}$ m long.

2 pieces of length $\frac{1}{2}$ fit into 1 metre, so 6 pieces fit into 3 metres $(3 \times 2 = 6)$ and $3 \div \frac{1}{2} = 6$

1. Answer the questions and complete the division statement.

   a) How many pieces of length $\frac{1}{3}$ fit into 1? _____3_____ $1 \div \frac{1}{3} =$ _____3_____

       How many pieces of length $\frac{1}{3}$ fit into 2? _2 × 3 = 6_ $2 \div \frac{1}{3} =$ _____6_____

       How many pieces of length $\frac{1}{3}$ fit into 5? _____ $5 \div \frac{1}{3} =$ _____

   b) How many pieces of length $\frac{1}{4}$ fit into 1? _____ $1 \div \frac{1}{4} =$ _____

       How many pieces of length $\frac{1}{4}$ fit into 3? _____ $3 \div \frac{1}{4} =$ _____

       How many pieces of length $\frac{1}{4}$ fit into 7? _____ $7 \div \frac{1}{4} =$ _____

   c) How many pieces of length $\frac{1}{a}$ fit into 1? _____ $1 \div \frac{1}{a} =$ _____

       How many pieces of length $\frac{1}{a}$ fit into 3? _____ $3 \div \frac{1}{a} =$ _____

       How many pieces of length $\frac{1}{a}$ fit into b? _____ $b \div \frac{1}{a} =$ _____

2. Find each quotient.

   a) $9 \div \frac{1}{5} =$ ___ × ___ = ___   b) $8 \div \frac{1}{4} =$ ___ × ___ = ___   c) $7 \div \frac{1}{6} =$ ___ × ___ = ___

   d) $8 \div \frac{1}{3} =$ ___   e) $6 \div \frac{1}{6} =$ ___   f) $5 \div \frac{1}{7} =$ ___   g) $7 \div \frac{1}{7} =$ ___   h) $8 \div \frac{1}{9} =$ ___

NS8-24 Dividing Whole Numbers by Fractions (continued)

How many strings of length $\frac{2}{5}$ m fit along a string of length 4 m?

Step 1: Calculate how many strings of length $\frac{1}{5}$ m fit along a string of length 4 m.

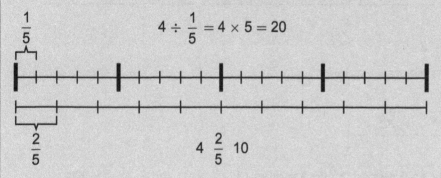

$$4 \div \frac{1}{5} = 4 \times 5 = 20$$

Step 2: Since $\frac{2}{5}$ is twice as long as $\frac{1}{5}$, only half as many will fit.

So divide the answer from Step 1 by 2: $20 \div 2 = 10$

3. Determine how many pieces will fit.

a) How many pieces of length $\frac{2}{3}$ fit into 4?

____12____ pieces of length $\frac{1}{3}$ fit into 4 so ____12____ $\div$ ____2____ = ____6____ pieces of length $\frac{2}{3}$ fit into 4.

b) How many pieces of length $\frac{2}{5}$ fit into 4?

_____ pieces of length $\frac{1}{5}$ fit into 4 so _____ $\div$ _____ = _____ pieces of length $\frac{2}{5}$ fit into 4.

c) How many pieces of length $\frac{3}{5}$ fit into 6?

_____ pieces of length $\frac{1}{5}$ fit into 6 so _____ $\div$ _____ = _____ pieces of length $\frac{3}{5}$ fit into 6.

d) How many pieces of length $\frac{a}{b}$ fit into c?

_____ pieces of length $\frac{1}{b}$ fit into c so _____ $\div$ _____ = _____ pieces of length $\frac{a}{b}$ fit into c.

4. Write each answer from Question 3 as a division statement.

a) $4 \div \frac{2}{3} = 6$ b)   c)   d)

5. Find each quotient.

a) $9 \div \frac{3}{4} =$ _____ $\times$ _____ $\div$ _____ = _____   b) $8 \div \frac{4}{5} =$ _____ $\times$ _____ $\div$ _____ = _____

c) $8 \div \frac{2}{7} =$ _____   d) $6 \div \frac{3}{4} =$ _____   e) $10 \div \frac{5}{6} =$ _____   f) $12 \div \frac{4}{5} =$ _____   g) $12 \div \frac{2}{5} =$ _____

NS8-24 Dividing Whole Numbers by Fractions *(continued)*

INVESTIGATION 1 ▶ The fractions $\frac{1}{3}$ and $\frac{2}{6}$ are equivalent. Does dividing by $\frac{1}{3}$ and dividing by $\frac{2}{6}$ result in the same answer?

A. Calculate each quotient.

i) $4 \div \frac{1}{3} =$ _____ $\times$ _____ $=$ _____

ii) $5 \div \frac{1}{3} =$ _____ $\times$ _____ $=$ _____

$4 \div \frac{2}{6} =$ _____ $\times$ _____ $\div$ _____ $=$ _____

$5 \div \frac{2}{6} =$ _____ $\times$ _____ $\div$ _____ $=$ _____

iii) $7 \div \frac{1}{3} =$ _____ $\times$ _____ $=$ _____

iv) $8 \div \frac{1}{3} =$ _____ $\times$ _____ $=$ _____

$7 \div \frac{2}{6} =$ _____ $\times$ _____ $\div$ _____ $=$ _____

$8 \div \frac{2}{6} =$ _____ $\times$ _____ $\div$ _____ $=$ _____

B. Does dividing by $\frac{1}{3}$ and dividing by $\frac{2}{6}$ result in the same answer? _____

INVESTIGATION 2 ▶ Does dividing by equivalent fractions always result in the same answer?

A. Write five fractions equivalent to $\frac{1}{2}$.

$$\frac{1}{2} = \frac{}{4} = \frac{}{6} = \frac{}{8} = \frac{}{10} = \frac{}{12}$$

B. Divide 3 by each fraction in your list from A.

$3 \div \frac{1}{2} = \frac{3 \times 2}{1} = 6$

$3 \div \frac{2}{4} = \frac{3 \times 4}{2} =$ _____

$3 \div \frac{}{6} =$ _____

$3 \div \frac{}{8} =$ _____

$3 \div \frac{}{10} =$ _____

$3 \div \frac{}{12} =$ _____

C. Does dividing by equivalent fractions always result in the same answer? _____

Explain why this is so. _____

_____

_____

_____

NS8-25 Operations with Fractions

1. Evaluate these expressions. Do the operation in brackets first.

a) $\dfrac{2}{3} + \left(\dfrac{1}{5} \times 4 \right) =$

b) $\left(\dfrac{2}{3} + \dfrac{1}{5} \right) \times 4 =$

c) $\dfrac{1}{5} + \left(\dfrac{4}{3} \div 2 \right) =$

d) $\left(\dfrac{1}{5} + \dfrac{4}{3} \right) \div 2 =$

e) $\dfrac{4}{3} - \left(\dfrac{2}{5} \times 2 \right) =$

f) $\left(\dfrac{4}{3} - \dfrac{2}{5} \right) \times 2 =$

g) $\dfrac{4}{3} - \left(\dfrac{2}{5} \div 2 \right) =$

h) $\left(\dfrac{4}{3} - \dfrac{2}{5} \right) \div 2 =$

2. Compare the problems that are similar in Question 1. Does the order you do the operations in affect the answer? _____

REMINDER ▶ Mathematicians have ordered the operations to avoid writing brackets all the time.

The order is:

1. Operations in brackets

2. Multiplication and division, from left to right

3. Addition and subtraction, from left to right

Examples: $5 - 3 \times \dfrac{2}{3} + 6 = 5 - 2 + 6$ but $(5 - 3) \times \left(\dfrac{2}{3} + 6 \right) = 2 \times \dfrac{20}{3}$

$\qquad\qquad\qquad\qquad = 3 + 6 \qquad\qquad\qquad\qquad\qquad\qquad = \dfrac{40}{3}$

$\qquad\qquad\qquad\qquad = 9 \qquad\qquad\qquad\qquad\qquad\qquad\quad = 13\dfrac{1}{3}$

---

3. Evaluate.

a) $\left(\dfrac{2}{3} + \dfrac{1}{2} \right) \times \dfrac{1}{4}$

b) $\dfrac{2}{3} + \dfrac{1}{2} \times \dfrac{1}{4}$

c) $\dfrac{3}{2} + \dfrac{1}{4} \times \dfrac{3}{4}$

d) $\dfrac{3}{2} \times \left(8 \div \dfrac{3}{4} \right)$

e) $\dfrac{5}{2} \div 5 \times \dfrac{4}{5}$

f) $\dfrac{5}{2} \div \left(5 \times \dfrac{4}{5} \right)$

g) $\dfrac{2}{3} + \dfrac{1}{2} - \dfrac{1}{4}$

h) $\dfrac{2}{3} + \left(\dfrac{1}{2} - \dfrac{1}{4} \right)$

i) $\dfrac{2}{3} - \dfrac{1}{4} + \dfrac{1}{2}$

j) $\dfrac{2}{3} - \left(\dfrac{1}{4} + \dfrac{1}{2} \right)$

k) $\dfrac{2}{3} - \dfrac{1}{4} \times \dfrac{1}{2}$

l) $\left(\dfrac{2}{3} - \dfrac{1}{4} \right) \times \dfrac{1}{2}$

4. Remove any brackets that are not necessary.

Note: In some expressions, all brackets will be necessary.

a) $\dfrac{2}{3} + \left(\dfrac{1}{2} - \dfrac{1}{3} \right)$

b) $\dfrac{2}{3} \times \left(\dfrac{1}{2} - \dfrac{1}{3} \right)$

c) $\left(\dfrac{1}{2} \times \dfrac{1}{3} \right) + \left(\dfrac{1}{3} - \dfrac{1}{4} \right)$

d) $\left[\dfrac{1}{2} - \left(\dfrac{1}{3} + \dfrac{1}{4} \right) \right] \times \dfrac{1}{5}$

NS8-26 Dividing Fractions by Fractions

1. a) Find each quotient.

i) $(12 \times 1) \div (2 \times 1) = \underline{\quad} \div \underline{\quad} = \underline{\quad}$ ii) $(12 \times 2) \div (2 \times 2) = \underline{\quad} \div \underline{\quad} = \underline{\quad}$

iii) $(12 \times 3) \div (2 \times 3) = \underline{\quad} \div \underline{\quad} = \underline{\quad}$ iv) $(12 \times 4) \div (2 \times 4) = \underline{\quad} \div \underline{\quad} = \underline{\quad}$

v) $(12 \times 5) \div (2 \times 5) = \underline{\quad} \div \underline{\quad} = \underline{\quad}$ vi) $(12 \times 6) \div (2 \times 6) = \underline{\quad} \div \underline{\quad} = \underline{\quad}$

vii) $\dfrac{12 \times 7}{2 \times 7} = \boxed{\dfrac{\quad}{\quad}} = \underline{\quad}$ viii) $\dfrac{12 \times 8}{2 \times 8} = \boxed{\dfrac{\quad}{\quad}} = \underline{\quad}$

b) What do you notice about your answers in part a)? _____

Why is that so? _____

_____

_____

_____

INVESTIGATION 1 ▶ In a division statement, multiplying both terms by the same whole number results in the same quotient.

Does multiplying both terms by **the same fraction** result in the same quotient?

A. Find each quotient.

a) $\left(12 \times \dfrac{1}{2}\right) \div \left(2 \times \dfrac{1}{2}\right) = \underline{\ 6\ } \div \boxed{\dfrac{2}{2}} = \underline{\ 6\ } \times \underline{\ 2\ } \div \underline{\ 2\ } = \underline{\ 6\ }$

b) $\left(12 \times \dfrac{1}{3}\right) \div \left(2 \times \dfrac{1}{3}\right) = \underline{\ 4\ } \div \boxed{\dfrac{2}{3}} = \underline{\ 4\ } \times \underline{\ 3\ } \div \underline{\ 2\ } = \underline{\quad}$

c) $\left(12 \times \dfrac{1}{4}\right) \div \left(2 \times \dfrac{1}{4}\right) = \underline{\quad} \div \boxed{\dfrac{\quad}{\quad}} = \underline{\quad} \times \underline{\quad} \div \underline{\quad} = \underline{\quad}$

d) $\left(12 \times \dfrac{1}{6}\right) \div \left(2 \times \dfrac{1}{6}\right) = \underline{\quad} \div \boxed{\dfrac{\quad}{\quad}} = \underline{\quad} \times \underline{\quad} \div \underline{\quad} = \underline{\quad}$

e) $\left(12 \times \dfrac{2}{3}\right) \div \left(2 \times \dfrac{2}{3}\right) = \underline{\quad} \div \boxed{\dfrac{\quad}{\quad}} = \underline{\quad} \times \underline{\quad} \div \underline{\quad} = \underline{\quad}$

B. What do you notice about your answers in A? _____

C. In a division statement, does multiplying both terms by the same fraction result in the same quotient? _____

NS8-26 Dicing Fractions by Fractions (continued)

NS8-26 **Dividing Fractions by Fractions** (continued)

The **reciprocal** of the fraction $\frac{a}{b}$ is the fraction $\frac{b}{a}$.

2. Write the reciprocal of each fraction.

   a) The reciprocal of $\frac{3}{4}$ is _____

   b) The reciprocal of $\frac{5}{3}$ is _____

   c) The reciprocal of $\frac{4}{7}$ is _____

   d) The reciprocal of $\frac{9}{2}$ is _____

3. If the fraction $\frac{a}{b}$ is less than 1, then its reciprocal is _____ than 1.

REMINDER ▶ $\frac{a}{b} \times \frac{b}{a} = 1$ for any a and b. Example: $\frac{3}{4} \times \frac{4}{3} = \frac{12}{12} = 1$

4. Translate the formula in the box into words:

   A fraction multiplied by its _____ is always _____.

REMINDER ▶ Dividing by 1 leaves a number unchanged.

Examples: $\qquad 5 \div 1 = 5 \qquad\qquad \frac{2}{3} \div 1 = \frac{2}{3} \qquad\qquad \frac{7}{5} \div 1 = \frac{7}{5}$

5. Multiply the reciprocals then divide by 1 to find the quotients.

   a) $\frac{5}{7} \div \left(\frac{3}{4} \times \frac{4}{3} \right)$

   b) $\frac{2}{3} \div \left(\frac{2}{5} \times \frac{5}{2} \right)$

   c) $\frac{3}{5} \div \left(\frac{2}{9} \times \frac{9}{2} \right)$

   $= \frac{5}{7} \div$ _____ $=$ _____

   $= \frac{2}{3} \div$ _____ $=$ _____

   $= \frac{3}{5} \div$ _____ $=$ _____

6. Fill in the blanks to make the quotients equal.

   a) $\frac{4}{5} \div \frac{3}{4} = \left(\frac{4}{5} \times \boxed{\frac{4}{3}} \right) \div \left(\frac{3}{4} \times \frac{4}{3} \right)$

   b) $\frac{3}{4} \div \frac{2}{5} = \left(\frac{3}{4} \times \boxed{-} \right) \div \left(\frac{2}{5} \times \frac{5}{2} \right)$

   c) $\frac{2}{3} \div \frac{1}{2} = \left(\frac{2}{3} \times \boxed{-} \right) \div \left(\frac{1}{2} \times \frac{2}{1} \right)$

   d) $\frac{2}{3} \div \frac{3}{5} = \left(\frac{2}{3} \times \boxed{-} \right) \div \left(\frac{3}{5} \times \frac{5}{3} \right)$

7. Look at your answer to Question 6 b). Explain why $\frac{3}{4} \div \frac{2}{5} = \frac{3}{4} \times \frac{5}{2}$.

NS8-26 Dividing Fractions by Fractions *(continued)*

8. Fill in the blanks to make the quotient equal to the product.

a) $\dfrac{2}{5} \div \dfrac{3}{7} = \dfrac{2}{5} \times \boxed{}$

b) $\dfrac{2}{3} \div \dfrac{2}{5} = \dfrac{2}{3} \times \boxed{}$

c) $\dfrac{7}{2} \div \dfrac{3}{5} = \dfrac{7}{2} \times \boxed{}$

d) $\dfrac{3}{4} \div \dfrac{2}{7} = \dfrac{3}{4} \times \boxed{}$

e) $\dfrac{2}{5} \div \dfrac{1}{6} = \dfrac{2}{5} \times \boxed{}$

f) $\dfrac{3}{4} \div \dfrac{3}{5} = \dfrac{3}{4} \times \boxed{}$

9. Finish writing the rule: $\dfrac{a}{b} \div \dfrac{c}{d} = \dfrac{a}{b} \times \underline{}$

10. Use your rule from Question 9 to find each quotient. Express your answer in lowest terms.

a) $\dfrac{3}{5} \div \dfrac{2}{3} = \dfrac{3}{5} \times \dfrac{3}{2} = \dfrac{9}{10}$

b) $\dfrac{3}{5} \div \dfrac{2}{5} =$

c) $\dfrac{1}{3} \div \dfrac{5}{6} =$

d) $\dfrac{1}{5} \div \dfrac{3}{8} =$

e) $\dfrac{5}{8} \div \dfrac{2}{3} =$

f) $\dfrac{6}{7} \div \dfrac{2}{3} =$

g) $\dfrac{8}{5} \div \dfrac{3}{2} =$

h) $\dfrac{8}{5} \div \dfrac{2}{3} =$

i) $\dfrac{1}{5} \div \dfrac{3}{5} =$

11. Divide by first changing all mixed numbers to improper fractions.

a) $3\dfrac{1}{2} \div \dfrac{2}{3} = \dfrac{7}{2} \div \dfrac{2}{3}$

$= \dfrac{7}{2} \times \dfrac{3}{2}$

$= \dfrac{21}{4}$

$= 5\dfrac{1}{4}$

b) $4\dfrac{1}{2} \div \dfrac{1}{4}$

c) $2\dfrac{2}{3} \div \dfrac{4}{9}$

d) $3\dfrac{3}{4} \div 7\dfrac{1}{2}$

e) $5\dfrac{6}{8} \div \dfrac{1}{4}$

f) $3 \div \dfrac{1}{10}$

g) $1\dfrac{1}{9} \div 1\dfrac{2}{3}$

h) $2 \div 1\dfrac{7}{9}$

12. Divide each fraction by itself. (Reduce your answer to lower terms.)

a) $\dfrac{3}{4} \div \dfrac{3}{4} = \dfrac{3}{4} \times \dfrac{4}{3}$

$= \dfrac{12}{12} = 1$

b) $\dfrac{4}{7} \div \dfrac{4}{7} =$

c) $\dfrac{8}{3} \div \dfrac{8}{3} =$

13. What do you notice about your answers to Question 12? Why is this so?

NS8-21 Word Problems

1. A foot is 12 inches. A yard is 3 feet. What fraction of a yard is 8 inches?

   Find what fraction of a foot is 8 inches: 8 inches is $\frac{8}{12}$ of a foot.

   Find what fraction of a yard is a foot: 1 foot is $\frac{1}{3}$ of a yard.

   So 8 inches $= \frac{8}{12} \times \frac{1}{3}$ of a yard $=$ _____ of a yard.

2. A year has _____ months. A decade has _____ years.
   What fraction of a decade is 8 months?

3. What fraction of a day is 45 minutes?

4. What fraction of a century is 13 weeks?

5. What fraction of a day is 40 seconds?

6. a) Bilal bought $\frac{7}{5}$ cups of flour. He used $\frac{3}{4}$ of it to bake a pie. How much flour did he use?
   b) Did Bilal use more or less than a cup of flour? How do you know?

7. Ron bought $\frac{8}{3}$ cups of sugar. He used $\frac{1}{4}$ of it to bake a cake. He then ate $\frac{3}{10}$ of the cake. How much sugar did he eat?

8. Sam biked $\frac{2}{3}$ km in 4 minutes. How far did he bike in 1 minute?

   $\frac{2}{3} \div 4 = \boxed{}$ km

9. A string of length $3\frac{1}{2}$ m is divided into 5 equal parts. How long is each piece?

   $3\frac{1}{2} \div 5 = \frac{7}{2} \div 5 = \boxed{}$ m $=$ _____ cm

10. A cake recipe used $1\frac{1}{3}$ cups sugar. The cake is divided into 8 pieces.
    How much sugar is in each piece?

11. Rosa bought $\frac{4}{5}$ kg of dry lasagne. Each person needs $\frac{2}{35}$ kg.
    How many people can she feed?

12. A string of length $4\frac{4}{5}$ m long is divided into pieces of length $\frac{3}{10}$ m.
    How many pieces are there?

NS8-28 Decimal Fractions

10, 100, 1 000, ... are **powers of 10**. In a **decimal fraction**, the denominator is a power of ten.

There are 100 squares on a **hundredths grid**.

1 one   1 tenth 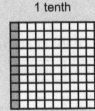   1 hundredth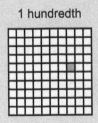

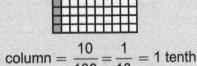

$$1 \text{ column} = \frac{10}{100} = \frac{1}{10} = 1 \text{ tenth} \qquad 1 \text{ square} = \frac{1}{100} = 1 \text{ hundredth}$$

1. Write two equivalent fractions for the shaded part of the grid.
   Remember: 1 column = 1 tenth.

   a) $\dfrac{2}{10} = \dfrac{}{100}$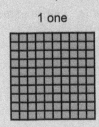

   b) $\dfrac{}{10} = \dfrac{}{100}$

   c) $\dfrac{}{10} = \dfrac{}{100}$

2. Write the fraction shown by the shaded part of the grid in two ways.

   a) $\dfrac{23}{100} =$

   $\dfrac{2}{10} + \dfrac{}{100}$

   b) $\dfrac{}{100} =$

   $\dfrac{}{10} + \dfrac{}{100}$

   c) $\dfrac{}{100} =$

   $\dfrac{}{10} + \dfrac{}{100}$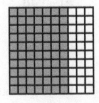

3. Shade the grid to show the fraction. Then write the fraction another way.

   a) $\dfrac{47}{100} =$

   $\dfrac{}{10} + \dfrac{}{100}$

   b) $\dfrac{92}{100} =$

   $\dfrac{}{10} + \dfrac{}{100}$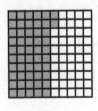

   c) $\dfrac{36}{100} =$

   $\dfrac{}{10} + \dfrac{}{100}$

4. Determine the equivalent fraction.

   a) $\dfrac{7}{10} = \dfrac{7 \times 10}{10 \times 10} = \dfrac{}{100}$

   b) $\dfrac{36}{100} = \dfrac{36 \times \underline{}}{100 \times \underline{}} = \dfrac{}{1000}$

   c) $\dfrac{4}{100} = \dfrac{4 \times \underline{}}{100 \times \underline{}} = \dfrac{}{1000}$

5. Write the equivalent fractions.

   a) $\dfrac{5}{10} = \dfrac{}{100} = \dfrac{}{1000}$

   b) $\dfrac{}{10} = \dfrac{80}{100} = \dfrac{}{1000}$

   c) $\dfrac{73}{100} = \dfrac{}{1000}$

   d) $\dfrac{540}{1000} = \dfrac{}{100}$

NS8-29 Place Value and Decimals

Decimals are a short way to write decimal fractions.

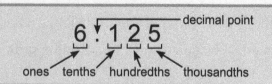

1. Write the decimal fraction in the place value chart. Then write the fraction as a decimal.

a) $\dfrac{5}{10} + \dfrac{4}{100} = \underline{} . \underline{}\,\underline{}$

ones	tenths	hundredths
0	5	4

b) $\dfrac{9}{10} + \dfrac{6}{100} + \dfrac{3}{1000} = \underline{} . \underline{}\,\underline{}\,\underline{}$

ones	tenths	hundredths	thousandths
0			

2. Write the value of the digit **8** in each decimal in words and as a fraction.

a) 0.4**8**   8 _____*hundredths*_____ or $\dfrac{8}{100}$

b) 0.34**8**   8 _____ or $\dfrac{8}{}$

c) 0.**8**76   8 _____ or $\dfrac{8}{}$

d) 0.3**8**   8 _____ or $\dfrac{8}{}$

3. Write the number shown in the place value chart as a decimal, using 0 as a placeholder.

a)

ones	tenths	hundredths
		8

$\underline{0} . \underline{0}\,\underline{8}$

b)

ones	tenths	hundredths	thousandths
			3

$\underline{} . \underline{}\,\underline{}\,\underline{}$

c)

ones	tenths	hundredths
		6

$\underline{} . \underline{}\,\underline{}$

d)

ones	tenths	hundredths	thousandths
			9

$\underline{} . \underline{}\,\underline{}\,\underline{}$

4. Write the number as a decimal. Use zeros as placeholders.

a) 6 tenths = $\underline{0} . \underline{}$

b) 2 tenths = $\underline{} . \underline{}$

c) 8 tenths = $\underline{} . \underline{}$

d) 6 hundredths = $\underline{0} . \underline{0}\,\underline{}$

e) 4 hundredths = $\underline{} . \underline{}\,\underline{}$

f) 3 hundredths = $\underline{} . \underline{}\,\underline{}$

g) 6 thousandths = $\underline{} . \underline{}\,\underline{}\,\underline{}$

h) 1 thousandths = $\underline{} . \underline{}\,\underline{}\,\underline{}$

i) 5 hundredths = $\underline{} . \underline{}\,\underline{}$

5. Write the number in expanded form as a decimal.

a) 3 tenths + 5 hundredths + 2 thousandths = $\underline{0} . \underline{}\,\underline{}\,\underline{}$

b) 7 tenths = $\underline{} . \underline{}$

c) 6 tenths + 4 hundredths = $\underline{} . \underline{}\,\underline{}$

d) 5 hundredths + 7 thousandths = $\underline{} . \underline{}\,\underline{}\,\underline{}$

e) 7 tenths + 5 thousandths = $\underline{} . \underline{}\,\underline{}\,\underline{}$

6. Put a decimal point in the number so the digit 3 has the value $\dfrac{3}{100}$.
Add zeros if you need to.

a) 2 3

b) 7 3 2

c) 7 6 5 3

d) 3

NS8-30 Decimals, Money, and Measurements

1. Complete the chart.

Drawing	Fraction	Decimal	Equivalent Decimal	Equivalent Fraction	Drawing
	$\dfrac{5}{10}$	0.5	0.50	$\dfrac{50}{100}$	
	$\dfrac{}{10}$	__.___	__.___	$\dfrac{}{100}$	

2. Fill in the missing numbers. Remember: $\dfrac{1}{10}=\dfrac{10}{100}$ and $\dfrac{1}{100}=\dfrac{10}{1000}$.

a) $0.8 = \dfrac{8}{10} = \dfrac{}{100} = 0.80$

b) $0.\underline{} = \dfrac{}{10} = \dfrac{40}{100} = 0.\underline{}.$

c) $0.\underline{} = \dfrac{}{10} = \dfrac{}{100} = 0.30$

d) $0.03 = \dfrac{3}{100} = \dfrac{}{1000} = 0.030$

e) $0.\underline{}\,\underline{} = \dfrac{2}{100} = \dfrac{}{1000} = 0.020$

f) $0.\underline{}\,\underline{} = \dfrac{}{100} = \dfrac{70}{1000} = 0.\underline{}\,\underline{}\,\underline{}$

3. How many tenths and hundreds are shaded? Write a fraction and a decimal to represent them.

a)

   ___47___ hundredths = ____ tenths ____ hundredths $\dfrac{47}{100} = 0.\underline{}\,\underline{}$

b)

   ____ hundredths = ____ tenths ____ hundredths $\dfrac{}{100} = 0.\underline{}\,\underline{}$

4. Write the fraction as a decimal.

a) $\dfrac{35}{100} = 0.\underline{}\,\underline{}$

b) $\dfrac{61}{100} = 0.\underline{}\,\underline{}$

c) $\dfrac{18}{100} = 0.\underline{}\,\underline{}$

d) $\dfrac{3}{100} = 0.\underline{}\,\underline{}$

5. Write the decimal in expanded form in two ways.

a) $0.52 =$ ____ tenths ____ hundredths

   $=$ ____ hundredths

b) $0.40 =$ ____ tenths ____ hundredths

   $=$ ____ hundredths

6. Write the number as a decimal.

a) 23 hundredths = 0. __ __

b) 61 hundredths = 0. __ __

c) 12 hundredths = 0. __ __

No unauthorized copying

NS8-30 Decimals, Money, and Measurements (continued)

7. Fill in the blanks.

   a) 428 thousandths = ____ tenths ____ hundredths ____ thousandths $\frac{428}{1000}$ = 0. __ __ __

   b) 762 thousandths = ____ tenths ____ hundredths ____ thousandths $\frac{}{1000}$ = 0. __ __ __

8. Write the fraction as a decimal.

   a) $\frac{268}{1000}$ = 0. __ __ __   b) $\frac{709}{1000}$ = 0. __ __ __   c) $\frac{63}{1000}$ = 0. __ __ __

9. Write the decimal in expanded form in two ways.

   a) 0.678 = ____ tenths ____ hundredths ____ thousandths = ____ thousandths

   b) 0.643 = ____ tenths ____ hundredths ____ thousandths = ____ thousandths

10. Write the number as a decimal.

   a) 765 thousandths = _0.765_   b) 194 thousandths = _____   c) 803 thousandths = _____

   d) 42 thousandths = _0.042_   e) 15 thousandths = _____   f) 75 thousandths = _____

11. Write the decimal as a fraction.

   a) 0.3   b) 0.57   c) 0.654   d) 0.45   e) 0.03

   f) 0.056   g) 0.002   h) 0.1   i) 0.704   j) 0.069

12. A **dime** is **one tenth** of a dollar. A **penny** is **one hundredth** of a dollar.

   Express the value of each decimal in four different ways.

   a) 0.64   b) 0.73

   6 dimes and 4 pennies   _____

   6 tenths and 4 hundredths   _____

   64 pennies   _____

   64 hundredths   _____

13. A **decimetre** is **one tenth** of a metre. A **centimetre** is **one hundredth** of a metre.

   Express the value of each measurement in four different ways.

   a) 0.28 m   b) 0.16 m

14. Keiko says 0.79 is greater than 0.9 because 79 is greater than 9. Can you explain her mistake?

15. What unit of measurement does the 5 in 0.725 m represent?

NS8-31 Decimals and Fractions Greater Than 1

The whole-number part of a decimal is the digits **to the left** of the decimal point.

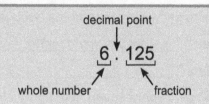

1. Underline the whole-number part of the decimal.

a) <u>54</u>.432   b) 876.4   c) 25.23   d) 8.034   e) 0.65   f) 90.005

2. Write the decimal in expanded form.

a) 7.5 = ____ ones + ____ tenths

b) 4.32 = ____ ones + ____ tenths + ____ hundredths

c) 56.426 = __5__ tens + __6__ ones + __4__ tenths + ____ hundredths + ____ thousandths

d) 67.04 = ____ tens + ____ ones + ____ tenths + ____ hundredths

e) 7.048 = ____ ones + ____ tenths + ____ hundredths + ____ thousandths

3. Write the number as a decimal.

a) 4 tens + 3 ones + 8 tenths + 5 hundredths + 2 thousandths = __ __ . __ __ __

b) 8 ones + 3 tenths + 2 hundredths + 7 thousandths = _____

c) 3 tens + 7 ones + 6 tenths + 9 hundredths = _____

d) 8 hundreds + 8 tens + 8 ones + 8 tenths + 8 hundredths = _____

4. Write the decimal in the place value chart.

	thousands	hundreds	tens	ones	tenths	hundredths	thousandths
a) 17.34			1	7	3	4	
b) 8.987							
c) 270.93							
d) 8 900.5							
e) 78.003							

5. Write the whole number and the hundredths or thousandths in each decimal.

a) 6.98 _____*six*_____ and _____*ninety-eight*_____ hundredths

b) 1.47 _____ and _____ hundredths

c) 32.005 _____ and _____ thousandths

d) 8.051 _____ and _____ thousandths

e) 80.105 _____ and _____ thousandths

NS8-31 **Decimals and Fractions Greater Than 1** (continued)

6. Fill in the blanks to show how to read the decimal.

   a) 6.8 is read as "_____*six and eight tenths*_____"

   b) 6.02 is read as "_____ and two _____"

   c) 27.89 is read as "twenty-seven and eighty-nine _____"

   d) 19.285 is read as "_____ and two hundred eighty-five _____"

A decimal can be written as a mixed number: $3.75 = 3\frac{75}{100}$

---

7. Write the number represented on the grids in three ways.

   a)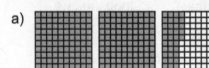

   __2__ ones __35__ hundredths   2 . __ __ $\dfrac{2}{100}$

   b)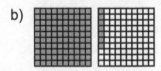

   ____ one ____ hundredths   __ . __ __ $\dfrac{}{100}$

   c)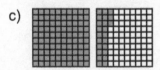

   ____ one ____ hundredths   __ . __ __ $\dfrac{}{100}$

   d)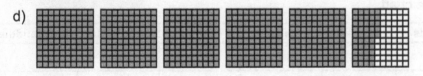

   ____ ones ____ hundredths   __ . __ __ $\dfrac{}{100}$

8. Write a mixed number for the decimal.

   a) 3.51   b) 1.67   c) 8.2   d) 9.163

   e) 31.35   f) 23.956   g) 1.9   h) 24.305

9. Write a decimal for the mixed number.

   a) $2\frac{17}{100}$ b) $1\frac{67}{100}$ c) $76\frac{7}{10}$ d) $5\frac{375}{1000}$ e) $3\frac{9}{100}$ f) $29\frac{5}{1000}$

10. Which is larger, 12.056 or $12\frac{52}{100}$? Explain.

NS8-32 Comparing and Ordering Tenths and Hundredths

This number line is divided into tenths. The number represented by point **A** is $2\frac{3}{10}$ or 2.3.

1. Write a fraction or a mixed number for each point.

A _____   B _____   C _____   D _____   E _____

2. a) Write a decimal for each mark on the number line.

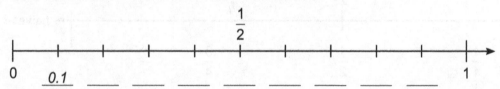

   b) Which decimal is equal to one half? $\frac{1}{2}$ = _____

3. Use the number line in Question 2 to say whether the decimal is closest
   to 0, $\frac{1}{2}$, or 1.

   a) 0.2 is closest to ____   b) 0.8 is closest to ____   c) 0.7 is closest to ____

   d) 0.9 is closest to ____   e) 0.3 is closest to ____   f) 0.1 is closest to ____

4. a) Mark each point with a dot and label the point with the correct letter.

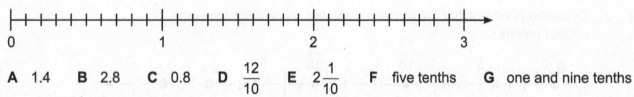

   A 1.4   **B** 2.8   **C** 0.8   **D** $\frac{12}{10}$ **E** $2\frac{1}{10}$ **F** five tenths   **G** one and nine tenths

   b) Use the number line to order the points from least to greatest.

   ___*F*___, ____, ____, ____, ____, ____, ____

5. a) This number line is divided into hundredths. Mark 0.50 on the number line.
In your notebook, explain how you decided where to mark this point.

0.10

0   1

b) Mark and label these points on the number line above. In your notebook, explain
the strategy you used to place each number on the line.

A 0.62   **B** $\dfrac{34}{100}$ **C** 0.04   **D** $\dfrac{51}{100}$

c) Use the number line to order the points from least to greatest. ____, ____, ____, ____

6. Use the number lines to compare the pairs of numbers below.
Write < (less than) or > (greater than) between each pair of numbers.

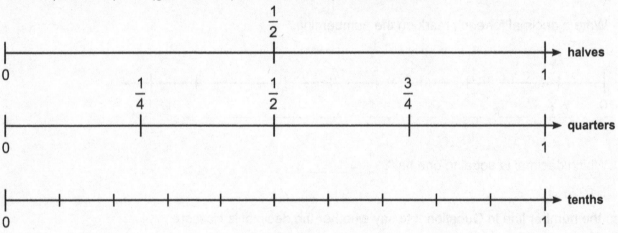

$\dfrac{1}{2}$

0   1   halves

$\dfrac{1}{4}$ $\dfrac{1}{2}$ $\dfrac{3}{4}$

0   1   quarters

0   1   tenths

0   1   hundredths

a) $0.8 \square \dfrac{3}{4}$ **b)** $0.6 \square \dfrac{7}{10}$ **c)** $0.7 \square \dfrac{1}{2}$ **d)** $0.3 \square \dfrac{1}{4}$

e) $0.6 \square \dfrac{1}{2}$ **f)** $0.23 \square \dfrac{1}{4}$ **g)** $0.08 \square \dfrac{1}{2}$ **h)** $\dfrac{3}{4} \square 65$

7. a) Circle the numbers that are placed on the line incorrectly. Draw the
correct point(s).

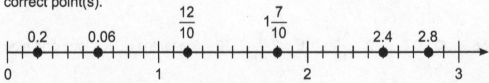

0.2   0.06 $\dfrac{12}{10}$ $1\dfrac{7}{10}$ 2.4   2.8

0   1   2   3

b) Write a number between each pair of numbers.

i) 0.2, _____, $\dfrac{12}{10}$ ii) $\dfrac{12}{10}$, _____, $1\dfrac{7}{10}$ iii) $1\dfrac{7}{10}$, _____, 2.5   iv) 2.5, _____, 2.8

NS8-33 Ordering Decimals and Fractions to Thousandths

1. Order the fractions from least to greatest. Use a common denominator.

   a) $\dfrac{50}{100}$ $\dfrac{4}{10} = \dfrac{}{100}$ $\dfrac{6}{10} = \dfrac{}{100}$

   b) $\dfrac{30}{100}$ $\dfrac{2}{10} =$ $\dfrac{9}{10} =$

   _____ , _____ , _____   _____ , _____ , _____

2. Write the decimal as a fraction with denominator 100 by first adding a zero to the decimal.

   a) $0.7 = \underline{\ 0.70\ } = \dfrac{70}{100}$ b) $0.9 = \underline{\hspace{1cm}} = \dfrac{}{100}$ c) $0.1 = \underline{\hspace{1cm}} = \dfrac{}{100}$

3. Add a zero to change decimal tenths to hundredths. Then circle the greatest decimal.

   a) 0.40   0.35   0.43   b) 0.74   0.6   0.5   c) 3.6   3.55   3.7

4. Order the fractions from least to greatest. Use a common denominator.

   a) $\dfrac{72}{1000}$ $\dfrac{64}{100} = \dfrac{}{1000}$ $\dfrac{68}{100} = \dfrac{}{1000}$

   b) $\dfrac{54}{100} = \dfrac{}{1000}$ $\dfrac{504}{1000}$ $\dfrac{5}{10} = \dfrac{}{100} = \dfrac{}{1000}$

   _____ , _____ , _____   _____ , _____ , _____

5. Write the decimal as a fraction with denominator 1 000 by first adding one or two zeros to the decimal.

   a) $0.65 = \underline{\hspace{1cm}} = \dfrac{}{1000}$ b) $0.83 = \underline{\hspace{1cm}} = \dfrac{}{1000}$ c) $0.3 = \underline{\hspace{1cm}} = \dfrac{}{1000}$

6. Add zero(s) to make the decimals decimal thousandths. Then circle the greatest decimal thousandth.

   a) 0.12   0.036   0.3   b) 0.2   0.69   0.082   c) 7.5   7.35   7.432

7. Write each decimal as an improper fraction with the denominator shown. Then order the decimals from greatest to least.

   a) $4.6 = \dfrac{46}{10}$ $4.7 = \dfrac{}{10}$ $4.3 = \dfrac{}{10}$

   b) $2.97 = \dfrac{297}{100}$ $2.05 = \dfrac{}{100}$ $2.78 = \dfrac{}{100}$

   $\underline{\ 4.7\ }$, _____ , _____   _____ , _____ , _____

   c) $1.3 = \dfrac{1300}{1000}$ $1.8 = \dfrac{}{1000}$ $1.6 = \dfrac{}{1000}$

   d) $7.2 = \dfrac{7200}{1000}$ $7.547 = \dfrac{}{1000}$ $7.85 = \dfrac{}{1000}$

   _____ , _____ , _____   _____ , _____ , _____

8. Write a decimal that matches each description.

   a) between 0.83 and 0.89   0. _____   b) between 0.6 and 0.70   0. _____

   c) between 0.385 and 0.39   0. _____   d) between 0.457 and 0.5   0. _____

9. Write the numbers in the place value chart. Then order the numbers from greatest to least.

    a) 0.242, 1.368, 1.70, 2.05

ones	tenths	hundredths	thousandths
0	2	4	2

    _____, _____, _____, _____

    b) 0.654, 0.555, 0.655, 0.554

ones	tenths	hundredths	thousandths

    _____, _____, _____, _____

10. Complete the number patterns.

    a) 7.5, 7.6, 7. __ , 7.8, 7.9, 8. __ , 8. __

    b) 10.5, 11.5, 12.5, _____, _____

    c) _____, 9.40, 9.35, _____, 9.25, 9.20

    d) 0.005, 0.010, 0.015, _____, 0.025, 0.030

    e) 25.6, _____, _____, 28.6, 29.6

    f) 50.63, 50.53, _____, 50.33, _____

11. Arrange the numbers in increasing order.

    a) 34.546, 34.456, 34.466

    _____, _____, _____

    b) 80.765, 80.756, 80.657

    _____, _____, _____

12. Arrange the numbers in decreasing order.

    a) 75.240, 75.704, 77.740

    _____, _____, _____

    b) 0.004, 0.040, 0.041, 4.001

    _____, _____, _____, _____

13. Write five decimals greater than 1.32 and less than 1.33.

14. Circle the greater number. Hint: First change all fractions and decimals to fractions with denominator 100 or 1 000. (Note: $4 \times 250 = 1\,000$)

    a) $\frac{1}{2}$ 0.51

    b) $\frac{4}{5}$ 0.85

    c) $\frac{3}{4}$ 0.734

15. Write the numbers in order from least to greatest. Explain how you found your answer.

    a) 0.7   0.34 $\frac{3}{5}$

    b) 0.817 $\frac{77}{100}$ $\frac{4}{5}$

    c) $\frac{3}{5}$ 0.425 $\frac{1}{2}$

16. How does knowing that $\frac{1}{4} = 0.25$ help you find the decimal form of $\frac{3}{4}$?

17. Explain how you know 0.635 is greater than $\frac{1}{2}$.

A Base Ten Model for Decimal Tenths and Hundredths

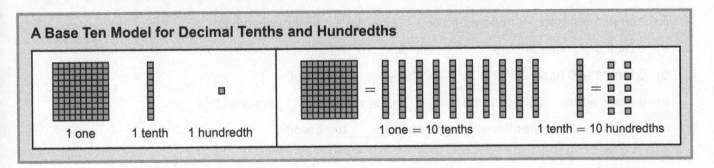

1 one   1 tenth   1 hundredth   1 one = 10 tenths   1 tenth = 10 hundredths

1. Regroup as many of the blocks as you can into bigger blocks. What decimal does each model represent?

a)

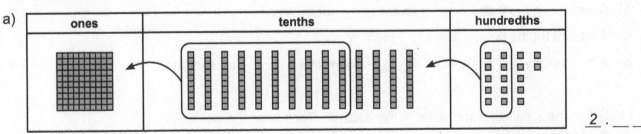

$\underline{\hspace{0.2cm}2\hspace{0.2cm}}$. __ __

b)

$\underline{\hspace{0.3cm}}$. __ __

c)

$\underline{\hspace{0.3cm}}$. __ __

2. Regroup.

a) 27 tenths = __2__ ones + ____ tenths   b) 74 hundredths = ____ tenths + ____ hundredths

c) 36 tenths = ____ ones + ____ tenths   d) 19 hundredths = ____ tenth + ____ hundredths

3. Regroup so that each place value has a single digit.

a) 3 ones + 14 tenths = __4__ ones + __4__ tenths

b) 7 tenths + 17 hundredths = ____ tenths + ____ hundredths

c) 6 hundredths + 11 thousandths = ____ hundredths + ____ thousandth

NS8-34 Regrouping Decimals (continued)

4. Exchange 1 tenth for 10 hundredths or 1 hundredth for 10 thousandths.

   a) 6 tenths + 0 hundredths = __5__ tenths + __10__ hundredths

   b) 8 tenths + 0 hundredths = ____ tenths + ____ hundredths

   c) 9 hundredths + 0 thousandths = ____ hundredths + ____ thousandths

   d) 3 tenths + 0 hundredths = ____ tenths + ____ hundredths

5. Exchange one of the larger unit for 10 of the smaller unit.

   a) 3 hundredths + 6 thousandths = __2__ hundredths + __16__ thousandths

   b) 6 tenths 4 hundredths = ____ tenths ____ hundredths

   c) 4 ones 9 tenths = ____ ones ____ tenths

   d) 8 hundredths + 1 thousandth = ____ hundredths + ____ thousandths

6. Underline the smallest place value in the decimal. Then write the decimal as an improper fraction.

   a) 2.<u>3</u> = $\frac{23}{10}$ b) 9.5 =   c) 5.6 =   d) 3.8<u>5</u> = $\frac{}{100}$ e) 2.18 =

   f) 9.96   g) 1.63 =   h) 1.93<u>4</u> = $\frac{}{1000}$ i) 5.735 =   j) 3.312 =

7. Add zeros to rewrite the whole number as decimal tenths, hundredths, and thousandths. Example: 2 = 2.0 = 2.00 = 2.000

   a) 8 = _____ = _____ = _____   b) 16 = _____ = _____ = _____

   c) 240 = _____ = _____ = _____

8. Regroup the whole number as ones, tenths, hundredths, and thousandths.

   a) 8 = _____ ones = _____ tenths = _____ hundredths = _____ thousandths

   b) 16 = _____ ones = _____ tenths = _____ hundredths = _____ thousandths

9. Complete the statements.

   a) 3.7 = _____ tenths   b) 7.2 = _____ tenths

   c) 15.4 = _____ tenths   d) 78.3 = _____ tenths

   e) 3.25 = _____ hundredths   f) 6.93 = _____ hundredths

   g) 3.25 = _____ thousandths   h) 6.93 = _____ thousandths

   i) 6.89 = _____ thousandths   j) 10.46 = _____ thousandths

NS8-35 Addition Strategies for Decimals

1. Write an addition statement that corresponds to the grids.

a) + =

0. _25_ + 0. ____ = 0. ____

b) + =

0. ____ + 0. ____ = 0. ____

2. Add by sketching a base ten model. Note: Use a hundreds block for a one and a tens block for a tenth.

a) $1.12 + 1.23$

b) $1.46 + 1.33$

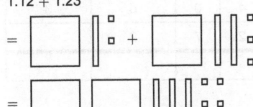

3. Use equivalent fractions to calculate the decimal sums.

a) $0.3 + 0.5 = \dfrac{3}{10} + \dfrac{}{10} = \dfrac{}{10} = 0.\underline{}$

b) $0.35 + 0.22 = \dfrac{}{100} + \dfrac{}{100} = \dfrac{}{100} = 0.\underline{}\,\underline{}$

c) $0.58 + 0.05 = \dfrac{}{100} + \dfrac{}{100} = \dfrac{}{100} = 0.\underline{}\,\underline{}$

d) $0.129 + 0.474 = \dfrac{}{1000} + \dfrac{}{1000} = \dfrac{}{1000} = 0.\underline{}\,\underline{}\,\underline{}$

4. Write the decimals as fractions with a common denominator to calculate the sums.

a) $0.27 + 0.6 = \dfrac{27}{100} + \dfrac{6}{10} = \dfrac{27}{100} + \dfrac{}{100} = \dfrac{}{100} = \underline{}.\underline{}\,\underline{}$

b) $0.57 + 0.765 = \dfrac{57}{100} + \dfrac{765}{1000} = \dfrac{}{1000} + \dfrac{765}{1000} = \dfrac{}{1000} = \underline{}.\underline{}\,\underline{}\,\underline{}$

c) $6.065 + 0.99 = \dfrac{}{1000} + \dfrac{}{100} = \dfrac{}{1000} + \dfrac{}{1000} = \dfrac{}{1000} = \underline{}.\underline{}\,\underline{}\,\underline{}$

5. Write both decimals using the smallest place value to calculate the sums.

a) $2.15 + 7.3$

= _215_ hundredths + _73_ tenths

= ____ hundredths + ____ hundredths

= ____ hundredths

= ____ . ____ ____

b) $4.064 + 2.94$

= ____ thousandths + ____ hundredths

= ____ thousandths + ____ thousandths

= ____ thousandths

= ____ . ____ ____ ____

NS8-35 Addition Strategies for Decimals (continued)

6. Add by adding each place value.

a) 3.3 + 2.4

$= (\underline{\ 3\ }$ ones $+ \underline{\ 3\ }$ tenths$) + (\underline{\ \ \ }$ ones $+ \underline{\ \ \ }$ tenths$)$

$= (\underline{\ 3\ }$ ones $+ \underline{\ 2\ }$ ones$) + (\underline{\ \ \ }$ tenths $+ \underline{\ \ \ }$ tenths$)$

$= \underline{\ \ \ }$ ones $+ \underline{\ \ \ }$ tenths $= \underline{\ \ }\ .\ \underline{\ \ }$

b) 5.6 + 1.3

$= (\underline{\ \ \ }$ ones $+ \underline{\ \ \ }$ tenths$) + (\underline{\ \ \ }$ ones $+ \underline{\ \ \ }$ tenths$)$

$= (\underline{\ \ \ }$ ones $+ \underline{\ \ \ }$ ones$) + (\underline{\ \ \ }$ tenths $+ \underline{\ \ \ }$ tenths$)$

$= \underline{\ \ \ }$ ones $+ \underline{\ \ \ }$ tenths $= \underline{\ \ }\ .\ \underline{\ \ }$

7. Add by adding each place value in the chart.

a)

tens	ones	tenths	hundredths
3	2	1	
+	6	7	8
		8	8

b)

ones	tenths	hundredths	thousandths
4	0	5	3
2	7	2	

8. Add by adding each place value. Regroup wherever necessary. Example:

ones	tenths
1	6
+ 4	7
5	13

$\underline{\ 13\ }$ tenths =

$\underline{\ \ \ }$ one + $\underline{\ \ \ }$ tenths,

so the sum is

6	3

a)

ones	tenths	hundredths
	6	3
+ 9	1	8

$\underline{\ \ \ }$ hundredths =

$\underline{\ \ \ }$ tenths + $\underline{\ \ \ }$ hundredths,

so the sum is

b)

ones	tenths	hundredths	thousandths
		5	3
+	4	2	9

$\underline{\ \ \ }$ thousandths =

$\underline{\ \ \ }$ hundredths + $\underline{\ \ \ }$ thousandths,

so the sum is

9. Use the place value chart to add the decimals. Then regroup.

a) 0.823 + 3.146 + 0.4

tens	ones	tenths	hundredths	thousandths
+				

Regroup:

b) 0.43 + 45.452 + 2.4

tens	ones	tenths	hundredths	thousandths
+				

Regroup:

BONUS ▶ Regroup twice to add: 5.412 + 11.035 + 2.357

NS8-36 Adding and Subtracting Decimals

1. Add the decimals.

a) 0.42 + 0.34

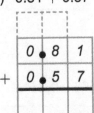

b) 5.71 + 4.26

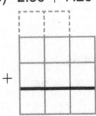

Adding Decimals

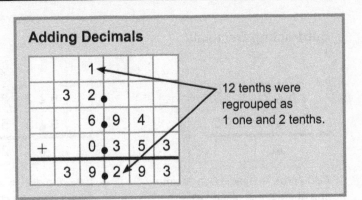

12 tenths were regrouped as 1 one and 2 tenths.

c) 0.516 + 0.473

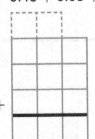

d) 9.317 + 0.162

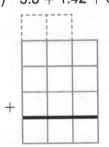

2. Add the decimals. Line up the decimal points. Put a decimal point in place ready for the answer.

a) 0.81 + 0.57

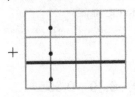

b) 2.56 + 7.26

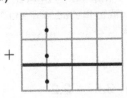

c) 0.583 + 1.254

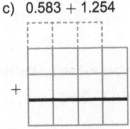

d) 4.444 + 5.078

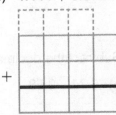

e) 0.43 + 0.08 + 0.42

f) 5.8 + 1.42 + 0.6

g) 1.278 + 0.56 + 6.304

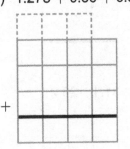

h) 0.9 + 0.99 + 0.999

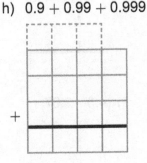

3. Add the decimals on grid paper.

a) 4.32 + 2.88

b) 3.64 + 5.48

c) 9.493 + 3.17

d) 0.87 + 0.027

e) 7.096 + 2.169 + 5.38

f) 0.077 + 2.84 + 0.699

g) 47.5 + 7.007 + 16.87

4. a) The mass of a nickel is 3.95 g and the mass of a penny is 2.35 g. What is the total mass of 2 nickels and 3 pennies?

b) The mass of a dime is 1.75 g, and the mass of a quarter is 4.4 g. What is heavier, 10 dimes or 4 quarters?

5. Bill adds 43.4 + 5.65 on grid paper. He gets 99.9. Is this the right answer? Explain Bill's mistake.

NS8-36 Adding and Subtracting Decimals *(continued)*

Subtracting Decimals

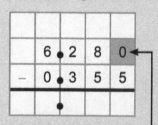

Add zeros to make each decimal end at the same place value.

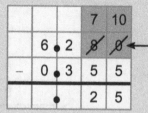

If the top digit in a column is **less than the digit below** it, take 1 from the column to the left and add 10 to the top digit.

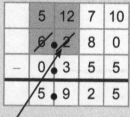

6. Subtract the decimals.

a) 0.43 – 0.21

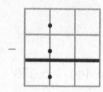

b) 0.86 – 0.24

c) 3.57 – 2.2

d) 6.39 – 0.35

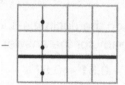

7. Subtract the decimals. Remember to line up the decimal points.

a) 0.71 – 0.58

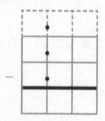

b) 5.62 – 3.56

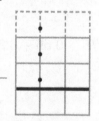

c) 7.156 – 4.25

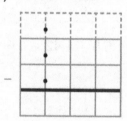

d) 2.563 – 0.271

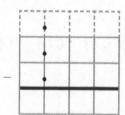

e) 4.5 – 2.67

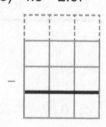

f) 31.1 – 23.2

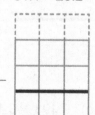

g) 7.455 – 6.78

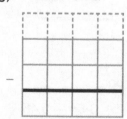

h) 5.207 – 1.239

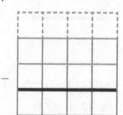

8. Subtract the decimals on grid paper.

a) 0.87 – 0.024   b) 9.435 – 3.12   c) 5.83 – 3.68   d) 4.58 – 2.72

9. What is the difference in the thickness of these coins?

a) a penny (1.45 mm) and a dime (1.22 mm)

b) a dollar (1.95 mm) and a quarter (1.58 mm)

NS8-37 Multiplying Decimals by 10

If a hundreds block represents 1 whole (1.0), then a tens block represents 1 tenth (0.1).

$10 \times 0.1 = 1.0$

10 tenths make 1 whole.

1. Multiply the number of tens blocks by 10. Draw the number of hundreds blocks you would have, then complete the multiplication sentence.

a)
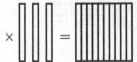

$10 \times 0.3 = \underline{\quad 3 \quad}$

b) $10 \times \ \ =$

$10 \times 0.2 = \underline{\qquad}$

c) $10 \times \ \ =$

$10 \times 0.6 = \underline{\qquad}$

2. To multiply by 10, shift the decimal one place to the right.

a) $10 \times 0.7 = \underline{\quad 7 \quad}$　　b) $10 \times 0.8 = \underline{\qquad}$　　c) $10 \times 1.5 = \underline{\qquad}$　　d) $10 \times 0.9 = \underline{\qquad}$

e) $10 \times 3.4 = \underline{\qquad}$　　f) $4.5 \times 10 = \underline{\qquad}$　　g) $15.6 \times 10 = \underline{\qquad}$　　h) $12.3 \times 10 = \underline{\qquad}$

i) $10 \times 3.07 = \underline{\quad 30.7 \quad}$　　j) $10 \times 3.78 = \underline{\qquad}$　　k) $10 \times 87.4 = \underline{\qquad}$　　l) $62.35 \times 10 = \underline{\qquad}$

To change metres to decimetres, multiply by 10.　　　　1 m = 10 dm

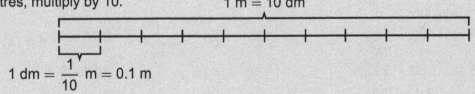

$1 \text{ dm} = \dfrac{1}{10} \text{ m} = 0.1 \text{ m}$

3. Find the answers.

a) $0.3 \text{ m} = \underline{\qquad} \text{ dm}$　　　　b) $0.7 \text{ m} = \underline{\qquad} \text{ dm}$　　　　c) $6.5 \text{ m} = \underline{\qquad} \text{ dm}$

4. 10×6 can be written as a sum: $6 + 6 + 6 + 6 + 6 + 6 + 6 + 6 + 6 + 6$.

Write 10×0.6 as a sum and skip count by 0.6 to find the answer.

5. A dime is a tenth of a dollar (10¢ = $0.10). Draw a picture or use money to show that $10 \times \$0.70 = \$7.00$.

NS8-38 Multiplying Decimals by 100 and 1 000

 = 1.0   □ = 0.01 ——————————————→ 100 × □ =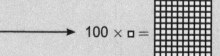

If a hundreds block represents 1 whole (1.0),
then a ones block represents 1 hundredth (0.01).

100 × 0.01 = 1.0
100 hundredths make 1 whole.

1. Write a multiplication sentence for each picture.

a) 100 × =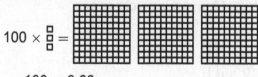

___100 × 0.03___ = _____

b) 100 × □ =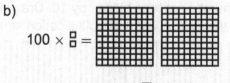

_____ = _____

The picture shows why the decimal shifts two places to the right when you multiply by 100.

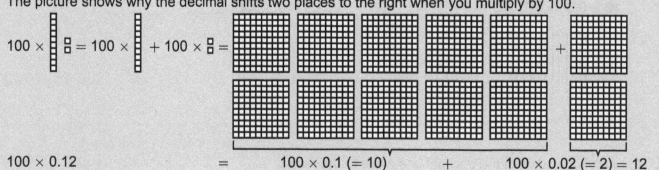

100 × 0.12   =   100 × 0.1 (= 10)   +   100 × 0.02 (= 2) = 12

2. To multiply by 100, shift the decimal two places to the right.

a) 100 × 0.6 = __60__   b) 4.5 × 100 = _____   c) 100 × 8.2 = _____

d) 100 × 7.3 = _____   e) 3.1 × 100 = _____   f) 100 × 7.0 = _____

g) 0.24 × 100 = _____   h) 100 × 0.86 = _____   i) 0.03 × 100 = _____

3. Multiply.

a) 100 × 0.02 = _____   b) 100 × 0.03 = _____   c) 0.73 × 100 = _____   d) 0.48 × 100 = _____

e) 100 × 3.72 = _____   f) 4.08 × 100 = _____   g) 100 × 0.34 = _____   h) 100 × 0.8 = _____

i) 2.4 × 100 = _____   j) 100 × 0.05 = _____   k) 1.24 × 100 = _____   l) 3.5 × 100 = _____

4. a) What do 1 000 thousandths add up to? _____   b) What is 1 000 × 0.001? _____

5. Look at your answer to Question 4 b).

How many places right does the decimal shift when you multiply by 1 000? _____

6. Multiply the numbers by shifting the decimal.

a) 1 000 × 0.83 = _____   b) 0.836 × 1 000 = _____   c) 1 000 × 7.436 = _____

d) 0.36 × 1 000 = _____   e) 1 000 × 3.45 = _____   f) 2.7 × 1 000 = _____

NS8-39 Dividing Decimals by 10 and 100

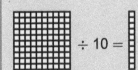 ÷ 10 = | 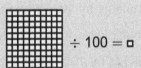 ÷ 10 = □   ÷ 100 = □

Divide 1 whole into 10 equal parts; each part is 1 tenth:

$1.0 \div 10 = 0.1$

Divide 1 tenth into 10 equal parts; each part is 1 hundredth:

$0.1 \div 10 = 0.01$

Divide 1 whole into 100 equal parts; each part is 1 hundredth:

$1.0 \div 100 = 0.01$

1. Complete each picture and write a division statement for it.

a) 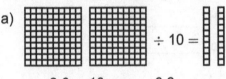 ÷ 10 =

     $\underline{\ 2.0 \div 10\ } = \underline{\ 0.2\ }$

b) 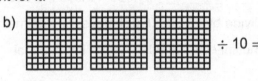 ÷ 10 =

     _____ = ____

c) ÷ 10 = □□

     $\underline{\ 0.2 \div 10\ } = $ ____

d)  ÷ 10 =

     _____ = ____

e) 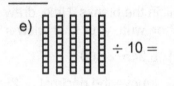 ÷ 10 =

     _____ = ____

f) 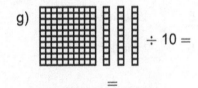 ÷ 10 = □□ □□□

     $\underline{\ 2.3 \div 10\ } = $ ____

g) ÷ 10 =

     _____ = ____

2. Division undoes multiplication. How do you undo multiplying by 10 or 100?

a) To multiply by 10, I move the decimal point _____ places to the _____,

     so to divide by 10, I move the decimal point _____ places to the _____.

b) To multiply by 100, I move the decimal point _____ places to the _____,

     so to divide by 100, I move the decimal point _____ places to the _____.

3. Shift the decimal one or two places to the left by drawing an arrow, then write the answer in the blank. Hint: If there is no decimal, add one to the right of the number first.

a) $0.5 \div 10 = $ _____   b) $0.8 \div 10 = $ _____   c) $0.7 \div 10 = $ _____   d) $4.1 \div 10 = $ _____

e) $36 \div 10 = $ _____   f) $71 \div 10 = $ _____   g) $0.6 \div 10 = $ _____   h) $23.4 \div 10 = $ _____

i) $3.0 \div 100 = $ _____   j) $8.1 \div 100 = $ _____   k) $0.8 \div 100 = $ _____   l) $51.3 \div 100 = $ _____

4. Explain why $1.00 \div 100 = 0.01$, using a dollar coin as a whole.

5. A wall 3.5 m wide is painted with 100 stripes of equal width. How wide is each stripe?

6. $6 \times 3 = 18$ and $18 \div 6 = 3$ are in the same fact family. Write a division statement in the same fact family as $10 \times 0.1 = 1.0$.

NS8-40 Multiplying and Dividing by Powers of 10

1. a) To multiply by 10, I move the decimal ___1___ place(s) to the _____right_____.

    b) To multiply by 1 000, I move the decimal _____ place(s) to the _____.

    c) To divide by 100, I move the decimal _____ place(s) to the _____.

    d) To divide by 10, I move the decimal _____ place(s) to the _____.

    e) To _____ by 1 000, I move the decimal _____ places to the left.

    f) To _____ by 10, I move the decimal _____ place to the left.

    g) To _____ by 100, I move the decimal _____ places to the right.

    h) To divide by 10 000 000, I move the decimal _____ places to the _____.

    i) To multiply by 100 000, I move the decimal _____ places to the _____.

2. Fill in the blanks. Next, draw arrows to show how you would shift the decimal.
    Then write your final answer in the grid.

    a) 6.345 × 100

    I move the decimal ___2___ places _____right_____.

    | | | 6 | . 3 | 4 | 5 | | | rough work |
    | | | 6 | 3 | 4 | . 5 | | | final answer |

    b) 7.8 ÷ 1 000

    I move the decimal ___3___ places _____left_____.

    | | | | | 7 | . 8 | | | rough work |
    | | . 0 | 0 | 7 | 8 | | | final answer |

    c) 238.567 × 1 000

    I move the decimal _____ places _____.

    | | 2 | 3 | 8 | . 5 | 6 | 7 | | rough work |
    | | | | | | | | | final answer |

    d) 200.75 ÷ 100

    I move the decimal _____ places _____.

    | | 2 | 0 | 0 | . 7 | 5 | | | rough work |
    | | | | | | | | | final answer |

    e) 0.401 × 100 000

    I move the decimal _____ places _____.

    | | | 0 | . 4 | 0 | 1 | | | rough work |
    | | | | | | | | | final answer |

    f) 23.683 ÷ 10 000

    I move the decimal _____ places _____.

    | | | 2 | 3 | . 6 | 8 | 3 | | rough work |
    | | | | | | | | | final answer |

3. Copy the numbers onto grid paper. Show how you would shift the decimal
    in each case.

    a) 2.78 × 1 000   b) 48.002 × 100   c) 0.054 × 10   d) 60.07 × 1 000   e) 0.08 × 10 000

    f) 0.845 ÷ 10   g) 180.67 ÷ 100   h) 89.07 ÷ 1 000   i) 19.34 ÷ 10 000   j) 0.06 ÷ 1 000

NS8-41 Multiplying Decimals by Whole Numbers

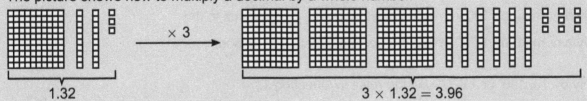

The picture shows how to multiply a decimal by a whole number.

$\times 3$ →

1.32

$3 \times 1.32 = 3.96$

Hint: Simply multiply each digit separately.

1. Multiply mentally.

a) $3 \times 1.23 =$ _____   b) $2 \times 3.4 =$ _____   c) $6 \times 2.01 =$ _____   d) $3 \times 4.2 =$ _____

e) $4 \times 1.21 =$ _____   f) $5 \times 4.1 =$ _____   g) $2 \times 7.13 =$ _____   h) $7 \times 8.01 =$ _____

2. Multiply by exchanging tenths for ones.

a) $7 \times 1.4 =$ __7__ ones + __28__ tenths = __9__ ones + __8__ tenths = __9.8__

b) $3 \times 4.6 =$ _____ ones + _____ tenths = _____ ones + _____ tenths = _____

c) $4 \times 5.7 =$ _____ ones + _____ tenths = _____ ones + _____ tenths = _____

d) $3 \times 6.9 =$ _____

3. Multiply by exchanging tenths for ones or hundredths for tenths.

a) $3 \times 3.61 =$ _____ ones + _____ tenths + _____ hundredths

= _____ ones + _____ tenths + _____ hundredths = _____

b) $4 \times 2.15 =$ _____ ones + _____ tenths + _____ hundredths

= _____ ones + _____ tenths + _____ hundredths = _____

4. Multiply. In some questions you will have to regroup twice.

a)
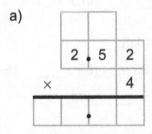

b)
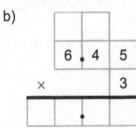

c)
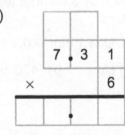

d)
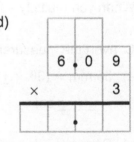

5. Find the products.

a) 6×4.6 b) 7×0.5 c) 8×5.2 d) 2×2.37 e) 3×35.6 f) 6×4.7

g) 5×2.8 h) 6×9.62 i) 4×5.96 j) 9×6.27 k) 4×46.82 l) 5×38.75

6. You can rewrite the product 70×3.6 as $10 \times 7 \times 3.6$. Use this method to find these products.

a) 50×3.1 b) 70×0.6 c) 40×9.67 d) 300×7.4 e) 600×0.3

NS8-42 Multiplying Decimals by 0.1, 0.01, and 0.001

1. To multiply a number by 10, move the decimal point __1__ place to the ___right___ .

   To multiply a number by 100, move the decimal point _____ places to the _____.

   To multiply a number by 1 000, move the decimal point _____ places to the _____.

2. a) Multiply by 10, 100, or 1 000. Use the rules in Question 1.

   $10 \times 0.1 =$ __1.0__ $100 \times 0.1 =$ _____ $1\,000 \times 0.1 =$ _____

   b) Rule: To multiply a number by 0.1, move the decimal point _____ place to the _____.

   c) Use your rule from part b) to find these products.

   i) $0.1 \times 0.1 =$ _____   ii) $0.01 \times 0.1 =$ _____   iii) $0.001 \times 0.1 =$ _____

   iv) $5 \times 0.1 =$ _____   v) $0.2 \times 0.1 =$ _____   vi) $0.07 \times 0.1 =$ _____

3. a) Multiply by moving the decimal point. Use the rules in Question 1.

   $10 \times 0.01 =$ _____ $100 \times 0.01 =$ _____ $1\,000 \times 0.01 =$ _____

   b) Rule: To multiply a number by 0.01, move the decimal point _____ places to the _____.

   c) Predict: To multiply a number by 0.001, move the decimal point _____ places to the _____.

   d) Use your rule from part b) and your prediction from part c) to determine these products. Use a calculator to check your answers.

   i) $0.1 \times 0.01 =$ _____   ii) $0.01 \times 0.01 =$ _____   iii) $0.3 \times 0.001 =$ _____

   iv) $2.5 \times 0.01 =$ _____   v) $13.9 \times 0.001 =$ _____   vi) $810.6 \times 0.001 =$ _____

4. Multiply.

   a) 0.05×0.01 b) 0.32×0.001 c) 50×0.01 d) 0.001×23.7

   e) 0.1×72.35 f) 0.01×853.2 g) $90\,014 \times 0.001$ **BONUS ▶** $17.03 \times 0.000\,01$

5. When you multiply a number n by a number less than 1, the product is _____ than n.

6. Convert the measurements. Use 1 mm = 0.1 cm, 1 cm = 0.01 m, 1 m = 0.001 km.

   a) 36 mm = (36 × __0.1__) cm   b) 470 cm = (470 × _____) m   c) 85 m = (85 × _____) km

   = _____ cm   = _____ m   = _____ km

7. a) Rewrite each decimal as a product with one factor that is 0.1, 0.01, or 0.001.

   i) $0.2 = 2 \times$ __0.1__   ii) $0.7 = 7 \times$ ____   iii) $0.03 =$ ____ $\times 0.01$ iv) $0.005 = 5 \times$ ____

   b) Rewrite the decimal as you did in part a). Then multiply.

   i) $16 \times 0.2 = 16 \times 2 \times 0.1$ ii) $75 \times 0.04 = 75 \times$ ____ $\times 0.01$ iii) $18 \times 0.005 = 18 \times$ ____ $\times 0.001$

   = ____ × 0.1   = ____ × 0.01   = ____ × 0.001

   = ____   = ____   = ____

NS8-43 Multiplying Decimals by Decimals

A place value after the decimal point is called a **decimal place**.

1. How many decimal places does each number have?

   a) 201.4 has _____   b) 72.03 has _____   c) 214.126 has _____   d) 80.023 007 has _____

2. a) Change each decimal to a fraction with denominator 10, 100, or 1 000.

   i) $0.2 =$ _____   ii) $0.02 =$ _____   iii) $0.12 =$ _____   iv) $5.1 =$ _____   v) $8.247 =$ _____

   b) Compare the number of zeros in the denominator of the fraction to the number of decimal places in the decimal. What do you notice?

3. Shade squares to show each amount. Find the product.

   a) 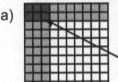 Shade 2 rows to show 2 tenths.
   Shade 3 columns to show 3 tenths.
    $\frac{6}{100}$

   $\frac{2}{10}$ of $\frac{3}{10}$ is $\frac{6}{100}$ so $\frac{2}{10} \times \frac{3}{10} = \frac{6}{100}$

   b) 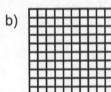 $\frac{2}{10} \times \frac{3}{5} =$

   c) 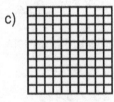 $\frac{7}{10} \times \frac{4}{10} =$

4. Write a multiplication sentence for each figure.

   a) 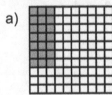 $\frac{7}{10} \times \frac{3}{10} = \frac{21}{100}$

   b) 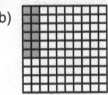 _____

   c) _____

   d) _____

5. Multiply the fractions (see p. 39).

   a) $\frac{3}{100} \times \frac{5}{10}$ b) $\frac{3}{10} \times \frac{5}{10}$ c) $\frac{3}{100} \times \frac{5}{100}$ d) $\frac{3}{1000} \times \frac{5}{10}$

6. Look at your answers to Question 5. When multiplying fractions with denominator 10, 100, 1 000, etc., how can you find the number of zeros in the denominator of the product?

7. a) To find each product, first change each decimal to a fraction and multiply using the rule for multiplying fractions. Then change your answer back into a decimal.

   i) $0.3 \times 0.7 = \frac{3}{10} \times \frac{7}{10} = \frac{21}{100} = 0.21$ ii) 0.5×0.4

   iii) 0.2×0.8 iv) 0.05×0.4 v) 0.05×0.03 vi) 0.02×0.007

   b) How can you find the number of decimal places in the product without multiplying?

NS8-43 Multiplying Decimals by Decimals (continued)

Example: 0.28×0.4	Step 1: Multiply the decimals as if they were whole numbers. $28 \times 4 \quad 112$	Step 2: 0.28 has 2 decimal places and 0.4 has 1 decimal place. So the product should have $2 + 1 = 3$ decimals places. $0.28 \times 0.4 \quad 0.112$

8. Using the rule given above, multiply the decimals in your notebook.

a) 0.5×0.8 b) 0.7×0.9 c) 0.2×0.6 d) 0.15×0.8 e) 0.26×0.3

f) 0.4×0.67 g) 0.32×0.9 h) 0.04×0.7 i) 0.2×0.7 j) 0.8×0.46

BONUS ▶ $0.4 \times 0.3 \times 0.02 \times 0.02 \times 0.003$

9. Round each decimal number to the first digit from the left that is not 0—this is called the **leading digit**.

a) $0.023\ 7 \approx \underline{\ 0.02\ }$ b) $0.003\ 89 \approx \underline{\qquad}$ c) $92.156 \approx \underline{\qquad}$ d) $0.007\ 777\ 77 \approx \underline{\qquad}$

10. Estimate the products.

a) $2.1 \times 6.8 \approx \underline{\qquad} \times \underline{\qquad} = \underline{\qquad}$ b) $6.54 \times 3.417 \approx \underline{\qquad} \times \underline{\qquad} = \underline{\qquad}$

c) 3.25×5.498 d) 15.125×2.064 e) 9.678×44.7 f) 35.78×46.72

11. Estimate the product, then place the decimal point correctly in each answer.

a) $7.8 \times 4 = 3\ 1\ 2$ b) $35.60 \times 4.8 = 1\ 7\ 0\ 8\ 8$

c) $5.25 \times 1.78 = 9\ 3\ 4\ 5$ d) $47.35 \times 3.187 = 1\ 5\ 0\ 9\ 0\ 4\ 4\ 5$

12. Estimate each product, then correct the answers that are wrong.

a) $3.4 \times 2.01 = 6\ .\ 8\quad 3\quad 4$ b) $3.4 \times 2.05 = 0\ .\ 6\quad 9\quad 7$

c) $3.4 \times 2.056 = 6\ .\ 9\quad 9\quad 0\quad 4$ d) $76.35 \times 11.23 = 8\quad 5\quad 7\ .\ 4\quad 1\quad 0\quad 5$

13. Multiply as if the numbers were whole numbers. Then estimate to place the decimal point.

a) 2.7×3.6 b) 6.8×0.73 c) 4.5×3.9

14. $a \times b = 0.24$. Write as many possible values for a and b as you can find.

15. Gus asks Katie and Anna to place the decimal point in the answer. $2.74 \times 32.5 = 8\quad 9\quad 0\quad 5$

Katie estimates $2.74 \times 32.5 \approx 3 \times 30 = 90$ and writes $8\quad 9\ .\ 0\quad 5$

Anna counts decimal places: $2 + 1 = 3$ and writes $8\ .\ 9\quad 0\quad 5$

a) Check on a calculator to see who is right.

$2.74 \times 32.5 = \underline{\qquad\qquad}$ so $\underline{\qquad\qquad}$ is right.

b) Calculate 274×325. What answer did you get? How does it compare to 8 905? Explain why counting decimal places gave the wrong answer in this case. Hint: What mistake did Gus make?

NS8-44 Multiplying Decimals by 2- and 3-Digit Decimals

1. Multiply in parts and finish the charts.

a) $6.5 \times 2.3 = \qquad 6.5 \times 2 \qquad + \qquad 6.5 \times 0.3$

$= (6 \times 2) + (0.5 \times 2) + (6 \times 0.3) + (0.5 \times 0.3)$

$= \underline{\quad 12 \quad} + \underline{\quad 1.0 \quad} + \underline{\quad 1.8 \quad} + \underline{\quad 0.15 \quad}$

$= \underline{\qquad 13.0 \qquad} + \underline{\qquad 1.95 \qquad}$

$= \underline{\qquad 14.95 \qquad}$

×	2	0.3
6	12	1.8
0.5	1	0.15

b) $7.4 \times 3.5 = 7.4 \times \underline{\qquad} + 7.4 \times \underline{\qquad}$

$= (7 \times \underline{\quad}) + (0.4 \times \underline{\quad}) + (7 \times \underline{\quad}) + (0.4 \times \underline{\quad})$

$= \underline{\quad} + \underline{\quad} + \underline{\quad} + \underline{\quad}$

$= \underline{\quad} + \underline{\quad}$

$= \underline{\quad}$

×	3	0.5
7		
0.4		

c) 9.3×2.8 Find the products of the parts.

×		

Add the products of the parts.

$9.3 \times 2.8 = \underline{\quad} + \underline{\quad} + \underline{\quad} + \underline{\quad}$

$= \underline{\quad} + \underline{\quad}$

$= \underline{\quad}$

d) 9.3×10.4 e) 20.5×10.2 f) 6.6×6.6 g) 100.7×2.3

2. Multiply. Estimate or count decimal places to place the decimal point.

a)

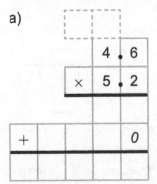

b)

c)

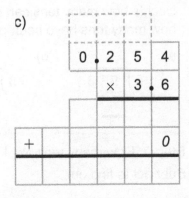

3. Multiply. Use long multiplication. Estimate or count decimal places to place the decimal point.

a) 2.8×3.6 b) 16.7×0.73 c) 5.205×1.4 d) 432.74×0.32 e) 9.452×4.6

4. Calculate using a calculator. Estimate to check your answer. Round answers to 2 decimal places.

a) 6.235×5.88 b) 78.401×31.72 c) 457.13×0.786 d) 2.222×2.222

NS8-45 Long Division — 3- and 4-Digit by 1-Digit

Problem: Divide 95 objects into 4 groups (95 ÷ 4).

Here is a base ten model of the problem.

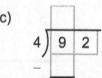

95 ÷ 4 →

?   ?   ?   ?

95 = 9 tens + 5 ones

Solve the problem using **long division**.

Step 1: Write the numbers like this: 4)95

the number of groups ↗   ↖ the number you are dividing

Step 2: How can you divide 9 tens blocks equally into the 4 groups?

You can divide 8 of the 9 tens blocks into 4 equal groups of size 2:

There are 2 tens blocks in each group. → 2 4)95

There are 4 groups.

2
4)95
8 ← 2 × 4 = 8 tens blocks placed

1. How many groups are you going to make? How many tens blocks can you put in each group?

   a) 4)91

   groups _____

   number of tens in each group _____

   b) 3)74

   groups _____

   number of tens in each group _____

   c) 6)85

   groups _____

   number of tens in each group _____

   d) 2)73

   groups _____

   number of tens in each group _____

2. Decide how many tens can be placed in each group. Then multiply to find out how many tens have been placed.

   a) 5)9 3

   b) 3)8 4

   c) 4)9 2

   d) 5)9 4

   e) 9)9 1

Step 3: How many tens blocks are left? Subtract to find out.

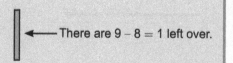

← There are 9 − 8 = 1 left over.

3. For each question, carry out the first **three** steps of long division.

   a) 5)6 2

   b) 4)4 8

   c) 2)8 7

   d) 3)6 4

   e) 5)8 5

   f) 7)8 3

NS8-45 Long Division — 3- and 4-Digit by 1-Digit *(continued)*

Step 4: There is 1 tens block left over, and there are 5 ones in 95.

So there are 15 ones left in total. Write the 5 beside the 1 to show this.

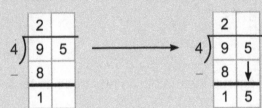

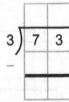

There are still 15 ones to place in 4 groups.

← There are still this many ones to place.

4. Carry out the first **four** steps of long division.

a) 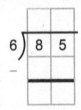 6)85

b) 8)97

c) 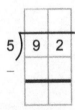 5)92

d) 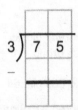 3)75

e) 3)73

Step 5: How many ones can you put in each group?

Divide to find out:

2 3 ← 15 ÷ 4 = **3** R ____
4)9 5
  8
  1 5

How many ones are left over?

5. Carry out the first **five** steps of long division.

a) 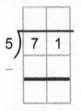 5)71

b) 4)57

c) 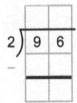 2)96

d) 3)93

e) 5)82

Steps 6 and 7: Find the number of ones left over.

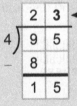

2 3
4)9 5
  8
  1 5
  1 2 ← There are 3 × 4 = 12 ones placed.
    3 ← There are 15 – 12 = 3 ones left over.

Long division and the model both show that **95 ÷ 4 = 23 with 3 left over.**

6. Carry out all the steps of long division on grid paper.

a)  6)83   b) 4)55   c) 3)95   d) 3)82   e) 4)69   f) 7)87

How to divide 334 objects into 2 groups using a base ten model and long division.

Base ten model of 334:

Step 1: Divide the hundreds into 2 groups.

remaining blocks

```
        1  ←── 1 hundreds block
  2 ) 3  3  4    in each group
  -  2  ←── 2 hundreds placed
        1  ←── 1 hundred left over
```

Step 2: Regroup the remaining hundreds as tens.

```
        1
  2 ) 3  3  4
  -  2  ↓
        1  3  ←── 13 tens
```

Step 3: Divide the tens into 2 groups.

```
        1  6  ←── 6 tens in each group
  2 ) 3  3  4
  -  2
        1  3
        1  2  ←── 12 tens placed
              1  ←── 1 ten left over
```

Step 4: Regroup and divide the remaining ones.

```
        1  6  7
  2 ) 3  3  4
  -  2
        1  3
        1  2
              1  4
              1  4
                 0
```

7. Divide.

a)
```
  5 ) 8  3  2
  -
  -
```

b)
```
  3 ) 6  4  5
  -
  -
```

c)
```
  6 ) 8  4  1
  -
  -
```

d)
```
  8 ) 9  7  8
  -
  -
```

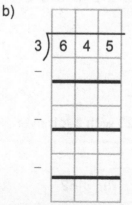
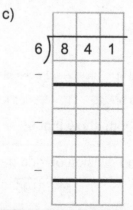
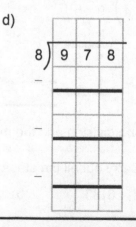

8. In each question below, there are fewer hundreds than the number of groups.

Write a zero in the hundreds position to show that no hundreds can be placed in equal groups. Then perform the division as if the hundreds had automatically been exchanged for tens.

a)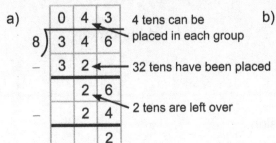

4 tens can be placed in each group

32 tens have been placed

2 tens are left over

b)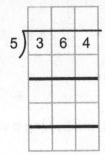

c)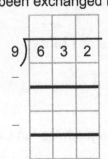

d)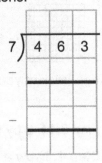

9. In each question below say how many tens or hundreds can be placed in 5 groups. Underline the place values you will divide by 5.

a) 5)315

31 tens

b) 5)726

7 hundreds

c) 5)623

d) 5)321

e) 5)892

f) 5)240

g) 5)987

h) 5)412

10. Divide.

a)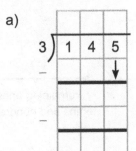

b)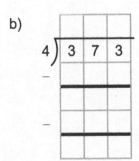

c)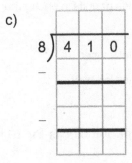

d)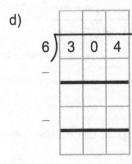

e)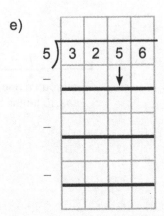

f)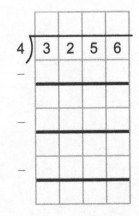

g)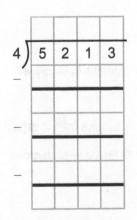

h)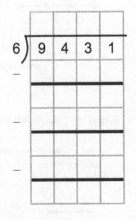

i) 9)784

j) 7)3 512

k) 8)312

l) 8)65 135

m) 2)7 463

n) 3)7 913

o) 5)6 417

p) 8)6 417

q) 6)6 417

r) 7)6 417

NS8-46 Dividing Decimals by Whole Numbers

You can divide a decimal by a whole number by making a base ten model. Here is what the blocks represent:

 = **1 one** or **1 unit**   = **1 tenth**   □ = **1 hundredth**

Keep track of your work using long division.

1. Find **3.14 ÷ 2** by making a base ten model and by long division.

   Step 1: Draw a base ten model for 3.14.

   Draw your model here.

   Step 2: Divide the largest (unit) blocks into 2 equal groups.

   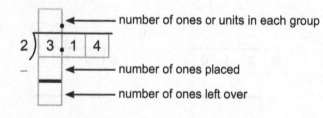

   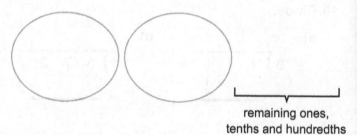

   remaining ones, tenths and hundredths

   Step 3: Exchange the leftover unit blocks for 10 tenths.

   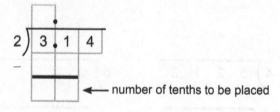

   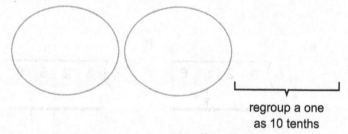

   regroup a one as 10 tenths

   Step 4: Divide the tenths blocks into 2 equal groups.

   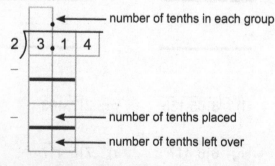

   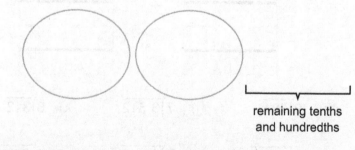

   remaining tenths and hundredths

NS8-46 Dividing Decimals by Whole Numbers *(continued)*

Step 5: Exchange the leftover tenth block for 10 hundredths.

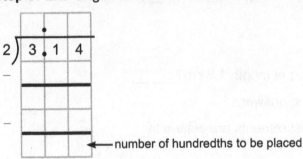

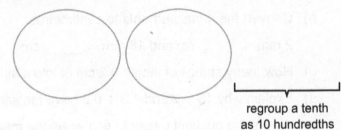

← regroup a tenth as 10 hundredths

← number of hundredths to be placed

Steps 6 and 7: Divide the hundredths into 2 equal groups.

← number of hundredths in each group

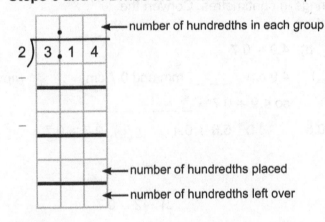

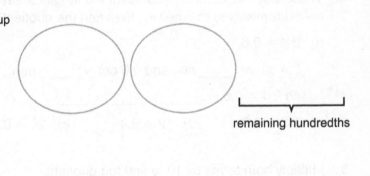

← remaining hundredths

← number of hundredths placed

← number of hundredths left over

2. Divide.

a)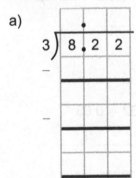

b)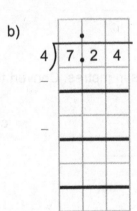

c)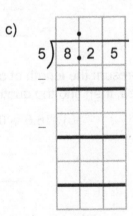

d)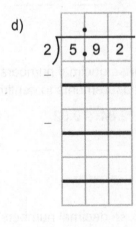

3. Divide.

a) $8\overline{)6.48}$ b) $9\overline{)8.1}$ c) $8\overline{)3.44}$ d) $9\overline{)6.21}$ e) $5\overline{)36.45}$

4. Five oranges cost $3.65. How much does each orange cost?

5. A regular octagon has a perimeter of 3.12 m. How long is each side?

6. Philip cycled 58.4 km in 4 hours. How many kilometres did he cycle in an hour?

7. Louise earned $95.36 in 8 hours. How much did she earn each hour?

8. Which is a better deal, 8 markers for $4.96 or 7 markers for $4.55.

NS8-47 Dividing Decimals by Decimals

1. a) How many strings of length 2 mm fit into a string of length 18 mm? _____

   b) Convert the measurements to centimetres.

      2 mm = _____ cm and 18 mm = _____ cm

   c) How many strings of length 0.2 cm fit into a string of length 1.8 cm? _____

   d) Explain why 18 ÷ 2 and 1.8 ÷ 0.2 have the same answer.

   e) Why is the quotient easier to find when the measurements are written in millimetres than in centimetres?

2. These decimal numbers represent the length of strings in centimetres. Convert the measurements to millimetres, then find the quotient.

   a) 2.4 ÷ 0.6   b) 4.9 ÷ 0.7

      2.4 cm = _____ mm and 0.6 cm = _____ mm   4.9 cm = _____ mm and 0.7 cm = _____ mm

      so 2.4 ÷ 0.6 = _____ ÷ _____ = _____   so 4.9 ÷ 0.7 = _____ ÷ _____ = _____

   c) 7.2 ÷ 0.9   d) 12 ÷ 0.4   e) 20 ÷ 0.5   f) 5.6 ÷ 0.4   g) 9.8 ÷ 0.7

3. Multiply both terms by 10 to find the quotient.

   a) 8.4 ÷ 0.6   b) 78 ÷ 0.6   c) 42 ÷ 0.7

      = _____ ÷ _____   = _____ ÷ _____   = _____ ÷ _____

      = _____   = _____   = _____

4. These decimal numbers represent the length of strings in metres. Convert the measurements to centimetres, then find the quotient.

   a) 2.84 ÷ 0.02   b) 16.5 ÷ 0.05   c) 7.32 ÷ 0.03

      = _____ ÷ _____   = _____ ÷ _____   = _____ ÷ _____

      = _____   = _____   = _____

5. These decimal numbers represent the length of strings in metres. Convert the measurements to millimetres, then find the quotient.

   a) 1.112 ÷ 0.008   b) 1.778 ÷ 0.007   c) 6.3 ÷ 0.009   d) 5.28 ÷ 0.006

6. Multiply both the dividend and divisor by 10, 100, or 1000 to change them to whole numbers. (Be sure to multiply both by the same number!) Then divide.

   a) 24 ÷ 0.4 = _____ ÷ _____   b) 51 ÷ 0.03 = _____ ÷ _____

      = _____   = _____

   c) 16 ÷ 0.2   d) 63 ÷ 0.07   e) 680 ÷ 0.4   f) 60 ÷ 0.005   g) 12 ÷ 0.003

   h) 4.5 ÷ 0.5   i) 0.08 ÷ 0.4   j) 0.48 ÷ 0.2   k) 62.8 ÷ 0.2   l) 8.8 ÷ 1.1

UNIT 2

Patterns and Algebra 1

PA8-1 Extending Patterns

1. These sequences were made by adding the same number to each term. Find the
   number, then extend the pattern.

   a) 1 , 4 , 7 , _____ , _____ , _____

   b) 2 , 8 , 14 , _____ , _____ , _____

   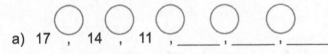
   c) 4 , 9 , 14 , _____ , _____ , _____

   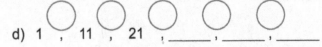
   d) 1 , 11 , 21 , _____ , _____ , _____

2. These sequences were made by subtracting the same number from each term.
   Find the number, then extend the pattern.

   a) 17 , 14 , 11 , _____ , _____ , _____

   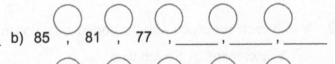
   b) 85 , 81 , 77 , _____ , _____ , _____

   c) 51 , 46 , 41 , _____ , _____ , _____

   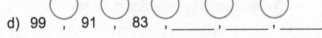
   d) 99 , 91 , 83 , _____ , _____ , _____

3. Find the numbers that are added or subtracted, then extend the pattern.

   Write a plus sign (+) if you add the number and a minus sign (−) if you subtract
   the number.

   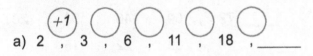
   a) 2 , 3 , 6 , 11 , 18 , _____

   b) 21 , 16 , 12 , 9 , 7 , _____

   c) 3 , 6 , 12 , 24 , 48 , _____

   d) 57 , 37 , 22 , 12 , 7 , _____

   e) 1 , 1 , 2 , 3 , 5 , 8 , 13 , 21 , 34 , _____ , _____ , _____

4. The sequence in Question 3 e) is called the **Fibonacci sequence**. How can you get

   each term from the previous two terms? _____

   _____ .

5. Find the gaps between the gaps and extend the patterns.

   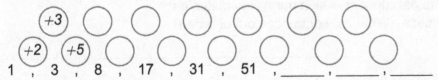
   1 , 3 , 8 , 17 , 31 , 51 , _____ , _____ , _____

PA8-2 Describing Patterns

1. Write the amount by which each term in the sequence increases (goes up) or decreases (goes down). Use a plus sign (+) if the sequence increases and a minus sign (−) if it decreases.

a) 3 , 7 , 5 , 12 , 8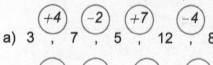

b) 4 , 9 , 5 , 14 , 19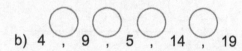

c) 2 , 9 , 10 , 20 , 29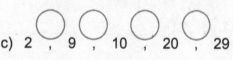

d) 4 , 6 , 8 , 7 , 12

e) 56 , 47 , 45 , 39 , 31

f) 45 , 54 , 59 , 63 , 55

2. Match each sequence with the correct description.

a) **A** increases by 5 each time
   B increases by different amounts

   _____ 11 , 16 , 21 , 26 , 31
   _____ 9 , 15 , 17 , 34 , 37

b) **A** increases by different amounts
   B increases by 7 each time

   _____ 12 , 19 , 26 , 33 , 40
   _____ 6 , 13 , 18 , 26 , 33

c) **A** decreases by the same amount
   B decreases by different amounts

   _____ 21 , 20 , 18 , 15 , 11
   _____ 13 , 10 , 7 , 4 , 1

d) **A** decreases by 13 each time
   B decreases by different amounts

   _____ 72 , 59 , 46 , 33 , 20
   _____ 48 , 35 , 22 , 15 , 3

BONUS ▶

A increases by 5 each time
B decreases by different amounts
C increases by different amounts

_____ 23 , 28 , 29 , 35 , 43
_____ 27 , 24 , 20 , 19 , 16
_____ 34 , 39 , 44 , 49 , 54

A increases and decreases
B increases by the same amount
C decreases by different amounts
D decreases by the same amount

_____ 41 , 39 , 35 , 23 , 7
_____ 10 , 14 , 23 , 19 , 11
_____ 38 , 36 , 34 , 32 , 30
_____ 28 , 31 , 34 , 37 , 40

3. Make 3 sequences that match the descriptions. Ask a partner to match each sequence with the correct description. (Write the sequences out of order!)

   A increases by 6 each time _____ _____

   B decreases by different amounts _____ _____

   C increases and decreases _____ _____

PA8-2 Describing Patterns *(continued)*

4. These sequences were made by multiplying each term by the same number.
Find the number, then extend the pattern.

a) 1 , 2 , 4 , _____ , _____

b) 50 , 100 , 200 , _____ , _____

c) 4 , 12 , 36 , _____ , _____

d) 3 , 30 , 300 , _____ , _____

5. These sequences were made by dividing each term by the same number. Find the
number, then extend the pattern.

a) 400 , 200 , 100 , _____ , _____

b) 96 , 48 , 24 , _____ , _____

c) 500 , 100 , 20 , _____

d) 1600 , 400 , 100 , _____

6. Write a rule for each pattern. Use the words **add**, **subtract**, **multiply**, or **divide**.

a) 3 , 6 , 12 , 24   ×2 ×2 ×2   *start at 3 and multiply by 2*

b) 5 , 8 , 11 , 14   +3 +3 +3   _____

c) 31 , 28 , 25 , 22   _____

d) 81 , 27 , 9 , 3   _____

e) 2, 10, 50, 250

f) 32, 16, 8, 4

g) 30 000, 3 000, 300, 30

h) 10, 200, 4 000, 80 000

7. Describe each pattern as **increasing**, **decreasing**, or **repeating**.

a) 2 , 4 , 8 , 16 , 32 , 64 _____

b) 4 , 8 , 0 , 4 , 8 , 0 _____

c) 30 , 28 , 26 , 24 , 23 _____

d) 2 , 6 , 10 , 14 , 17 _____

e) 11 , 9 , 6 , 11 , 9 , 6 _____

f) 63 , 58 , 53 , 48 , 43 _____

PA8-3 T-tables

Claude makes an **increasing pattern** with squares. He records the number of squares in each figure in a chart or T-table. He also records the number of squares he adds each time he makes a new figure.

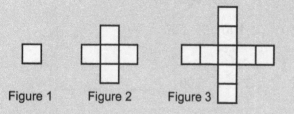

Figure 1   Figure 2   Figure 3

Figure	Number of Squares
1	1
2	5
3	9

4
4
→ Number of squares added each time

The number of squares in the figures are 1, 5, 9, … Claude writes a rule for this number pattern:
Rule: Start at 1 and add 4 each time.

1. Claude makes other increasing patterns with squares.

   How many squares does he add to make each new figure? Write your answers in the circles. Then write a rule for the pattern.

   a)
Figure	Number of Squares
1	2
2	7
3	12

   Rule: Start at _____ and add _____.

   b)
Figure	Number of Squares
1	2
2	9
3	16

   Rule:

   c)
Figure	Number of Squares
1	1
2	4
3	7

   Rule:

2. Extend the number pattern. How many squares would be used in Figure 6?

   a)
Figure	Number of Squares
1	6
2	11
3	16
4	
5	
6	

   b)
Figure	Number of Squares
1	2
2	6
3	10
4	
5	
6	

   c)
Figure	Number of Squares
1	3
2	9
3	15
4	
5	
6	

PA8-3 T-tables *(continued)*

3. At the end of Week 1, Ryan has $150 in his savings account.
   He spends $15 each week.

   a) How much money will he have left at the end of Week 5?

   _____

   b) At the end of which week will he have no money left?

   _____

Week	Savings
1	$150
2	
3	
4	
5	

4. The water in a rain barrel is 18 cm deep at 5 p.m. If 3 cm of rain fall each hour,
   how deep is the water at 9 p.m.?

5. A marina rents kayaks for $8 for the first hour and $6 for every hour after that.
   How much would it cost to rent a kayak for 6 hours?

6. a) Copy and complete the chart for these figures: 1   2   3

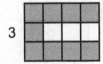

Figure	Number of light squares	Number of dark squares	Total number of squares
1	1	5	6
2			
3			

   b) How many dark squares will be needed for a figure with 7 light squares?
   c) How many squares will be needed for a figure with 15 dark squares?

7. The chart shows how much fuel an airplane burns as it travels.

Time (minutes)	Fuel (kL)	Distance from Airport (km)
0	150	3 600
30	143	3 150
60	136	2 700

   a) How much fuel will be left in the airplane after $2\frac{1}{2}$ hours?

   b) How far from the airport will the plane be after 3 hours?

   c) How much fuel will be left in the airplane when it reaches the airport?

8. Halley's Comet returns to Earth every 76 years. It was last seen in 1986.

   a) List the next three dates it will return to Earth.
   b) When was the first time Halley's comet was seen in the 1900s?

PA8-4 Patterns (Advanced)

1. Here are some number pyramids:

 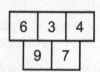

Can you find the rule used to make the patterns in the pyramids? Describe it here:

_____

2. Using the rule you described in Question 1, find the missing numbers:

a)

b)

c)

d)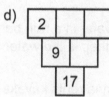

e)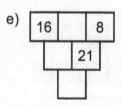

f)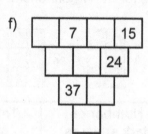

g)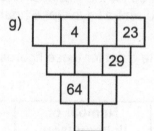

h)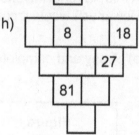

3. **Pascal's Triangle** is made using the rule above, but with all 1s on the outer part of the pyramid.

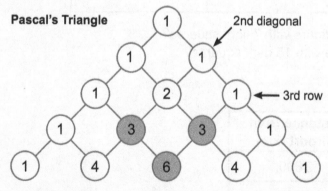

Pascal's Triangle — 2nd diagonal — 3rd row

a) Create Pascal's Triangle in your notebook, up to 7 rows.

b) What is the 3rd number in the 9th row of Pascal's Triangle? Hint: Extend the pattern in the 3rd diagonal.

c) Add the numbers in each of the first five rows of Pascal's Triangle. What pattern do you see in the sums?

d) Using the pattern you found in part c), predict the sum of the numbers in the 8th row.

PA8-5 Variables

A **numeric expression** is a combination of numbers, operation signs, and sometimes brackets, that represents a quantity. For example, these expressions all represent 10:

$7 + 3$ $\qquad\qquad$ $12 - 2$ $\qquad\qquad$ $100 \div 10$ $\qquad\qquad$ $(4 + 1) \times 2$

1. Calculate each expression.

a) $1 + 3 + 4 =$ _____   b) $3 \times 4 =$ _____   c) $2 \times 2 \times 2 =$ _____   d) $5 + 2 =$ _____

An **equation** is a mathematical statement that has two expressions representing the same quantity separated by an equal sign. Example: $12 - 2 = 100 \div 10$

2. Circle two expressions from Question 1 that represent the same quantity.

Write an equation using those two expressions. _____

A **variable** is a letter or symbol (such as x, n, or h) that represents a number. An **algebraic expression** is a combination of one or more variables that may include numbers, operation signs, and brackets.

Examples of algebraic expressions: $\qquad$ $5 \times (t + 7)$ $\qquad$ $n \div 5$ $\qquad$ $(3 + z) \div 5 - y$

3. Make your own example of an algebraic expression. _____

In the product of a number and a variable, the multiplication sign is usually dropped.

Example: $3 \times t = t \times 3$ are both written as $3t$.

4. Rewrite these expressions without multiplication signs.

a) $3 \times s =$ _____3s_____   b) $n \times 5 + 2 =$ ___5n + 2___   c) $12 - 4 \times r =$ _____

d) $7 \times a - 3 =$ _____   e) $b \times 4 - 3 =$ _____   f) $5 + 6 \times w =$ _____

5. Rewrite these expressions with multiplication signs.

a) $3h =$ ___3 × h___   b) $2 - 3g =$ _____   c) $3f + 4 =$ _____

6. It costs $5 per hour to rent a pair of skis. Write an algebraic expression for the cost of renting skis for...

a) h hours: __5 × h__ or __5h__   b) t hours: _____ or _____   c) x hours: _____ or _____

7. A **flat fee** is a fixed charge that doesn't depend on how long you rent an item. Example: A company charges a flat fee of $7 to rent a boat, plus $3 for each hour the boat is used.

Write an expression for the amount you would pay to rent a boat for...

a) h hours
Hourly rate: $4
Flat fee: $5

____4h + 5____

b) t hours
Hourly rate: $3
Flat fee: $8

_____

c) w hours
Hourly rate: $5
Flat fee: $6

_____

PA8-5 Variables *(continued)*

> When replacing a variable with a number in a product, we use brackets.
>
> Example: To substitute 7 for n in $3n = 3 \times n$, we write $3(7) = 3 \times 7$.

8. Write the number 2 in each bracket and evaluate.

a) $5(\underline{\ 2\ }) = \underline{\ 5 \times 2\ } = \underline{\ 10\ }$ b) $3(\underline{\ 2\ }) = \underline{\ 3 \times 2\ } = \underline{\quad}$ c) $4(\underline{\quad}) = \underline{\quad} = \underline{\quad}$

d) $2(\underline{\quad}) + 5$ e) $4(\underline{\quad}) - 2$ f) $6(\underline{\quad}) + 3$

$= \underline{\quad\quad} = \underline{\quad\quad}$ $= \underline{\quad\quad} = \underline{\quad\quad}$ $= \underline{\quad\quad} = \underline{\quad\quad}$

9. Replace n with 2 in each expression.

a) $4n + 3$
$= 4(2) + 3$
$= 8 + 3$
$= 11$

b) $5n + 1$

c) $3n - 2$

d) $2n + 3$

10. A company charges a flat fee of $6 to rent a pair of skis plus $3 for each hour you use the skis. The total cost is given by the expression $3h + 6$. Find the cost of renting a pair of skis for…

a) 4 hours

b) 2 hours

c) 5 hours

d) 7 hours

$3(4) + 6$
$= 12 + 6$
$= 18$

11. Replace the variable with the given value and evaluate. This is called **substitution**.

a) $5h + 2, h = 3$

b) $2n + 3, n = \dfrac{1}{2}$

c) $5t - 2, t = 0.8$

$5(3) + 2$
$= 15 + 2$
$= 17$

d) $3m + 9, m = \dfrac{2}{3}$

e) $9 - 2z, z = 4$

f) $3n + 2, n = 0.6$

12. Evaluate each expression.

a) $2n + 3, n = 5$

b) $2t + 3, t = 5$

c) $3 + 2n, n = 5$

$2(5) + 3$
$= 10 + 3 = 13$

13. a) What do you notice about your answers in Question 12? _____

b) Why is that so? _____

PA8-6 Substituting Fractions and Decimals for Variables

1. Replace the variables with the given fraction and evaluate. Write your answer as a mixed or proper fraction.

a) $2x$, $x = \dfrac{1}{3}$

$x = 2(\dfrac{1}{3}) = \dfrac{2}{3}$

b) $u + 5$, $u = \dfrac{5}{7}$

c) $3r$, $r = \dfrac{2}{5}$

d) $s + 6$, $s = \dfrac{3}{5}$

e) $3x + 2$, $x = \dfrac{5}{8}$

f) $z - 2$, $z = \dfrac{13}{5}$

g) $5z - 1$, $z = \dfrac{3}{5}$

h) $3v - 2$, $v = \dfrac{4}{5}$

i) $2h - 1$, $h = \dfrac{2}{3}$

j) $4t + 1$, $t = \dfrac{3}{8}$

k) $5t - 6$, $t = \dfrac{7}{4}$

l) $3w - 8$, $w = 2\dfrac{3}{4}$

2. Replace the variables with the given decimal and evaluate. Write your answer as a decimal.

a) $6x$, $x = 0.5$

$6x = 6(0.5)$
$\quad = 3.0$

b) $9p$, $p = 4.2$

c) $w - 2$, $w = 3.7$

d) $z + 4$, $z = 5.83$

e) $4x + 3$, $x = 1.3$

f) $3m - 5$, $m = 4.75$

g) $3t - 2$, $t = 0.8$

h) $4z - 5$, $z = 2.31$

3. a) Which parts from Questions 1 and 2 have the same answer? _____ and _____

   b) Why are these parts the same?

4. Sandwiches cost $3 and drinks cost $2. The cost of s sandwiches and d drinks is $3s + 2d$.

   Find the cost of the following amounts:

   a) 5 sandwiches and 4 drinks

   $3s + 2d = 3(5) + 2(4)$
   $\qquad\quad = 15 + 8$
   $\qquad\quad = 23$

   b) 6 sandwiches and 6 drinks

   c) 2 sandwiches and 7 drinks

   The cost is __$23__

   The cost is _____

   The cost is _____

PA8-6 Substituting Fractions and Decimals for Variables *(cont'd)*

5. Replace the variables with the given values and evaluate.

   a) $3x + 5y$, $x = 6$ and $y = 2$

   $3(6) + 5(2)$
   $= 18 + 10$
   $= 28$

   b) $4x - y$, $x = 5$ and $y = 3$

   c) $4x - y$, $x = 0.5$ and $y = 1$

   d) $7x + 2y$, $x = \dfrac{1}{3}$ and $y = \dfrac{2}{3}$

   e) $3x + 4y - 2z$, $x = 5$, $y = 2$, $z = 7$

   f) $2x - 3y + 5z$, $x = 5$, $y = \dfrac{1}{3}$, $z = 3$

   g) $2x + y - 3z$, $x = \dfrac{2}{5}$, $y = \dfrac{2}{3}$, $z = \dfrac{1}{6}$

   h) $5x - 3y + 2z$, $x = 3$, $y = \dfrac{1}{3}$, $z = 5$

6. Which two parts of Question 5 have the same answer? _____ and _____

   BONUS ▶ Why are these two parts the same? _____

7. Write an expression for the total value, v, in cents, of these coins:

   a) n nickels   <u> $5n$ </u>

   b) w nickels   _____

   c) n nickels and d dimes   _____

   d) a quarters and b pennies   _____

   e) a quarters, b dimes, c nickels, and d pennies   _____

8. Use your expression from Question 7 e). How much money, in cents, is 3 quarters, 4 dimes, 7 nickels and 8 pennies? Show your work.

9. Write an expression for the maximum number of points to be scored on a 10-question test if Questions 1, 2, and 3 are each worth m points, Questions 4 and 5 are each worth p points, and Questions 6 to 10 are each worth r points.

10. Natalia needs to buy 14 sandwiches, 12 pizzas, and 40 drinks for a party.

    a) If sandwiches cost $s, pizzas cost $p, and drinks cost $d, write an expression for the total cost of the food.

    b) Company A charges $2 for each sandwich, $7 for each pizza, and $1 for each drink. How much would Natalia pay if she bought the food at Company A?

    c) Company B charges $2.50 for each sandwich, $6.80 for each pizza, and $0.95 for each drink. How much would Natalia pay if she bought the food at Company B?

    d) Where should Natalia buy the food for the party—Company A or Company B? Why?

PA8-7 Solving Equations — Guess and Check

Only one value of x will make the equation $x + 3 = 7$ true.

Finding the value of a variable that makes an equation true is called **solving for the variable**.

1. a) Calculate $3n (= 3 \times n)$ and $3n - 5$ for each value of n given in the chart.

n	2	3	4	5	6	7	8	9	10	11	12
$3n$	6	9	12								
$3n - 5$	1	4	7								

b) Use the chart to solve for n.

i) $3n - 5 = 16$

n = _____

ii) $3n - 5 = 25$

n = _____

iii) $3n - 5 = 10$

n = _____

iv) $3n - 5 = 31$

n = _____

REMINDER ▶ Division is often written in fractional form:

$$12 \div 4 = \frac{12}{4} \qquad 15 \div 5 = \frac{15}{5} \qquad x \div 3 = \frac{x}{3} \qquad w \div 7 = \frac{w}{7}$$

2. a) Calculate $x \div 4 \left(= \frac{x}{4}\right)$ and then $\frac{x}{4} + 5$ for each value of x given in the chart.

x	0	4	8	12	16	20	24	28	32	36	40	44
$\frac{x}{4}$	0	1	2	3	4							
$\frac{x}{4} + 5$	5	6	7	8								

b) Use the chart to solve for x.

i) $\frac{x}{4} + 5 = 7$

x = _____

ii) $\frac{x}{4} + 5 = 15$

x = _____

iii) $\frac{x}{4} + 5 = 13$

x = _____

iv) $\frac{x}{4} + 5 = 9$

x = _____

3. Substitute $n = 8$ into the expression on the left side of the equation. Then decide if n needs to be greater than 8, less than 8, or equal to 8 to make the equation true.

a) $3n + 2 = 29$

$3(8) + 2 = $ ___26___ is ___less than___ 29.

So n should be ___greater than___ 8.

b) $2n + 3 = 19$

$2(8) + 3 = $ _____ is _____ 19.

So n should be _____ 8.

c) $\frac{n}{2} + 6 = 9$

$\frac{8}{2} + 6 = $ _____ is _____ 9.

So n should be _____ 8.

d) $\frac{n}{4} + 7 = 10$

$\frac{8}{4} + 7 = $ _____ is _____ 10.

So n should be _____ 8.

No unauthorized copying

Patterns and Algebra 1

PA8-7 Solving Equations — Guess and Check (continued)

4. Solve for n by guessing small values for n, checking, and revising.

   a) $3n + 2 = 8$

   $n =$ _____

   b) $5n - 2 = 13$

   $n =$ _____

   c) $\dfrac{n}{3} + 5 = 7$

   $n =$ _____

   d) $\dfrac{n}{2} - 5 = 3$

   $n =$ _____

5. Sara solves $7x + 11 = 67$ and gets $x = 8$.

   a) Verify Sara's answer.

   b) What value for t solves $7t + 11 = 67$? _____

   c) What value for x solves $11 + 7x = 67$? _____

   How do you know? _____

   d) What value for x solves $67 = 7x + 11$? _____

   How do you know? _____

6. Circle the equations that are just another way of writing $8x + 3 = 51$.

   $3 + 8x = 51$ $8t + 3 = 51$ $3w + 8 = 51$ $8 + 3x = 51$

   $51 = 3 + 8x$ $51 = 8w + 3$ $r \times 8 + 3 = 51$ $51 = 3 + 8t$

   $3 + 8r = 51$ $51 + 8r = 3$ $8z + 3 = 51$ $8z + 51 = 3$

7. Solve these equations by guessing, checking, and revising.

   a) $2 + 7x = 23$

   $x =$ _____

   b) $3 + 5x = 38$

   $x =$ _____

   c) $8 + 2x = 26$

   $x =$ _____

   d) $5 + 3n = 20$

   $n =$ _____

   e) $3 + 5x = 18$

   $x =$ _____

   f) $23 = 7u + 2$

   $u =$ _____

   g) $7u + 5 = 40$

   $u =$ _____

   h) $30 = 3 + 9n$

   $n =$ _____

8. Circle the two equations from Question 7 that are the same, but just written differently.

9. **BONUS** ▶ Solve this equation for x and y: $2x + 1 = 7 = 4y - 1$.

   EXTRA CHALLENGE ▶ Both x and y are whole numbers. How many solutions can you find for $2x + 1 = 4y - 1$?

PA8-7 Solving Equations — Guess and Check (continued)

10. a) Solve each equation by guessing, checking, and revising.

$2x = 8$ $2x + 1 = 9$ $2x + 2 = 10$ $2x + 3 = 11$

$x =$ _____ $x =$ _____ $x =$ _____ $x =$ _____

b) What do you notice about your answers in part a)? _____

Why is this the case? _____

_____

c) Which problem from part a) was easiest to solve? _____

Why? _____

d) Write another equation that has the same answer as the equations in part a).

_____

e) Fill in the box so that the equation has the same answer as the equations in part a).

$2x - \boxed{} = 5$

11. Do $3x = 15$ and $3x - 2 = 13$ have the same answer? How do you know?

12. a) Solve each equation by guessing, checking, and revising.

i) $2x + 1 = 5$ ii) $4x + 2 = 10$ iii) $6x + 3 = 15$ iv) $8x + 4 = 20$

$x =$ _____ $x =$ _____ $x =$ _____ $x =$ _____

b) What do you notice about your answers in part a)? _____

Why is this the case? _____

_____

13. Do $3x - 1 = 11$ and $15x - 5 = 55$ have the same answer? How do you know?

14. All these equations have the same answer. Write the missing numbers.

$3x = 15$ $3x + \boxed{} = 16$ $3x + 4 = \boxed{}$

$3x - \boxed{} = 11$ $6x + \boxed{} = 32$ $\boxed{} x = 150$

PA8-8 Solving Equations — Preserving Equality

1. Write the number that makes each equation true.

   a) $8 + 4 - \boxed{} = 8$ b) $8 \times 3 \div \boxed{} = 8$ c) $8 \div 2 \times \boxed{} = 8$ d) $8 - 5 + \boxed{} = 8$

2. Write the operation that makes each equation true.

   a) $7 + 2 \bigcirc 2 = 7$ b) $8 \times 3 \bigcirc 3 = 8$ c) $12 \div 2 \bigcirc 2 = 12$ d) $15 - 4 \bigcirc 4 = 15$

3. Write the operation and number that make each equation true.

   a) $17 + 3 \underline{\ \ -3\ \ } = 17$ b) $20 \div 4 \underline{\ \ \ \ \ \ } = 20$ c) $18 + 2 \underline{\ \ \ \ \ \ } = 18$

   d) $6 \div 2 \underline{\ \ \ \ \ \ } = 6$ e) $6 \times 2 \underline{\ \ \ \ \ \ } = 6$ f) $6 - 2 \underline{\ \ \ \ \ \ } = 6$

4. How could you undo each action to get back to the number you started with?

   a) add 4 _____ *subtract 4* _____

   b) multiply by 3 _____

   c) divide by 2 _____

   d) subtract 7 _____

5. Start with the number 3. Do the operations in order and then undo them in backwards order.

Add 7	_____10_____		Subtract 7	_____
Multiply by 2	_____20_____		Divide by 2	_____
Subtract 5	_____		Add 5	_____
Divide by 3	_____	⟶	Multiply by 3	_____

   Did you finish with the number you started with? _____

6. Start with the number 11. Do the operations in order and then undo them in backwards order.

Add 4	_____15_____		_____	_____
Divide by 3	_____		_____	_____
Subtract 1	_____		_____	_____
Multiply by 4	_____	⟶	*Divide by 4*	_____

   Did you finish with the number you started with? _____

7. Start with 3. Multiply by 2. Then add 4.

   Circle the sequence of operations that will get you back where you started (that is, back to 3).

   Divide your answer by 2, then subtract 4.   *Subtract 4 from your answer, then divide by 2.*

PA8-8 Solving Equations — Preserving Equality *(continued)*

> Remember: The variable x represents a number, so you can treat it like a number.
>
> | Operation | Result | Operation | Result |
> |---|---|---|---|
> | Add 3 to x | $x + 3$ | Multiply 3 by x | $3 \times x = 3x$ |
> | Add x to 3 | $3 + x$ | Multiply x by 3 | $x \times 3 = 3x$ |
> | Subtract 3 from x | $x - 3$ | Divide x by 3 | $x \div 3 = \dfrac{x}{3}$ |
> | Subtract x from 3 | $3 - x$ | Divide 3 by x | $3 \div x = \dfrac{3}{x}$ |

8. Show the result of each operation.

a) Multiply x by 7 ___$7x$___

b) Add 4 to x ___$x + 4$___

c) Subtract 5 from x _____

d) Subtract x from 5 _____

e) Divide x by 10 _____

f) Divide 9 by x _____

g) Multiply 8 by x _____

h) Add x to 9 _____

BONUS ▶ Add x to y _____

9. What happens to the variable x?

a) $2x$ ___*Multiply by 2*___

b) $3x$ _____

c) $x + 4$ _____

d) $x - 5$ _____

e) $\dfrac{x}{3}$ _____

f) $\dfrac{6}{x}$ _____

g) $4 - x$ _____

BONUS ▶ $x + x$ _____

10. Write the correct operation and number to get back to the variable.

a) $n + 3$ ___-3___ $= n$

b) $n \times 3$ _____ $= n$

c) $5m$ _____ $= m$

d) $x - 5$ _____ $= x$

e) $x + 7$ _____ $= x$

f) $\dfrac{x}{14}$ _____ $= x$

g) $\dfrac{z}{5}$ _____ $= z$

h) $7y$ _____ $= y$

i) $r + 8$ _____ $= r$

11. Circle the expressions that always equal m, for any number m. Check your answers for $m = 5$.

$7m - 7$ $\qquad$ $7m \div 7$ $\qquad$ $m \div 7 \times 7$ $\qquad$ $7 \div m \times 7$ $\qquad$ $7 + m - 7$ $\qquad$ $7 - m + 7$

12. Solve for x by doing the same thing to both sides of the equation. Check your answer.

a) $3x \quad = 12$ ◄——— Check by replacing
$3x \div 3 = 12 \div 3$ $\quad$ x with your answer:
$x \quad = 4$ $\qquad$ $3(4) = 12$

b) $x - 4 = 11$

c) $4x = 20$

d) $x + 5 = 8$

e) $3 + x = 9$

f) $\dfrac{x}{6} = 3$

g) $5x = 15$

h) $x - 7 = 10$

i) $2x = 18$

j) $\dfrac{x}{2} = 3$

k) $x + 1 = 20$

l) $10x = 90$

m) $9x = 54$

n) $x + 26 = 53$

PA8-9 Solving Equations — Two Operations

1. Jason does some operations to the secret number x. He gets 37 every time. Write an equation and then work backwards to find x.

   a) **Perform Jason's operations**

Start with x	x
Multiply by 5	$5x$
Add 7	$5x + 7$
Get 37	$5x + 7 = 37$

   Work backwards to find x

Write the equation again	$5x + 7 = 37$
Undo adding 7 by subtracting 7	$5x + 7 - 7 = 37 - 7$
Write the new equation	$5x = 30$
Undo multiplying by 5 by dividing by 5	$5x \div 5 = 30 \div 5$
Write the new equation	$x = 6$

   You solved for x!

   Check your answer by doing the operations in order:

   Start with your answer: __6__ Multiply by 5: __30__ Add 7: __37__ Do you get 37? __Yes__

   b) **Perform Jason's operations**

Start with x	x
Multiply by 8	_____
Add 5	_____
Get 37	_____

   Work backwards to find x

Write the equation again	_____
Undo adding 5 by subtracting 5	_____
Write the new equation	_____
Undo multiplying by 8 by dividing by 8	_____
Write the new equation	_____

   You solved for x!

   Check your answer by doing the operations in order:

   Start with your answer: _____ Multiply by 8: _____ Add 5: _____ Do you get 37? _____

   c) **Perform Jason's operations**

Start with x	x
Multiply by 4	_____
Subtract 3	_____
Get 37	_____

   Work backwards to find x

Write the equation again	_____
Undo subtracting 3 by adding 3	_____
Write the new equation	_____
Undo multiplying by 4 by dividing by 4	_____
Write the new equation	_____

   You solved for x!

   Check your answer by doing the operations in order:

   Start with your answer: _____ Multiply by 4: _____ Subtract 3: _____ Do you get 37? _____

PA8-9 Solving Equations — Two Operations (continued)

2. Jason does some operations to the secret number x. He gets 10. Write an equation and then work backwards to find x.

a) **Perform Jason's operations**   **Work backwards to find x**

Start with x	x	Write the equation again		$\dfrac{x}{6}$ 3 10
Divide by 6	$\dfrac{x}{6}$	Undo adding 3 by subtracting 3		$\dfrac{x}{6} + 3 - 3 = 10 - 3$
Add 3	$\dfrac{x}{6} + 3$	Write the new equation		$\dfrac{x}{6} = 7$
Get 10	$\dfrac{x}{6} + 3 = 10$	Undo dividing by 6 by multiplying by 6		$\dfrac{x}{6}(6) = 7(6)$
		Write the new equation		$x = 42$
		You solved for x!		

Check your answer by doing the operations in order:

Start with your answer: __42__ Divide by 6: __7__ Add 3: __10__ Do you get 10? __Yes__

b) **Perform Jason's operations**   **Work backwards to find x**

Start with x	x	Write the equation again	
Divide by 4	_____	Undo subtracting 1 by adding 1	_____
Subtract 1	_____	Write the new equation	_____
Get 10	_____	Undo dividing by 4 by multiplying by 4	_____
		Write the new equation	_____
		You solved for x!	

Check your answer by doing the operations in order:

Start with your answer: _____ Divide by 4: _____ Subtract 1: _____ Do you get 10? _____

c) **Perform Jason's operations**   **Work backwards to find x**

Start with x	x	Write the equation again	
Divide by 5	_____	Undo adding 2 by subtracting 2	_____
Add 2	_____	Write the new equation	_____
Get 10	_____	Undo dividing by 5 by multiplying by 5	_____
		Write the new equation	_____
		You solved for x!	

Check your answer by doing the operations in order:

Start with your answer: _____ Divide by 5: _____ Add 2: _____ Do you get 10? _____

3. Solve for the variable by undoing each operation in the equation.

a) $8x + 3 = 27$

$8x + 3 - 3 = \underline{\quad 27 \quad} - \underline{\quad 3 \quad}$

$8x = \underline{\qquad}$

$8x \div 8 = \underline{\qquad} \div \underline{\qquad}$

$x = \underline{\qquad}$

b) $4h - 3 = 37$

$4h - 3 + 3 = 37 + \underline{\qquad}$

$4h = \underline{\qquad}$

$4h \div 4 = \underline{\qquad} \div \underline{\qquad}$

$h = \underline{\qquad}$

c) $\frac{x}{3} + 2 = 9$

$\frac{x}{3} + 2 - 2 = \underline{\quad 9 \quad} - \underline{\quad 2 \quad}$

$\frac{x}{3} = \underline{\quad 7 \quad}$

$\frac{x}{3}(3) = \underline{\quad 7 \quad} (\underline{\quad 3 \quad})$

$x = \underline{\quad 21 \quad}$

d) $\frac{x}{2} + 3 = 9$

$\frac{x}{2} + 3 - 3 = \underline{\qquad} - \underline{\qquad}$

$\frac{x}{2} = \underline{\qquad}$

$\frac{x}{2}(2) = \underline{\qquad} (\underline{\qquad})$

$x = \underline{\qquad}$

e) $3s - 4 = 29$ f) $2t + 3 = 11$ g) $\frac{x}{3} + 5 = 7$ h) $\frac{x}{2} - 4 = 7$

4. Write an expression for the amount of money (in dollars) that each person earns.

a) Katie earns \$1 for every 3 phone calls she makes and she makes x calls. $\underline{\quad \frac{x}{3} \quad}$

b) Ru earns \$3 for every call he makes and he makes m calls. $\underline{\qquad}$

c) Sylvia earns \$1 for every 5 people she serves and she serves p people. $\underline{\qquad}$

d) Tim earns \$5 for every person he serves and he serves p people. $\underline{\qquad}$

5. a) A store charges \$3 each hour to rent a pair of roller blades. Write an expression (using h for hours) for the cost of renting the roller blades. $\underline{\qquad}$

b) Mary rented the roller blades for 4 hours. How much did she pay? $\underline{\qquad}$

c) Sue paid \$15 to rent the roller blades. How many hours did she rent the roller blades for? $\underline{\qquad}$

6. Kim has \$35 in savings. She earns \$1 for every 5 clients she serves.

a) Write an expression for the total amount she will have saved after serving x clients. $\underline{\qquad}$

b) How much will she have saved after serving 100 clients? $\underline{\qquad}$

c) How many clients does she have to serve to be able to buy a shirt for \$90? $\underline{\qquad}$

7. a) For which part of Question 6 did you **substitute** for x? $\underline{\qquad}$

b) For which part of Question 6 did you **solve** for x? $\underline{\qquad}$

PA8-10 Solving Equations — Advanced

> The expression 3×2 is short for $2 + 2 + 2$. Similarly, the expression $3x$ is short for $x + x + x$.

1. Write $6x$ in three ways.

   a) $6x = \underbrace{x + x + x}_{} + \underbrace{x + x + x}_{}$

   $6x = \quad 3x \quad + \quad 3x$

   b) $6x = \underbrace{x + x}_{} + \underbrace{x + x + x + x}_{}$

   $6x = \qquad + \qquad$

   c) $6x = \underbrace{x}_{} + \underbrace{x + x + x + x + x}_{}$

   $6x = \qquad + \qquad$

2. Add.

   a) $3x + 5x = \underline{\quad 8x \quad}$ b) $4x + 3x = \underline{\qquad}$ c) $7x + x = \underline{\qquad}$ d) $4x + 2x + 3x = \underline{\qquad}$

3. Group the x's together, then solve the equation for x.

   a) $2x + 5x = 21$ b) $5x + 4x + 2 = 20$ c) $6x + x - 4 = 31$ d) $3x + 2x - 2 = 23$

4. Fill in the blanks.

   a) $3 - 3 = \underline{\qquad}$ b) $8 - 8 = \underline{\qquad}$ c) $132 - 132 = \underline{\qquad}$ d) $x - x = \underline{\qquad}$

   e) $3 + 3 - 3 = \underline{\qquad}$ f) $7 + 7 - 7 = \underline{\qquad}$ g) $5 + 5 - 5 = \underline{\qquad}$ h) $x + x - x = \underline{\qquad}$

> Every time you see a number or variable subtracted by itself in an equation (Examples: $3 - 3$, $5 - 5$, $8 - 8$, $x - x$), you can cross out both numbers or variables because they will add to 0. Crossing out parts of an equation that make 0 is called **cancelling**.

5. Fill in the blanks by crossing out numbers or variables that add 0 to the equation.

   a) $4 + \cancel{3} - \cancel{3} = \underline{\quad 4 \quad}$ b) $5 + 2 - 2 = \underline{\qquad}$ c) $7 + 1 - 1 = \underline{\qquad}$ d) $8 + 6 - 6 = \underline{\qquad}$

   e) $3 + 7 - 3 = \underline{\qquad}$ f) $2 + 9 - 2 = \underline{\qquad}$ g) $4 + 3 - 3 + 7 - 7 + 6 - 6 = \underline{\qquad}$

   h) $5 + 2 - 2 + 4 - 5 = \underline{\qquad}$ i) $7 + x - x = \underline{\qquad}$ j) $x + 12 - x = \underline{\qquad}$

   k) $x + x - x = \underline{\qquad}$ l) $x + x + x - x = \underline{\qquad}$ m) $x + x - x + x + x + x - x - x = \underline{\qquad}$

6. Rewrite these expressions as sums of individual variables and then cancel. Write what's left.

   a) $5x - 2x = \underline{\quad 3x \quad}$
   $x + x + x + \cancel{x} + \cancel{x} - \cancel{x} - \cancel{x}$

   b) $4x - x = \underline{\qquad}$

   c) $5x - x + 2x = \underline{\qquad}$

7. Solve these expressions without writing them as sums of individual x's.

   a) $7x - 5x = \underline{\qquad}$ b) $8x - 4x = \underline{\qquad}$ c) $4x - 2x + 3x = \underline{\qquad}$ d) $9x - 3x + 4x = \underline{\qquad}$

8. Group the x's together, then solve for x.

   a) $8x - 3x + x - 2 = 28$ b) $5x + x - x - 2x + 4 = 19$ c) $7x + 4 - 2x - 3 = 26$

PA8-11 Modelling Equations

A triangle has a mass of x kg and a circle has a mass of 1 kg.

1. Draw triangles and circles to show each mass (given in kg).

   a) $x + 2$

   △○○

   b) $3(x + 2)$

   △○○
   △○○
   △○○

   c) $2x + 3$

   d) $2(x + 3)$

   e) $4(x + 1)$

2. Draw a picture for each expression and write a new expression without brackets.

   a) $2(x + 3)$

   △○○○
   △○○○

   $2x + 6$

   b) $3(x + 1)$

   _____

   c) $2(x + 5)$

   _____

   d) $3(x + 4)$

   _____

   e) $4(x + 2)$

   _____

   f) $4(x + 4)$

   g) $3(x + 5)$

   h) $5(x + 3)$

   i) $2(x + 4)$

   j) $6(x + 1)$

   _____   _____   _____   _____   _____

3. Finish the equation.

   a) $3(x + 1) = 3x +$ _____

   b) $3(x + 2) = 3x +$ _____

   c) $3(x + 3) = 3x +$ _____

   d) $3(x + 4) = 3x +$ _____

   e) $3(x + 5) = 3x +$ _____

   f) $3(x + b) = 3x +$ _____

   g) $2(x + 3) = 2x +$ _____

   h) $4(x + 1) = 4x +$ _____

   i) $6(x + 2) = 6x +$ _____

   j) $4(x + 5) =$ _____ $+$ _____

   k) $5(x + 3) =$ _____ $+$ _____

   l) $a(x + b) =$ _____ $+$ _____

4. Write the expression on the left without brackets. Then solve the equation.

   a) $3(x + 2) = 18$
   $3x + 6 = 18$
   $3x + 6 - 6 = 18 - 6$
   $3x = 12$
   $x = 4$

   b) $2(x + 5) = 14$

   c) $5(x + 2) = 35$

   BONUS ▶ $2(x + 2) + 3(x + 1) = 27$

PA8-11 Modelling Equations *(continued)*

A triangle has a mass of *x* kg and a circle has a mass of 1 kg.

5. Scale A is balanced. Write the equation for each scale.

a)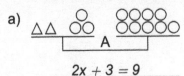

$$2x + 3 = 9$$

b)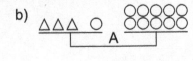

c)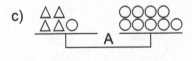

6. Write the equation that Scale A shows. Draw Scale B so that it balances only the triangles from Scale A, and write the new equation.

a)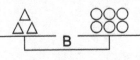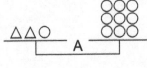

$$3x + 2 = 8 \qquad 3x = 6$$

b)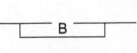

7. Scale B is balanced and has only triangles on one side and only circles on the other. Divide the circles into the number of groups given by the number of triangles. Show on Scale C what balances 1 triangle.

a)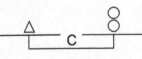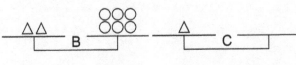

$$3x = 6 \qquad x = 2$$

b)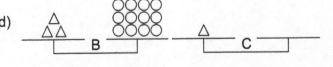

c)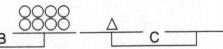

d)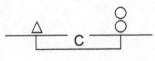

8. Scale A is balanced. Draw scales B and C as in Questions 2 and 3. Write the new equations.

a)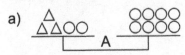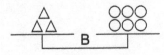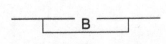

b)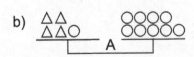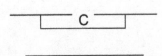

9. Draw Scales A, B, and C to model the process of solving the equation $3x + 5 = 11$.

No unauthorized copying   **Patterns and Algebra 1**

UNIT 3

Number Sense 2

NS8-48 Perfect Squares

1. Find the factors of each number below by drawing all the non-congruent rectangles (with whole number side lengths) that have an area equal to the number.

Example:

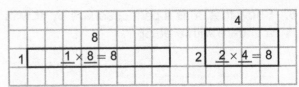

So the factors of 8 are: 1, 2, 4, and 8.

a) 4   b) 5   c) 6

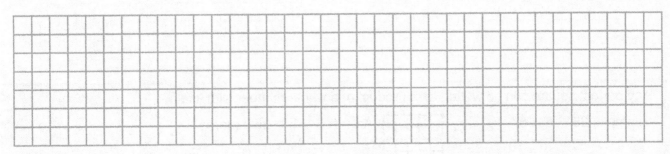

d) 7   e) 8   f) 9

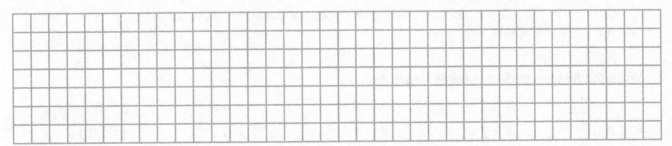

2. For which numbers in Question 1 could you draw a square? _____

> A number larger than 0 is called a **perfect square** if you can draw a square with whole number side lengths having that area.

3. a) Draw squares with side lengths 1, 2, 3, 4, and 5 on the grid.

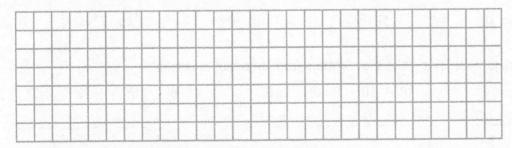

b) Write the first five perfect squares larger than 0.

_____ _____ _____ _____ _____

4. Explain why a square with an area of 20 cm² does not have a whole number side length.

5. Can a prime number be a perfect square? Explain.

NS8-48 **Perfect Squares** (continued)

6. Show that 36 is a perfect square by drawing a square with area 36.

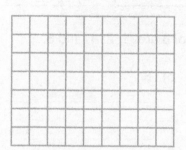

7. Show that 10 is not a perfect square by drawing all non-congruent rectangles with area 10.

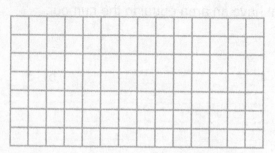

Any perfect square can be written as a product of a whole number with itself.

Example: $25 = 5 \times 5$.   Area $= 5 \times 5 = 25$ squares

NOTE: Since $0 = 0 \times 0$, we say that 0 is a perfect square even though you cannot draw a square with area 0.

---

8. Write the first ten perfect squares larger than 0.

$1 \times 1 =$ _____ $2 \times 2 =$ _____ $3 \times 3 =$ _____ $4 \times 4 =$ _____ $5 \times 5 =$ _____

$6 \times 6 =$ _____ $7 \times 7 =$ _____ $8 \times 8 =$ _____ $9 \times 9 =$ _____ $10 \times 10 =$ _____

When we multiply a number by itself, we get a perfect square. This process is called **squaring the number**. Example: 6 squared is $6 \times 6 = 36$. We write $6^2 = 36$. (The 2 is because we multiplied two 6s.)

---

9. Write each perfect square as a product and evaluate it.

a) $5^2 = 5 \times 5 = 25$ b) $3^2 =$ c) $8^2 =$ d) $0^2 =$ e) $7^2 =$

10. Calculate the perfect squares. Then write the numbers from smallest to largest.

a) 3^2 5^2 4^2 b) 10^2 8^2 9^2 c) 5^2 12^2 7^2

    9   25   16   _____ _____ _____   _____ _____ _____

    9   16   25   _____ _____ _____   _____ _____ _____

d) 3^2 5   10 4^2 2^2 e) 50 7^2 9^2 8^2 85

_____ _____ _____ _____ _____   _____ _____ _____ _____ _____

_____ _____ _____ _____ _____   _____ _____ _____ _____ _____

NS8-49 Factors of Perfect Squares

To list all the factors of a given number (the pairs of numbers that multiply to give that number), stop when you get a number that is already part of a pair.

1. Make a chart to find all the pairs of numbers that multiply to give each number.

a) 20

1st	2nd
1	20
2	10
3	
4	5
5	Done!

b) 12

1st	2nd

c) 15   d) 14   e) 25
f) 5   g) 26   h) 30
i) 42   j) 72   k) 63
l) 100   m) 64   n) 91

A **factor rainbow** for a number pairs the factors that multiply to give that number.

Factor rainbow for 9

9: 1 2 3 4 5 6 7 8 9

Factor rainbow for 10

10: 1 2 3 4 5 6 7 8 9 10

2. Finish the factor rainbow for each number.

6: 1 2 3 4 5 6   **8:** 1 2 3 4 5 6 7 8   **12:** 1 2 3 4 5 6 7 8 9 10 11 12

As a shortcut to making a factor rainbow, we can leave out all numbers that are not factors.

Example:

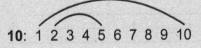

6: 1 2 3 6

3. Using the shortcut, make a factor rainbow for each number from 1 to 20.
For the numbers from 11 to 20, you will need to list the factors first.

1: 1

2: 1 2

3: 1 3

4: 1 2 4

5: 1 5

6: 1 2 3 6

7: 1 7

8: 1 2 4 8

9: 1 3 9

10: 1 2 5 10

11:

12:

13:

14:

15:

16:

17:

18:

19:

20:

No unauthorized copying

NS8-49 Factors of Perfect Squares (continued)

4. a) Look at your answers to Question 3. Which numbers have an odd number of factors?

_____, _____, _____, and _____.

b) Extend the sequence of numbers you found in part a) by using the gaps between the numbers.

◯　　　◯　　　◯　　　◯　　　◯

_____ , _____ , _____ , _____ , _____ , _____

Do you recognize the numbers in the sequence? What are they called? _____

c) All perfect squares have an odd number of factors. Why?

Hint: Look at the factor rainbows from Question 3. When is there a factor that is paired up with itself?

d) Write the reverse (see p. 116) of the statement from part c). Is it also true?

INVESTIGATION ▶ Which numbers have exactly 3 factors?

A. Explain why any number with exactly 3 factors is a perfect square.

B. List all the factors of the first 10 perfect squares greater than 0.

Perfect Square	Factors
$1 = 1^2$	1
$4 = 2^2$	1, 2, 4
$9 = 3^2$	1, 3, 9
$16 = 4^2$	1, 2, 4, 8, 16
$25 = 5^2$	
$36 = 6^2$	
$49 = 7^2$	
$64 = 8^2$	
$81 = 9^2$	
$100 = 10^2$	

C. Which perfect squares between 1 and 100 have exactly 3 factors?

_____^{2} , _____^{2} , _____^{2} , and _____^{2}

D. What are the prime numbers between 1 and 10?

_____ , _____ , _____ , and _____

E. Compare your answers to parts C. and D. What do you notice?

F. Make a conjecture about which numbers have exactly 3 factors.

G. Use your conjecture to find the first 3 numbers greater than 100 that have exactly 3 factors.

NS8-50 Square Roots of Perfect Squares

The number 5 is called the **square root** of 25 because 25 is the **square** of 5.

We write $\sqrt{25}$ 5 because 25 5^2 5 × 5.

Square roots are numbers, so you can add, subtract, multiply, and divide them.

1. Find the square root by writing the same number in each box.

   a) 9 = ☐ × ☐   b) 49 = ☐ × ☐   c) 0 = ☐ × ☐   d) 25 = ☐ × ☐

2. Evaluate.

   a) $\sqrt{49}$ = __7__   b) $\sqrt{16}$ = ____   c) $\sqrt{9}$ = ____   d) $\sqrt{36}$ = ____

   e) $\sqrt{1}$ = ____   f) $\sqrt{100}$ = ____   g) $\sqrt{81}$ = ____   h) $\sqrt{64}$ = ____

3. Evaluate.

   a) $\sqrt{25} + \sqrt{4}$ b) $\sqrt{36} \times \sqrt{25}$ c) $\sqrt{64} - \sqrt{9}$ d) $\sqrt{100} \div \sqrt{4}$ e) $\sqrt{49} + \sqrt{64}$
       = 5 + 2 = 7

   f) $\sqrt{36} - \sqrt{25}$ g) $\sqrt{36} \div \sqrt{4}$ h) $\sqrt{36} + \sqrt{25} - \sqrt{1}$ **BONUS** ▶ $\sqrt{25} + \sqrt{16} \times \sqrt{9}$

4. Order these numbers from smallest to largest.

   a) $\sqrt{49}$ $\sqrt{64}$ $\sqrt{25}$ $\sqrt{9}$ $\sqrt{16}$ b) $\sqrt{100}$ 3^2 5 4^2 $\sqrt{4}$ $\sqrt{8^2}$

5. Evaluate the two expressions. Then write = (equal) or ≠ (not equal) in the box.

   a) $\sqrt{4 \times 9}$ $\boxed{=}$ $\sqrt{4} \times \sqrt{9}$ b) $\sqrt{9 + 16}$ ☐ $\sqrt{9} + \sqrt{16}$

       = $\sqrt{36}$ = __2__ × __3__   = $\sqrt{\quad}$ = __ + __

       = __6__   = __6__   = __   = __

   c) $\sqrt{169 - 25}$ ☐ $\sqrt{169} - \sqrt{25}$ d) $\sqrt{100 \div 4}$ ☐ $\sqrt{100} \div \sqrt{4}$

       = $\sqrt{\quad}$ = __ − __   = $\sqrt{\quad}$ = __ ÷ __

       = __   = __   = __   = __

6. The factor rainbow for each perfect square is shown. Find the square root.

   a)

   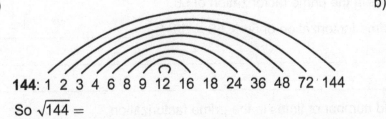

   144: 1 2 3 4 6 8 9 12 16 18 24 36 48 72 144

   So $\sqrt{144}$ =

   b)

   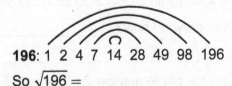

   196: 1 2 4 7 14 28 49 98 196

   So $\sqrt{196}$ =

7. a) How can you find the square root of a perfect square by looking at its factor rainbow?

   b) Draw a factor rainbow for 225 and find $\sqrt{225}$.

NS8-51 Prime Factorizations of Perfect Squares

1. Find the prime factorization of each perfect square by first finding the prime factorization of its square root.

a) 144
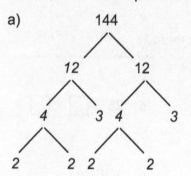

b) 196
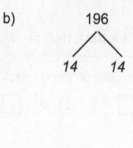

c) 64

d) 225
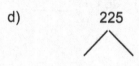

e) 256
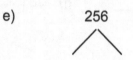

f) 400

2. How many times does the prime number 2 occur in the prime factorization of each number and its square root in Question 1?

a) $144 = 2 \times 2 \times 3 \times 2 \times 2 \times 3$ and $12 = 2 \times 2 \times 3$ So 2 occurs __4__ times in 144 and __2__ times in 12.

b) $196 =$ and $14 =$ So 2 occurs _____ times in 196 and _____ times in 14.

c) $64 =$ and _____ $=$ So 2 occurs _____ times in 64 and _____ times in _____.

d) $256 =$ and _____ $=$ So 2 occurs _____ times in 256 and _____ times in _____.

e) $225 =$ and _____ $=$ So 2 occurs _____ times in 225 and _____ times in _____.

f) $400 =$ and _____ $=$ So 2 occurs _____ times in 400 and _____ times in _____.

3. The prime number 2 occurs three times in the prime factorization of 56.

How many times will 2 occur in the prime factorization of $56 \times 56 = 56^2$? _____

How do you know? _____

_____

4. Can the prime number 2 occur an **odd** number of times in the prime factorization of a perfect square? Explain. _____

_____

NS8-51 Prime Factorizations of Perfect Squares (continued)

INVESTIGATION ▶ Can any prime number occur an odd number of times in the prime factorization of a perfect square?

A. $18 = 2 \times 3 \times 3$ so $18^2 = 18 \times 18 =$ _____

The prime number 3 occurs two times in the prime factorization of 18.

How many times does it occur in the prime factorization of $18^2 = 18 \times 18$? _____

B. $250 = 2 \times 5 \times 5 \times 5$ so $250^2 = 250 \times 250 =$ _____

The prime number 5 occurs three times in the prime factorization of 250.

How many times does it occur in the prime factorization of $250^2 = 250 \times 250$? _____

C. a) **Double** the number of times each prime factor occurs. Then use a calculator to find the **square root** of the result. In parts iii)–vii) you have to find the factors first.

   i) $45 = 3 \times 3 \times 5$ $\underline{3 \times 3 \times 3 \times 3 \times 5 \times 5}$ $= \underline{\quad 2025 \quad}$ and $\sqrt{2025} = \underline{\quad 45 \quad}$

   ii) $28 = 2 \times 2 \times 7$ _____ $= $_____ and $\sqrt{\quad} = $____

   iii) 48   iv) 35   v) 91   vi) 27   vii) 63

  b) What do you notice? _____

D. a) **Halve** the number of times each prime factor occurs, then find the **square** of the result. In parts iii)–vii) you have to find the factors first.

   i) $144 = 2 \times 2 \times 2 \times 2 \times 3 \times 3$ $\underline{2 \times 2 \times 3}$ $= \underline{\quad 12 \quad}$ and $\underline{\quad 12 \quad}^2 = \underline{\quad 144 \quad}$

   ii) $324 = 2 \times 2 \times 3 \times 3 \times 3 \times 3$ _____ $= $_____ and _____$^2 = $_____

   iii) 5625   iv) 576   v) 1936   vi) 11 025   vii) 27 225

  b) What do you notice? _____

E. Explain why a number is a perfect square if all its prime factors occur an even number of times in its prime factorization.

5. Which numbers are perfect squares? Find their prime factorizations to decide.

  a) 6 300   b) 6 400   c) 2 268   d) 243   e) 729   f) 1 296

6. a) Extend the pattern.

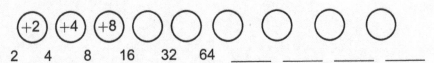

    2   4   8   16   32   64   ____   ____   ____   ____

  b) Find the prime factorization of all 10 terms in the pattern.

  c) Circle the perfect squares in the pattern in part a).

  d) Will the 100th term be a perfect square? How do you know?

UNIT 4

Measurement 1

ME8-1 Part-to-Part and Part-to-Whole Ratios

There are 3 circles for every 2 squares. The **ratio** of circles to squares is **3 : 2** or **3 to 2**.

1. Write the ratio of circles to squares.

a)

There are 2 circles for every ___ square.

The ratio of circles to squares is ___:___.

b)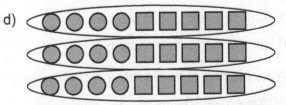

There are 2 circles for every ___ squares.

The ratio of circles to squares is ___:___.

c)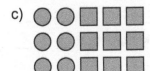

There are 2 circles for every ___ squares.

The ratio of circles to squares is ___:___.

d)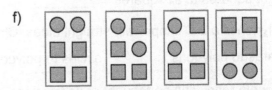

There are 4 circles for every ___ squares.

The ratio of circles to squares is ___:___.

e)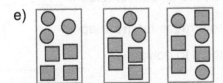

There are 3 circles for every ___ squares.

The ratio of circles to squares is ___:___.

f)

There are 2 circles for every ___ squares.

The ratio of circles to squares is ___:___.

Each group has 3 circles and 2 squares.
So ◯ : ▢ = 3 : 2.

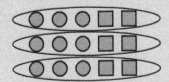

Each group has the same number of shapes.
3 groups have circles and 2 groups have squares.

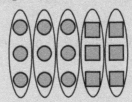

The ratio ◯ : ▢ is 3 : 2

The two sets have the same total number of circles and triangles, so the ratios ◯ : ▢ are the same!

---

g)

There is 1 circle for every ___ squares.

The ratio of circles to squares is ___:___.

h)

There are 3 circles for every ___ squares.

The ratio of circles to squares is ___:___.

ME8-1 Part-to-Part and Part-to-Whole Ratios (continued)

A **ratio** is a comparison of two or more numbers.
A **part-to-part ratio** compares one part to another part.
  Example: The ratio of squares to triangles is
    2 to 3, or 2 : 3.

A **part-to-whole ratio** compares one part to the whole.
  Example: The ratio of squares to total shapes is 2 to 7, or 2 : 7.

2. a) Write the part-to-part ratios for these shapes.

   i) squares to circles = _4_ : _3_   ii) triangles to circles = ___ : ___

   iii) dark squares to light squares = ___ : ___   iv) light circles to dark circles = ___ : ___

   v) light circles to dark squares = ___ : ___   vi) light shapes to dark shapes = ___ : ___

   b) Write the part-to-whole ratios for the shapes.

   i) circles to all shapes = _3_ : _8_   ii) squares to all shapes = ___ : ___

   iii) light shapes to all shapes = ___ : ___   iv) dark circles to all circles = ___ : ___

   v) light squares to all squares = ___ : ___   vi) dark circles to all dark shapes = ___ : ___

   c) A polygon is a 2-D shape with straight sides. Circle the part-to-whole ratios for the shapes.

   squares to polygons   circles to polygons   triangles to polygons

Part-to-whole ratios can be thought of as fractions.

EXAMPLE:

The ratio of squares to shapes is 2 : 7, so $\frac{2}{7}$ of the shapes are squares.

The ratio of light squares to all squares is 1 : 4, so $\frac{1}{4}$ of the squares are light.

3. Write the part-to-whole ratios from Question 2 b) as fractions.

   i) __$\frac{3}{8}$__ of the _shapes_ are _____.   ii) _____ of the _____ are _____.

   iii) _____ of the _____ are _____.   iv) _____ of the _____ are _____.

   v) _____ of the _____ are _____.   vi) _____ of the _____ are _____.

4. Circle the part-to-whole ratios. Underline the part-to-part ratios.

   a) vowels in **band** : letters in **band**   b) vowels in **blog** : consonants in **blog**   c) buses : trucks

   d) school days : days of the week   e) days in January : days in September   f) school buses : buses

5. A part-to-part ratio cannot be thought of as a fraction. Why not?

6. The ratio of circles to triangles is 94 : 93. Are there more circles or triangles? How do you know?

ME8-2 Equivalent Ratios

Two ratios are equivalent if they compare the same quantities.

There are 4 circles for every 3 squares. There are 8 circles for every 6 squares.
The ratio of circles to squares is 4 : 3 or 8 : 6.

4 : 3 and 8 : 6 are **equivalent ratios**.

1. Find two equivalent ratios for each picture.

a)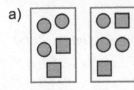

⬤ : ◻ = 3 : ___ = 6 : ___

b)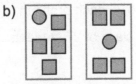

⬤ : ◻ = 1 : ___ = 2 : ___

c)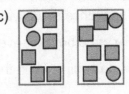

⬤ : ◻ = 2 : ___ = 4 : ___

2. Every word in the phrases below has 2 consonants and 1 vowel.
   Write equivalent ratios for the ratio 2 : 1 by counting all the consonants and vowels.

   a) the dog

   2 : 1 = ___ : ___

   b) the big dog

   2 : 1 = ___ : ___

   c) the dog was wet

   2 : 1 = ___ : ___

   d) the big dog got wet

   2 : 1 = ___ : ___

   e) the big fat dog was dry but got all wet

   2 : 1 = ___ : ___

3. a) Write a word that has 1 consonant for every vowel and a total of...

   i) 2 letters. _____   ii) 4 letters. _____   iii) 6 letters. _____

   b) Write two more equivalent ratios.   1 : 1 = ___ : ___ = ___ : ___

   c) Can you write a 9-letter word that has a ratio of consonants to vowels equal to 1 : 1? Explain.

4. a) Draw 15 circles and squares so that the ratio of circles to squares is 2 : 3.
      Hint: Repeatedly draw 2 circles and 3 squares until you have 15 shapes.

   b) Write an equivalent ratio for 2 : 3 by counting all the circles and squares. 2 : 3 = ___ : ___

To create equivalent ratios, multiply each term in the ratio by the same number.

2 : 1	=	(2 × 2) : (1 × 2)	=	(2 × 3) : (1 × 3)	=	(2 × 4) : (1 × 4)
2 : 1	=	4 : 2	=	6 : 3	=	8 : 4

5. Starting with the given ratio, write a sequence of four equivalent ratios.

   a) 3 : 4 = _6_ : _8_ = ___ : ___ = ___ : ___

   b) 3 : 7 = ___ : ___ = ___ : ___ = ___ : ___

   c) 5 : 8 = ___ : ___ = ___ : ___ = ___ : ___

   d) 3 : 10 = ___ : ___ = ___ : ___ = ___ : ___

ME8-2 Equivalent Ratios *(continued)*

There are 3 boys for every 2 girls in a class of 20 students.

To find out how many boys are in the class,

write out a sequence of equivalent ratios.

Stop when the terms of the ratio add to 20.

Boys		Girls	Total
3	:	2	5
6	:	4	10
9	:	6	15
12	:	**8**	**20**

12 boys + 8 girls = 20 students, so there are 12 boys in the class.

6. Write a sequence of equivalent ratios to solve each problem.

   a) There are 5 boys for every 4 girls in a class of 27 students.
      How many girls are in the class?

	Boys		Girls	Total
	5	:	4	9
	10	:		

   b) There are 2 red marbles for every 7 blue marbles in a box.

      If the box holds 45 marbles, how many of the marbles are blue?

   c) A recipe for punch calls for 3 L of orange juice for every 4 L of mango juice.
      How many litres of orange juice are needed to make 21 L of punch?

A part-to-part ratio can sometimes be changed to a part-to-whole ratio or fraction.

Example: There are 2 circles for every 5 triangles in a set of circles and triangles.

So there are 2 circles for every 7 shapes.

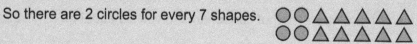

The ratio of circles to triangles is 2 : 5, so $\frac{2}{7}$ of the shapes are circles.

---

7. An aquarium has red and blue fish. Change each part-to-part ratio to a part-to-whole fraction.

   a) The ratio of blue fish to red fish is 3 : 2.

   b) The ratio of red fish to blue fish is 3 : 5.

   _____

   c) The ratio of blue fish to red fish is 4 : 3.

   d) The ratio of red fish to blue fish is 2 : 7.

   _____

8. A team's **win : loss** ratio is **5 : 2**. There are no ties. What fraction of the games did the team win?

9. Tania collects rock and jazz CDs. The ratio **rock CDs : jazz CDs = 4 : 7**.

   What fraction of Tania's CDs are rock CDs?

ME8-3 Solving Proportions

A **proportion** is an equation that shows two equivalent ratios. Example: $1 : 4 = 2 : 8$

When a proportion has a missing number (Example: $1 : 4 = \_\_\_ : 8$), finding the missing number is called **solving the proportion.**

1. Multiply the first term by the same number the second term was multiplied by.

   a) $4 : 5 = \_\_\_ : 20$

   b) $1 : 5 = \_\_\_ : 25$

   c) $2 : 5 = \_\_\_ : 20$

   d) $6 : 7 = \_\_\_ : 35$

   d) $3 : 4 = \_\_\_ : 16$

   f) $2 : 3 = \_\_\_ : 12$

2. Solve the proportion.

   a) $15 : 25 = 60 : \_\_\_$ b) $5 : 9 = \_\_\_ : 45$ c) $3 : 5 = 15 : \_\_\_$ d) $3 : 5 = \_\_\_ : 15$

To create an equivalent ratio with each term a smaller number, divide each term in the ratio by the same number. This is called simplifying the ratio. Example: $40 : 35 = 40 \div 5 : 35 \div 5$

$$= 8 : 7$$

3. Simplify each ratio.

   a) $6 : 24 = \_\_\_ : 8$ b) $9 : 21 = 3 : \_\_\_$ c) $60 : 100 = : \_\_\_ 50$ d) $70 : 30 = 35 : \_\_\_$

A ratio is in lowest terms when the numbers in the ratio are as small as they can be.

To write the ratio $30 : 36$ in lowest terms:

Step 1: Find the prime factorizations of 30 and 36. $30 = 2 \times 3 \times 5$

$36 = 2 \times 2 \times 3 \times 3$

Step 2: Find the greatest common factor (GCF) of 30 and 36. GCF $= 2 \times 3 = 6$.

Step 3: Divide each term in the ratio by the GCF to write the ratio in lowest terms.

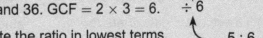

4. a) Write the prime factorization of each number.

   i) $10 = $ _____   ii) $12 = $ _____   iii) $30 = $ _____   iv) $75 = $ _____

   b) Find the GCF of each pair.

   i) 10 and 12   ii) 10 and 30   iii) 10 and 75   iv) 12 and 30   v) 12 and 75   vi) 30 and 75

   _____   _____   _____   _____   _____   _____

   c) Write each ratio in lowest terms by dividing both terms by their GCF.

   i) $10 : 12$ ii) $10 : 30$ iii) $10 : 75$ iv) $12 : 30$ v) $12 : 75$ vi) $75 : 30$

   _____   _____   _____   _____   _____   _____

5. Write each ratio in lowest terms.

   a) $25 : 35$ b) $21 : 6$ c) $20 : 12$ d) $14 : 21$ e) $84 : 27$ f) $90 : 75$

ME8-3 Solving Proportions *(continued)*

6. Write the ratio that is complete in lowest terms. Then find the missing number to make the ratios equivalent.

a) $8 : 10 = \underline{\ 4\ } : \underline{\ 5\ }$

so $8 : 10 = \underline{\ 12\ } : 15$

b) $4 : 6 = \underline{\ \ \ } : \underline{\ \ \ }$

so $4 : 6 = 6 : \underline{\ \ \ }$

c) $60 : 100 = \underline{\ \ \ } : \underline{\ \ \ }$

so $60 : 100 = \underline{\ \ \ } : 45$

7. Solve the proportions. Begin by writing the ratio that is complete in lowest terms.

a) $40 : 50 = \underline{\ \ \ } : \underline{\ \ \ }$

$= \underline{\ \ \ } : 30$

b) $70 : 100 = \underline{\ \ \ } : \underline{\ \ \ }$

$= \underline{\ \ \ } : 30$

c) $50 : 75 = \underline{\ \ \ } : \underline{\ \ \ }$

$= \underline{\ \ \ } : 24$

d) $6 : 24 = \underline{\ \ \ } : \underline{\ \ \ }$

$= \underline{\ \ \ } : 16$

e) $11 : 22 = \underline{\ \ \ } : \underline{\ \ \ }$

$= 5 : \underline{\ \ \ }$

f) $\underline{\ \ \ } : 7 = \underline{\ \ \ } : \underline{\ \ \ }$

$= 6 : 3$

g) $30 : 9 = \underline{\ \ \ } : \underline{\ \ \ }$

$= 50 : \underline{\ \ \ }$

h) $\underline{\ \ \ } : 25 = \underline{\ \ \ } : \underline{\ \ \ }$

$= 4 : 10$

i) $72 : 18 = \underline{\ \ \ } : \underline{\ \ \ }$

$= \underline{\ \ \ } : 7$

8. The ratio 3 506 : 5 259 in lowest terms is 2 : 3. What is the ratio 5 259 : 3 506 in lowest terms? How do you know?

INVESTIGATION ▶ $\frac{1}{3}$ of the students are girls. What is the ratio of girls to boys?

A. i) If there is 1 girl, there are _____ students altogether, so _____ are boys.

ii) If there are 2 girls, there are _____ students altogether, so _____ are boys.

iii) If there are 3 girls, there are _____ students altogether, so _____ are boys.

iv) If there are 4 girls, there are _____ students altogether, so _____ are boys.

v) If there are 5 girls, there are _____ students altogether, so _____ are boys.

B. What is the ratio of girls to boys in each case?

i) 1 : _____   ii) 2 : _____   iii) 3 : _____   iv) 4 : _____   v) 5 : _____

C. Are the ratios in part B equivalent?

D. Work backwards to check your work. Start with the ratios of girls to boys you found in part B. What fraction of the students are girls?

E. What is the ratio of girls to boys in the classes of Ms. X and Mr. Y?

Ms. X: $\frac{2}{5}$ of the students are girls.   Mr. Y: $\frac{5}{8}$ of the students are girls.

F. Whose class from part E has more girls than boys?

How can you tell from the fraction? How can you tell from the ratio?

ME8-4 Word Problems

		cats	dogs

> **PROBLEM ▶** In a pet shop, there are 3 cats for every 4 dogs. If there are 12 dogs in the shop, how many cats are there?

SOLUTION ▶ Write the names of the two things being compared.

Write the quantities under the names, as a ratio.

Re-read the question to determine which quantity is given and which is unknown. Write this information in a new row under the right names.

Solve the proportion.

        cats   dogs

        3 : 4

        ? : 12

        3 : 4 = ? : 12

? = 9, so there are 9 cats in the shop.

1. Nine bus tickets cost $19. How many bus tickets can you buy with $57?

2. Mike can run 3 laps in 5 minutes. How many laps can he do in 20 minutes?

3. Jared can run 4 laps in 10 minutes. How long will it take Jared to run 6 laps?

4. The ratio of boys to girls in a class is 5 : 6. If there are 20 boys, how many girls are there?

5. Two out of every 5 students at school are in the art program.
   There are 300 students in total. How many are in the art program?

6. Four out of 7 students like rap music. If 280 students like rap music, how many students are there in total?

7. There are 2 rap songs for every 3 rock songs on Will's MP3 player.
   There are a total of 120 rock songs. How many rap songs are there?

8. A muffin recipe calls for 2.5 cups of flour for 12 muffins. Jean wants to make 30 muffins. How much flour will she need?

9. The ratio of students in string band to students in brass band is 3 : 4. There are 36 students in the brass band. How many students are in the string band?

10. In a zoo, 2 out of every 3 gorillas are female. There are 15 gorillas in the zoo. How many male gorillas are there?

11. There are 3 green chromis fish for every 5 clown fish in an aquarium.

    a) If there are 30 clown fish, how many green chromis fish are there?

    b) If there are 30 green chromis fish, how many clown fish are there?

12. Irene has 64 jazz CDs and 80 rock CDs. Is the ratio of jazz CDs to rock CDs 3 : 4 or 4 : 5?

UNIT 5

Number Sense 3

NS8-52 Gains and Losses

1. Write a plus sign (+) if the net result is a gain. Write a minus sign (–) if the net result is a loss.

   a) a gain of $5 __+__

   b) a loss of $3 _____

   c) a gain of $4 _____

   d) a gain of $2 and a loss of $5 __–__

   e) a gain of $3 and a loss of $1 _____

   f) a loss of $3 and a gain of $4 _____

   g) a loss of $6 and a gain of $2 _____

2. Write each sequence of gains and losses using numbers and signs (+ and –).

   a) a gain of $3 and a loss of $5 __+3 – 5__

   b) a loss of $2 and a gain of $8 _____

   c) a loss of $4 and a gain of $3 _____

   d) a gain of $6 and a loss of $5 _____

   e) a loss of $5, a gain of $8, a loss of $2, then a gain of $1 _____–5 + 8 – 2 + 1_____

   f) a gain of $3, a gain of $5, a loss of $6, then a gain of $2 _____

   g) a loss of $5, a loss of $8, a gain of $10, then a gain of $5 _____

   h) a gain of $4, a loss of $3, a loss of $2, then a gain of $5 _____

3. Decide whether each sequence of gains and losses is a net gain (+) or a net loss (–).

   a) $+5 - 3$ __+__

   b) $+3 - 5$ _____

   c) $-2 + 4$ _____

   d) $-5 + 1$ _____

   e) $+8 - 7$ _____

   f) $+5 - 9$ _____

   g) $-4 + 5$ _____

   h) $-3 + 2$ _____

   i) $-9 + 5$ _____

4. How much was gained or lost overall? Use + for a gain, – for a loss, and 0 for no gain or loss.

   a) $+6 - 5 =$ __+1__

   b) $-4 + 3 =$ _____

   c) $+5 - 5 =$ _____

   d) $-6 + 6 =$ _____

   e) $-3 + 5 =$ _____

   f) $+8 - 12 =$ _____

   g) $+3 + 2 =$ _____

   h) $-4 - 1 =$ _____

   i) $-5 - 2 =$ _____

   j) $-5 + 2 =$ _____

   k) $+5 - 2 =$ _____

   l) $+5 + 2 =$ _____

   m) $+3 - 8 =$ _____

   n) $-6 + 2 =$ _____

   o) $+7 - 2 =$ _____

   p) $-5 + 7 =$ _____

   q) $-4 + 4 =$ _____

   r) $+7 - 7 =$ _____

5. Group the gains (+'s) and losses (–'s) together. Then say how much was gained or lost overall.

   a) $+4 - 3 + 2 =$ ____$+4 + 2 - 3$____

   $=$ ____$+6 - 3$____

   $=$ ____$+3$____

   b) $-3 + 4 - 2 =$ _____

   $=$ _____

   $=$ _____

   c) $-5 + 7 - 3 =$ _____

   $=$ _____

   $=$ _____

   d) $+8 - 5 + 2 =$ _____

   $=$ _____

   $=$ _____

e) $+5-4+6 =$ _____

  $=$ _____

  $=$ _____

f) $+4-6+3 =$ _____

  $=$ _____

  $=$ _____

6. Circle all the gains first. Then group the gains (+'s) and losses (−'s).

   Then say how much was gained or lost overall.

   a) $-5-1 +3 -2 +4 +6 -4 =$ ___ $+3+4+6-5-1-2-4$ ___

      $=$ ___ $+13-12$ ___

      $=$ ___ $+1$ ___

   b) $+6+3-4-5-8+2-1 =$ _____

      $=$ _____

      $=$ _____

   c) $-4+5+6-3-2+8-5+1-4 =$ _____

      $=$ _____

      $=$ _____

When the same number is gained and lost, the two numbers add 0 to the equation, so we can **cancel** them.

7. Cancel the numbers that make 0. Then write the total gain or loss.

   a) $-\cancel{3}+4+\cancel{3} =$ ___ $+4$ ___

   b) $-3-2+3 =$ _____

   c) $+5+4-5 =$ _____

   d) $-5-4+5 =$ _____

   e) $-6+7+6 =$ _____

   f) $-5+5+2 =$ _____

   g) $+3+4-4 =$ _____

   h) $-8-5+5 =$ _____

   i) $-5-8+5 =$ _____

   j) $+8-5+2+5-2 =$ _____

   k) $-3+4+2+3-2 =$ _____

   l) $-5+5-6+3-3 =$ _____

   m) $-4-3+2+3-2 =$ _____

   n) $-5-4+4-3+5 =$ _____

   o) $+4-5-4-2+5 =$ _____

   p) $-\cancel{3}+\cancel{2}+4-5-\cancel{2}+\cancel{6}+\cancel{3}-\cancel{6} =$ ___ $+4-5$ ___

      these cancel $=$ ___ -1 ___

   q) $-5+2+6-2+3+4+5-3 =$ _____

      $=$ _____

   r) $+8-11-4+6-2+11-6-4 =$ _____

      $=$ _____

   s) $-4-3+2-7+4+2+3 =$ _____

      $=$ _____

8. Find the mistake in the cancelling. Circle the two numbers that should not have been cancelled.

   $-\cancel{3}+\cancel{4}+\cancel{2}+6-\cancel{2}+\cancel{3}+\cancel{4}-\cancel{7}+\cancel{7} = +6$

NS8-53 Integers

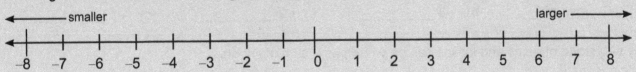

An **integer** is any one of these numbers: ..., –4, –3, –2, –1, 0, 1, 2, 3, 4, ...

Sometimes the numbers 1, 2, 3, 4, ... are written +1, +2, +3, +4, ...

An integer is **less than** another integer if it is **farther left** on the number line.

←——— smaller   larger ——→

-8 -7 -6 -5 -4 -3 -2 -1 0 1 2 3 4 5 6 7 8

1. Write three integers that are less than zero. _____ _____ _____

Integers that are **greater than 0** are called **positive**. Integers that are **less than 0** are called **negative**.

2. Circle the integers that are positive.   +4   7   –3   9   +2   +8   –5   –13

3. Circle the least integer in each pair.

   a) –3 or +5   b) –6 or –3   c) 7 or 5   d) –4 or –6
   e) 7 or –2   f) +8 or +3   g) –5 or –4   h) –7 or –9

4. Write < (less than) or > (greater than) in each box.

   a) +3 ☐ +7   b) –5 ☐ +4   c) 7 ☐ –2   d) –4 ☐ –6   e) –2 ☐ –10

5. Write two integers that are between –7 and –2. _____ and _____

6. Mark each integer on the number line with an X and label it with the correct letter.

   A +5   **B** –3   **C** +7   **D** –4   **E** –6

   -8   0   8

7. Put the integers into the boxes in **increasing** order.

   +5   –3   +10   –7   –2   ☐ ☐ ☐ ☐ ☐

8. Put the temperatures into the boxes in order from warmest to coldest.

   13°C   –18°C   23°C   –17°C   –48°C   ☐ ☐ ☐ ☐ ☐

9. a) If $0 < a < b$, mark possible places for a and b on the number line.

   b) Mark $-a$ and $-b$ on the same number line.

   0

   c) Write the correct symbol (< or >) in each box.

   If $0 < a < b$, then 0 ☐ $-a$ ☐ $-b$.

NS8-54 Adding Integers

A negative integer can represent a loss and a positive integer can represent a gain.

1. Write the gain or loss represented by the integer.

   a) –6 _loss of 6_   b) +3 _____   c) –2 _____   d) +7 _____

Any sequence of gains and losses can be written as a sum of integers.

Example: $-3 + 4 - 5 = (-3) + (+4) + (-5)$

$\qquad\qquad\qquad = (-3) + 4 + (-5).$

---

2. Write each sequence of gains and losses as a sum of integers.

   a) $+4 - 3 - 5$ _____$4 + (-3) + (-5)$_____   b) $-2 + 6 - 3$ _____

   c) $+3 + 2 - 7$ _____   d) $+5 - 3 - 4$ _____

   e) $-3 + 1 + 5$ _____   f) $-3 + 4 - 2$ _____

3. Write each sum of integers as a sequence of gains and losses.

   a) $(+3) + (-4) = $ _$+3 - 4$_   b) $(+3) + (+4) = $ _____   c) $(-3) + (+4) = $ _____   d) $(-3) + (-4) = $ _____

   e) $(+a) + (-b) = $ _____   f) $(+a) + (+b) = $ _____   g) $(-a) + (+b) = $ _____   h) $(-a) + (-b) = $ _____

4. Add the integers by first writing the sum as a sequence of gains and losses.

   a) $(+5) + (-2) = $ _$+5 - 2$_   b) $(-3) + (+4) = $ _____   c) $(-5) + (-4) = $ _____

   $\qquad\qquad\quad = $ _$+3$_ $ = $ _____ $ = $ _____

   d) $(+2) + (+6) = $ _____   e) $(-2) + (-9) = $ _____   f) $(-9) + (+7) = $ _____

   $\qquad\qquad\quad = $ _____ $ = $ _____ $ = $ _____

   g) $(+5) + (-2) + (+3) = $ _$+5 - 2 + 3$_   h) $(-5) + (+4) + (+2) = $ _____

   $\qquad\qquad\qquad = + $ _8_ $ - $ _2_ $ = $ _$+6$_ $ = + $ ___ $ - $ ___ $ = $ ___

   i) $3 + (-5) + (-2) + 6$ j) $(-2) + (-3) + 4 + 1$ k) $4 + 0 + (-5) + (-3)$ l) $3 + 2 + (-2) + (-3)$

Integers that add to 0 are called **opposite integers**.

Example: +3 and –3 are opposite integers because $(+3) + (-3) = +3 - 3 = 0$.

---

5. Write the opposite of each integer.

   a) The opposite of +2 is _____ .

   b) The opposite of –5 is _____ .

   c) The opposite of 3 is _____ .

   d) The opposite of –142 is _____ .

   BONUS ▶ The opposite of 0 is _____ .

NS8-54 **Adding Integers** *(continued)*

6. Add the integers by cancelling the opposite integers.

a) $(\cancel{+5}) + (\cancel{-5}) + (+3) = $ ___+3___

b) $(-5) + 3 + (-3) = $ _____

c) $(+5) + (-3) + (+3) = $ _____

d) $(-3) + (+5) + (-5) = $ _____

e) $(+4) + (-2) + (+2) = $ _____

f) $(+4) + (-4) + (+2) = $ _____

g) $(-6) + 6 + (-3) = $ _____

h) $(+7) + (-7) + (+4) = $ _____

All integers can be written as sums of +1s or –1s.

Examples: $3 = (+1) + (+1) + (+1) = 1 + 1 + 1$ $-3 = (-1) + (-1) + (-1) = -1 - 1 - 1$

---

7. Write each number as a sum of +1s and –1s. Then find the sum by cancelling pairs of +1s and –1s.

a) $(+4) + (-2) = $ ___+ 2___

$+ 1 + 1 + \cancel{1} + \cancel{1} - \cancel{1} - \cancel{1}$

b) $(-2) + (-1) = $ _____

c) $(+3) + (-4) = $ _____

d) $(+4) + (-2) = $ _____

e) $(+2) + (+3) = $ _____

f) $(-2) + (-3) = $ _____

g) $(-3) + (-2) = $ _____

h) $(-3) + (+3) = $ _____

8. Add the integers mentally.

Hint: Start by writing + or – to show whether you have a net gain or a net loss.

REMEMBER Two losses add to a bigger loss. $-7 - 2 = -9$

A gain and a loss cancel each other. $-8 + 6 = -2$

---

a) $(+5) + (-6)$

=

b) $(+2) + (-8)$

=

c) $(+3) + (+5)$

=

d) $(-2) + (-4)$

=

e) $(-7) + (+10)$

=

f) $(-4) + (+4)$

=

g) $(-3) + (-7)$

=

h) $(-2) + (-6)$

=

i) $(-4) + (-8)$

=

j) $(-5) + (+3)$

=

k) $(-4) + (-5)$

=

l) $(-17) + (+20)$

=

9. Decide whether each statement is true or false. If you circle false, give a counter-example.

a) The sum of two negative integers is negative.   **T   F**

b) If you add a negative integer to a positive integer, the result is negative.   **T   F**

NS8-55 Adding Integers on a Number Line

To add a negative integer, **move left**.

Example: $(+3) + (-4) = +3 - 4$, so subtract 4 from +3. Start at +3 and move left 4 places.

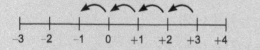

$$(+3) + (-4) = (-1)$$

To add a positive integer, **move right**.

Example: $(-2) + (+4) = -2 + 4$, so add 4 to -2. Start at -2 and move right 4 places.

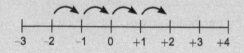

$$(-2) + (+4) = (+2)$$

1. Use a number line to add the integers.

a) $(+4) + (-6) = $ _____

b) $(-3) + (-2) = $ _____

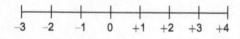   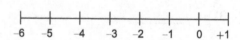

c) $(+1) + (+2) = $ _____

d) $(-4) + (+2) = $ _____

   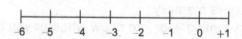

e) $(+4) + (-4) = $ _____

f) $(-3) + (+3) = $ _____

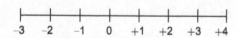   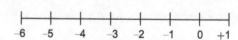

INVESTIGATION ▶ Does adding integers in a different order affect the answer?

A. Draw a number line to add the integers in different orders.

a) $(-3) + (-5)$ and $(-5) + (-3)$ b) $(+8) + (-2)$ and $(-2) + (+8)$

c) $(-3) + (-7)$ and $(-7) + (-3)$ d) $(-6) + (+2)$ and $(+2) + (-6)$

e) $(+3) + (-4) + (+2) + (-5) + (+1)$ and $(+3) + (+2) + (+1) + (-4) + (-5)$

B. Look at your answers in part A. Does adding integers in a different order affect the answer?

2. Use a number line to continue the pattern.

a) $+11, +8, +5, +2,$ _____, _____, _____   b) $-10, -8, -6, -4,$ _____, _____, _____

NS8-56 Subtracting Integers

Subtraction undoes addition, so to subtract an integer, do the opposite of what you would do to add the integer.

Example: (−5) − (−2)   To add (−2), move __2__ units to the _____*left*_____ .
To subtract (−2), move __2__ units to the _____*right*_____ .

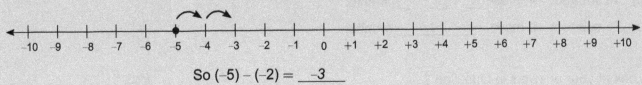

So (−5) − (−2) = __−3__

1. Use a number line to subtract.

a) (+5) − (−3)

To add (−3), move _____ units _____ .
To subtract (−3), move _____ units _____ .

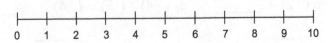

So (+5) − (−3) = _____

b) (+6) − (+2)

To add (+2), move _____ units _____ .
To subtract (+2), move _____ units _____ .

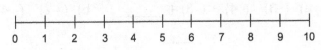

So (+6) − (+2) = _____

c) (−6) − (+4)

To add (+4), move _____ units _____ .
To subtract (+4), move _____ units _____ .

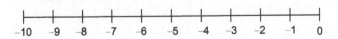

So (−6) − (+4) = _____

d) (−4) − (−3)

To add (−3), move _____ units _____ .
To subtract (−3), move _____ units _____ .

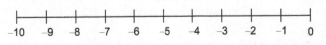

So (−4) − (−3) = _____

e) (+2) − (+5)

To add (+5), move _____ units _____ .
To subtract (+5), move _____ units _____ .

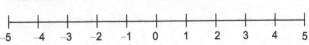

So (+2) − (+5) = _____

f) (+3) − (−1)

To add (−1), move _____ units _____ .
To subtract (−1), move _____ units _____ .

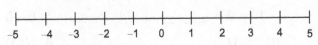

So (+3) − (−1) = _____

g) (−2) − (−3)

To add (−3), move _____ units _____ .
To subtract (−3), move _____ units _____ .

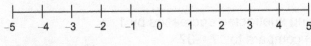

So (−2) − (−3) = _____

h) (−2) − (+3)

To add (+3), move _____ units _____ .
To subtract (+3), move _____ units _____ .

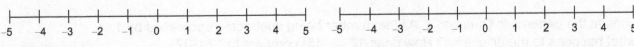

So (−2) − (+3) = _____

NS8-56 Subtracting Integers *(continued)*

2. Would you move **left** or **right** on a number line?

   a) To add +4, move _____ 4 units.

   b) To add –4, move _____ 4 units.

   c) To subtract +4, move _____ 4 units.

   c) To subtract –4, move _____ 4 units.

3. Look at your answers in Question 2.

   a) Subtracting +4 gives the same result as adding _____ so ▢ – (+4) = ▢ + _____ .

   b) Subtracting –4 gives the same result as adding _____ so ▢ – (–4) = ▢ + _____ .

4. Write each difference as a sum and then calculate the answer.

   a) $(-3) - (-4) = (-3) + $ _____   b) $(+2) - (+4) = (+2) + $ _____   c) $(+4) - (-5) = (+4) + $ _____

         = _____   = _____   = _____

   d) $(-3) - (+4) = (-3) + $ _____   e) $(-1) - (+4) = (-1) + $ _____   f) $(+3) - (-7) = (+3) + $ _____

         = _____   = _____   = _____

5. Write the correct integer in the blank.

   a) $x - (-3) = x + $ _____   b) $x - (+7) = x + $ _____   c) $x - (-25) = x + $ _____

6. Subtract by continuing the patterns.

   a) $10 - 4 = $ _____   b) $6 - 4 = $ _____   c) $15 - 4 = $ _____

          $10 - 3 = $ _____ $6 - 3 = $ _____ $15 - 3 = $ _____

          $10 - 2 = $ _____ $6 - 2 = $ _____ $15 - 2 = $ _____

          $10 - 1 = $ _____ $6 - 1 = $ _____ $15 - 1 = $ _____

          $10 - 0 = $ _____ $6 - 0 = $ _____ $15 - 0 = $ _____

       $10 - (-1) = $ _____ $6 - (-1) = $ _____ $15 - (-1) = $ _____

       $10 - (-2) = $ _____ $6 - (-2) = $ _____ $15 - (-2) = $ _____

       $10 - (-3) = $ _____ $6 - (-3) = $ _____ $15 - (-3) = $ _____

       $10 - (-4) = $ _____ $6 - (-4) = $ _____ $15 - (-4) = $ _____

   $10 - (-36) = $ _____ $6 - (-36) = $ _____ $15 - (-36) = $ _____

7. Look at the patterns in Question 6. As the number being subtracted decreases by 1, what happens to the difference? How does $17 - (-15)$ compare to $17 - 0$?

NS8-57 Subtraction Using a Thermometer

What does 2 – 5 mean on a thermometer?

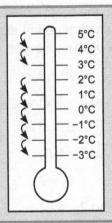

Look at 5 – 2.
If the temperature is 5° and drops 2°, the temperature becomes **5 – 2 = 3°**.

Now switch the 2 and the 5.
If the temperature is 2° and drops 5°, the temperature becomes **2 – 5 = –3°**.

1. Use the thermometer model to calculate each expression.

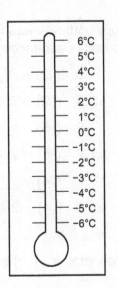

   a) If the temperature is 4° and the temperature drops 3°,
      the temperature becomes 4 – 3 = _____°.

      If the temperature is 3° and the temperature drops 4°,
      the temperature becomes 3 – 4 = _____°.

   b) If the temperature is 5° and the temperature drops 1°,
      the temperature becomes 5 – 1 = _____°.

      If the temperature is 1° and the temperature drops 5°,
      the temperature becomes 1 – 5 = _____°.

   c) 6 – 4 = _____ and 4 – 6 = _____

   d) 5 – 4 = _____ and 4 – 5 = _____

   e) 4 – 1 = _____ and 1 – 4 = _____

   f) 6 – 3 = _____ and 3 – 6 = _____

   g) 6 – 2 = _____ and 2 – 6 = _____

2. a) Look at your answers in Question 1. In general, how does $a - b$ compare to $b - a$?

   _____

   b) Use your answer to part a) to predict 98 – 101: _____

   c) Check your prediction on a calculator. Were you correct? _____

3. Use the thermometer model to subtract.

   a) (–2) – 3 = _____ and (–3) – 2 = _____   b) (–1) – 4 = _____ and (–4) – 1 = _____

   c) (–4) – 2 = _____ and (–2) – 4 = _____   d) (–5) – 1 = _____ and (–1) – 5 = _____

4. Look at your answers in Question 3.

   How does (–a) – b compare to (–b) – a? _____

   How do both of these compare to a + b? _____

NS8-57 Subtraction Using a Thermometer *(continued)*

5. Use the thermometer model to subtract the positive integer from the negative integer. Then change the sign (as you did in Question 2) to subtract the negative integer from the positive integer.

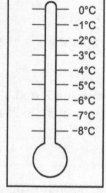

a)　　$(-2) - 3 = \underline{\ -5\ }$

　　so $3 - (-2) = \underline{\ +5\ }$

b)　　$(-1) - 4 = \underline{\hspace{2cm}}$

　　so $4 - (-1) = \underline{\hspace{2cm}}$

c)　　$-5) - 2 = \underline{\hspace{2cm}}$

　　so $2 - (-5) = \underline{\hspace{2cm}}$

d)　　$(-3) - 4 = \underline{\hspace{2cm}}$

　　so $4 - (-3) = \underline{\hspace{2cm}}$

e)　　$(-4) - 2 = \underline{\hspace{2cm}}$

　　so $2 - (-4) = \underline{\hspace{2cm}}$

f)　　$(-6) - 2 = \underline{\hspace{2cm}}$

　　so $2 - (-6) = \underline{\hspace{2cm}}$

6. Copy your answers from Question 5. How can you get the same answer by adding instead of subtracting? Write the correct positive integer in the blank.

a)　　$3 - (-2) = \underline{\ +5\ }$

　　so $3 - (-2) = 3 + \underline{\ (+2)\ }$

b)　　$4 - (-1) = \underline{\hspace{2cm}}$

　　so $4 - (-1) = 4 + \underline{\hspace{2cm}}$

c)　　$2 - (-5) = \underline{\hspace{2cm}}$

　　so $2 - (-5) = 2 + \underline{\hspace{2cm}}$

d)　　$4 - (-3) = \underline{\hspace{2cm}}$

　　so $4 - (-3) = 4 + \underline{\hspace{2cm}}$

e)　　$2 - (-4) = \underline{\hspace{2cm}}$

　　so $2 - (-4) = 2 + \underline{\hspace{2cm}}$

f)　　$2 - (-6) = \underline{\hspace{2cm}}$

　　so $2 - (-6) = 2 + \underline{\hspace{2cm}}$

7. In general, $a - (-b)$ gives the same result as $a + \underline{\hspace{2cm}}$.

8. Change the subtraction of a negative integer to the addition of a positive integer.

a)　$4 - (-3) = 4 + \underline{\hspace{1.5cm}}$

　　　$= \underline{\hspace{1.5cm}}$

b)　$5 - (-5) = 5 + \underline{\hspace{1.5cm}}$

　　　$= \underline{\hspace{1.5cm}}$

c)　$6 - (-3) = 6 + \underline{\hspace{1.5cm}}$

　　　$= \underline{\hspace{1.5cm}}$

d)　$(-2) - (-1) = (-2) + \underline{\hspace{1.5cm}}$

　　　$= \underline{\hspace{1.5cm}}$

e)　$(-3) - (-4) = -3 + \underline{\hspace{1.5cm}}$

　　　$= \underline{\hspace{1.5cm}}$

f)　$(-2) - (-5) = -2 + \underline{\hspace{1.5cm}}$

　　　$= \underline{\hspace{1.5cm}}$

> To subtract positive integers, imagine moving down the thermometer.
>
> To subtract negative integers, add their opposites or move up the thermometer.

9. a)　$(-3) - 5 = \underline{\hspace{1.5cm}}$

b)　$(-3) - (-5) = \underline{\hspace{1.5cm}}$

c)　$(-2) - (-4) = \underline{\hspace{1.5cm}}$

d)　$4 - 5 = \underline{\hspace{1.5cm}}$

e)　$(-8) - 3 = \underline{\hspace{1.5cm}}$

f)　$4 - (-5) = \underline{\hspace{1.5cm}}$

g)　$2 - 7 = \underline{\hspace{1.5cm}}$

h)　$2 - (-7) = \underline{\hspace{1.5cm}}$

i)　$-2 - (-7) = \underline{\hspace{1.5cm}}$

j)　$(-2) - 7 = \underline{\hspace{1.5cm}}$

k)　$(-7) - 2 = \underline{\hspace{1.5cm}}$

l)　$7 - (-2) = \underline{\hspace{1.5cm}}$

NS8-58 More Gains and Losses

REMEMBER **Sums of integers** can be written as sequences of gains and losses.

$$+5+(+3) = +5+3 \qquad +2+(-5) = +2-5 \qquad -3+(-2) = -3-2$$

Differences of integers may also be written as sequences of gains and losses.

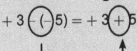 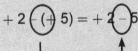

Taking away a loss gives a gain	Taking away a gain gives a loss

$$+(+ \longrightarrow +$$
$$+(- \longrightarrow -$$
$$-(+ \longrightarrow -$$
$$-(- \longrightarrow +$$

1. Rewrite each expression as a sequence of gains and losses.

   a) $+3+(-5)$ b) $-4-(+2)$ c) $-5-(-6)$ d) $+3-(-5)+(-4)+(+2)-(+6)$

   $\quad = +3-5 \qquad\qquad = \qquad\qquad\qquad = \qquad\qquad\qquad\qquad =$

2. Simplify each expression and then add to find the result.

   a) $+3+(+2)$ b) $-5+(-3)$ c) $+2-(+3)$ d) $-4-(-6)$

   $\quad = \qquad\qquad\qquad = \qquad\qquad\qquad = \qquad\qquad\qquad =$

   $\quad = \qquad\qquad\qquad = \qquad\qquad\qquad = \qquad\qquad\qquad =$

   e) $-11-(-6)$ f) $+14+(-8)$ g) $-3+(+7)$ h) $-25-(-5)$

   i) $-2+(-3)+(+4)$ j) $+3+(-5)+4$ k) $-9-(+8)-(-12)$ l) $-4+5-(-6)+(-3)$

3. Draw a number line from -10 to $+10$ and mark a number that is...

   A 2 less than 0   **B** 3 less than 4   **C** 3 greater than -1 **D** 5 greater than -2

   E halfway between $+2$ and $+6$ **F** an equal distance from -8 and -2

   G the same distance from 0 as -9 **H** twice as far from zero as -4

4. Solve the puzzle by placing the same integer in each shape.

   a) $\square + \square + \square = -6$ b) $\bigcirc + \bigcirc + \bigcirc = -30$

5. If you were to spin the spinner twice and add the two results...

   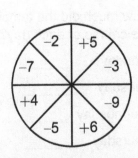

   a) What is the highest total you could score? _____

   b) What is the lowest total you could score? _____

   c) What is the largest possible difference between the two scores?

   _____

   d) How could you score zero? _____

NS8-59 Word Problems

1. In this square, the integers in each row, column, and two diagonals (these include the centre box) add up to +3.

   Fill in the missing integers.

+5		–3
–2		

2. The chart shows the average temperatures in winter and summer for three Canadian cities.

   Find the range of average temperatures for each city.

City	Average Winter Temp (°C)	Average Summer Temp (°C)	Range
Toronto	–5	20	
Montreal	–10	21	
Vancouver	–3	23	

3. The chart shows the average temperature on 5 planets.

   a) Write the temperatures in order from least to greatest.

   b) What is the difference between the highest and the lowest average temperature?

   c) Which planet has an average temperature 200°C lower than Earth?

Earth	+20°C
Venus	+470°C
Saturn	–180°C
Mercury	+120°C
Jupiter	– 50°C

4. When a plane takes off, the temperature on the ground is 20°C. The temperature outside the plane decreases by 5°C for every 1 000 m it climbs above the ground.

   a) What is the temperature outside the plane when it is 5 000 m above the ground?

   b) What will the temperature outside the plane be when it is 5 400 m above the ground?

5. A cup of hot chocolate has a temperature of +98°C. When Guled adds an ice cube, the temperature decreases by 1°C. Guled writes (+98) + (–7) to find the temperature after adding 7 ice cubes.

   a) How would Guled find the temperature after adding 12 ice cubes? (+98) + _____ = _____

   b) Guled's hot chocolate has 5 ice cubes and a temperature of +93°C. How would Guled find the temperature after **removing** 3 ice cubes?

6. How much did the temperature change in the course of each day?

   Monday _____

   Tuesday _____

   Wednesday _____

   Thursday _____

	Daily Low Temp (°C)	Daily High Temp (°C)
Monday	–8	+2
Tuesday	–10	–8
Wednesday	–4	0
Thursday	–17	–5

NS8-60 Multiplying Integers

> REMEMBER Multiplication is a short form for repeated addition.
>
> Example: $4 \times 5 = 5 + 5 + 5 + 5 = 20$
>
> When you multiply a negative integer and a positive integer, you can think of repeated addition.
>
> Example: $4 \times (-5) = (-5) + (-5) + (-5) + (-5) = -20$

1. Write each product as repeated addition. Then find the answer.

   a) $3 \times (-5) =$

   b) $2 \times (-7) =$

   c) $4 \times (-3) =$

   d) $4 \times (-2) =$

   e) $5 \times (-6) =$

   f) $3 \times (-8) =$

2. Look at your answers in Question 1. How does $a \times (-b)$ compare to $a \times b$?

3. Calculate $a \times (-b)$ by first calculating $a \times b$.

   a) $2 \times 7 =$ _____

   so $2 \times (-7) =$ _____

   b) $3 \times 4 =$ _____

   so $3 \times (-4) =$ _____

   c) $5 \times 6 =$ _____

   so $5 \times (-6) =$ _____

   d) $9 \times (-8) =$ _____

   e) $8 \times (-7) =$ _____

   f) $10 \times (-2) =$ _____

> The **distributive law** tells us how multiplication relates to addition and subtraction.
>
> For positive numbers a, b, and c,
>
> $a \times (b + c) = a \times b + a \times c$
>
> $a \times (b - c) = a \times b - a \times c$
>
> $(a + b) \times c = a \times c + b \times c$
>
> $(a - b) \times c = a \times c - b \times c$
>
> Examples:
>
> $2 \times (3 + 4) = 2 \times 7 = 14$ and $2 \times 3 + 2 \times 4 = 6 + 8 = 14$
>
> $2 \times (7 - 3) = 2 \times 4 = 8$ and $2 \times 7 - 2 \times 3 = 14 - 6 = 8$
>
> $(2 + 7) \times 3 = 9 \times 3 = 27$ and $2 \times 3 + 7 \times 3 = 6 + 21 = 27$
>
> $(7 - 2) \times 3 = 5 \times 3 = 15$ and $7 \times 3 - 2 \times 3 = 21 - 6 = 15$

4. Use the distributive law to rewrite each product.

   a) $2 \times (5 + 3)$

   $= 2 \times 5 + 2 \times 3$

   b) $3 \times (4 - 2)$

   $=$

   c) $(5 - 2) \times 3$

   $=$

   d) $(4 + 2) \times 5$

   $=$

   e) $(8 - 3) \times 3$

   $=$

   f) $4 \times (3 - 2)$

   $=$

   g) $(9 - 4) \times 2$

   $=$

   h) $(4 + 3) \times 6$

   $=$

   i) $(5 - 2) \times 3$

   $=$

NS8-60 Multiplying Integers (continued)

INVESTIGATION 1 ▶

Does the distributive law, $a \times (b - c) = a \times b - a \times c$, hold even when $b - c$ is negative?

A. Calculate both sides and then write = (equal) or ≠ (not equal) in the box.

i) $3 \times (2 - 5) \Box 3 \times 2 - 3 \times 5$

ii) $2 \times (4 - 10) \Box 2 \times 4 - 2 \times 10$

iii) $5 \times (1 - 4) \Box 5 \times 1 - 5 \times 4$

iv) $10 \times (2 - 7) \Box 10 \times 2 - 10 \times 7$

B. Choose your own positive integers a, b, and c, with b less than c (so that $b - c$ is negative).

$a = \underline{\hspace{1cm}}, b = \underline{\hspace{1cm}}, c = \underline{\hspace{1cm}}$

Calculate $a \times (b - c)$ and $a \times b - a \times c$. Does the distributive law hold?

Mathematicians defined multiplication so that the distributive law would hold for negative numbers too.

Here's how to calculate the product of a negative integer with a positive integer. $-3 \times 4 = ?$

Step 1: Write the negative integer as a difference between any two positive integers.

$-3 = 2 - 5$, so
$-3 \times 4 = (2 - 5) \times 4$

Step 2: Use the distributive law.

$= 2 \times 4 - 5 \times 4 = 8 - 20 = -12$

---

5. Calculate each product of a negative integer with a positive integer by using the distributive law.

a) $(-2) \times 5 = (1 - 3) \times 5$
$= 1 \times 5 - 3 \times 5$
$= 5 - 15$
$= -10$

b) $(-4) \times 7 = (1 - 5) \times 7$
$= 1 \times 7 - 5 \times 7$

c) $(-3) \times 5 = (0 - 3) \times 5$
$= 0 \times 5 - 3 \times 5$

d) $(-5) \times 3 = (0 - 5) \times 3$

e) $(-8) \times 3 = (2 - 10) \times 3$

f) $(-8) \times 3 = (0 - 8) \times 3$

6. Which product did you find twice in Question 5? Did you get the same answer both ways? Was one way easier? Explain.

7. Look at your answers to Question 5. How does $(-a) \times b$ compare to $a \times b$?

INVESTIGATION 2 ▶ How does $(-a) \times b$ compare to $a \times (-b)$?

A. Fill in the table. Use your own choice of a and b in the last row of the table.

a	b	−a	−b	(−a) × b	a × (−b)
2	3	-2	-3	$(-2) \times 3 = -6$	$2 \times (-3) = -6$
4	5				
5	3				

B. Compare the last two columns. What do you notice?

8. Calculate each product.

a) $(-3) \times 7 = \underline{\hspace{1cm}}$

b) $(-5) \times 4 = \underline{\hspace{1cm}}$

c) $(-2) \times 7 = \underline{\hspace{1cm}}$

d) $(-5) \times 8 = \underline{\hspace{1cm}}$

e) $(-6) \times 3 = \underline{\hspace{1cm}}$

f) $(-9) \times 8 = \underline{\hspace{1cm}}$

NS8-60 Multiplying Integers *(continued)*

Since mathematicians defined multiplication with negative integers to satisfy the distributive law, we can use the distributive law to find the product of two negative integers.

$$(-3) \times (-2) = (-3) \times (5 - 7) \longleftarrow \text{since } -2 = 5 - 7$$
$$= (-3) \times 5 - (-3) \times 7 \longleftarrow \text{since multiplication distributes over subtraction}$$
$$= -15 - (-21)$$
$$= -15 + 21$$
$$= +6$$

9. Calculate $(-2) \times (-5)$ by replacing -5 by various differences of positive integers.

a) $(-2) \times (-5) = (-2) \times (3 - 8)$

   $= (-2) \times 3 - (-2) \times 8$

   $= (-6) - (-16)$

   $= -6 + 16$

   $= +10$

b) $(-2) \times (-5) = (-2) \times (1 - 6)$

c) $(-2) \times (-5) = (-2) \times (0 - 5)$

10. Look at your answers in Question 9. Did you get the same answer all three ways? Was one way easiest? Explain.

11. Follow the steps to multiply negative integers a different way.

a) $(-2) \times (-3)$

   i) Explain why $(-2) \times (3 + (-3))$ equals zero.

   ii) Expand the expression in i) using the distributive law:

   $(-2) \times (3 + (-3)) = \underline{\hspace{1cm}} + \underline{\hspace{1cm}}$

   iii) Explain why $(-2) \times 3$ and $(-2) \times (-3)$ are opposite integers.

   iv) $(-2) \times 3 = \underline{\hspace{1cm}}$

   so $(-2) \times (-3) = \underline{\hspace{1cm}}$

b) $(-3) \times (-4)$

   i) Explain why $(-3) \times (4 + (-4))$ equals zero.

   ii) Expand the expression in i) using the distributive law:

   $(-3) \times (4 + (-4)) = \underline{\hspace{1cm}} + \underline{\hspace{1cm}}$

   iii) Explain why $(-3) \times 4$ and $(-3) \times (-4)$ are opposite integers.

   iv) $(-3) \times 4 = \underline{\hspace{1cm}}$

   so $(-3) \times (-4) = \underline{\hspace{1cm}}$

12. Look at your answers in Questions 9 and 11. How does $(-a) \times (-b)$ compare to $a \times b$?

13. Find the products.

a) $(-3) \times (-5) =$

b) $(-4) \times (-9) =$

c) $(-8) \times (-3) =$

d) $(-2) \times (-5) =$

e) $(-4) \times (-8) =$

f) $(-7) \times (-9) =$

g) $(-8) \times (-6) =$

h) $(-5) \times (-11) =$

14. Multiply mentally.

a) $3 \times (-9) =$

b) $-2 \times 2 =$

c) $(-7) \times (-8) =$

d) $4 \times (-6) =$

e) $-6 \times 7 =$

f) $(-9) \times (-4) =$

g) $-4 \times 6 =$

h) $(-9) \times (-9) =$

NS8-61 Dividing Integers

If you know how to multiply negative numbers, then you can divide negative numbers too!

REMEMBER Since $4 \times 3 = 12$ then $12 \div 3 = 4$ and $12 \div 4 = 3$.

1. Write two division statements from each multiplication statement.

a) $4 \times 3 = 12$

$\underline{12 \div 3 = 4}$

$\underline{12 \div 4 = 3}$

b) $(-4) \times 3 = (-12)$

$\underline{(-12) \div 3 = -4}$

$\underline{(-12) \div (-4) = 3}$

c) $(-4) \times (-3) = 12$

_____

_____

d) $4 \times (-3) = (-12)$

_____

_____

e) $3 \times 2 = 6$

_____

_____

f) $(-3) \times 2 = (-6)$

_____

_____

g) $(-3) \times (-2) = 6$

_____

_____

h) $3 \times (-2) = (-6)$

_____

_____

2. Find the quotients by finding the missing number in the product.

a) $\underline{\hspace{1cm}} \times 2 = 10$ so $10 \div 2 = \underline{\hspace{1cm}}$

b) $\underline{\hspace{1cm}} \times (-3) = (-6)$ so $(-6) \div (-3) = \underline{\hspace{1cm}}$

c) $\underline{\hspace{1cm}} \times (-2) = 8$ so $8 \div (-2) = \underline{\hspace{1cm}}$

d) $\underline{\hspace{1cm}} \times 2 = 6$ so $6 \div 2 = \underline{\hspace{1cm}}$

e) $\underline{\hspace{1cm}} \times 3 = (-15)$ so $(-15) \div 3 = \underline{\hspace{1cm}}$

f) $\underline{\hspace{1cm}} \times 4 = (-20)$ so $(-20) \div 4 = \underline{\hspace{1cm}}$

g) $\underline{\hspace{1cm}} \times (-3) = 9$ so $9 \div (-3) = \underline{\hspace{1cm}}$

h) $\underline{\hspace{1cm}} \times (-6) = (-18)$ so $(-18) \div (-6) = \underline{\hspace{1cm}}$

3. Look at your answers in Question 2. What is the sign of the quotient in each case?

a) I divided $(+) \div (+)$ in parts __*a)*__ and __*d)*__ .

The answers were __5__ and __3__ .

So $(+) \div (+) = \underline{\hspace{1cm}}$.

b) I divided $(-) \div (+)$ in parts _____ and _____ .

The answers were _____ and _____ .

So $(-) \div (+) = \underline{\hspace{1cm}}$.

c) I divided $(+) \div (-)$ in parts _____ and _____ .

The answers were _____ and _____ .

So $(+) \div (-) = \underline{\hspace{1cm}}$.

d) I divided $(-) \div (-)$ in parts _____ and _____ .

The answers were _____ and _____ .

So $(-) \div (-) = \underline{\hspace{1cm}}$.

4. Find the following quotients.

a) $(-20) \div 5 =$

b) $(-54) \div (-6) =$

c) $(-72) \div (-9) =$

d) $80 \div (-10) =$

e) $(-16) \div 4 =$

f) $(+30) \div (+6) =$

g) $(-40) \div (-8) =$

h) $(+72) \div 6 =$

5. Use a calculator to find the quotients.

a) $75 \div (-15) =$

b) $(-84) \div (-12) =$

c) $(-78) \div 13 =$

NS8-62 Relating Fractions and Division

 $\frac{1}{2}$ is one whole divided into 2 parts, so $\frac{1}{2} = 1 \div 2$.

1. a) $\frac{1}{5} = 1 \div$ ____   b) $\frac{1}{4} =$ ____ $\div$ ____   c) $\frac{1}{8} =$ ____ $\div$ ____

2. a) Explain why $24 \div 2$ is three times $8 \div 2$.   b) Explain why $3 \div 8$ is three times $1 \div 8$.

   c) Explain why $3 \div 8$ is $3 \times \frac{1}{8}$.   d) Explain why $3 \div 8 = \frac{3}{8}$.

3. Use $\frac{a}{b} = a \div b$ to write the fraction as a decimal. Keep dividing until the remainder is 0.

   a) $\frac{1}{5} = 1 \div 5$ b) $\frac{3}{5} =$ ___ $\div$ ___   c) $\frac{4}{10} =$ ___ $\div$ ___   d) $\frac{2}{4} =$ ___ $\div$ ___   e) $\frac{4}{8} =$ ___ $\div$ ___

   So, $\frac{1}{5} = 0.$___   So, $\frac{3}{5} = 0.$___   So, $\frac{4}{10} = 0.$___   So, $\frac{2}{4} = 0.$___   So, $\frac{4}{8} = 0.$___

   f) $\frac{5}{2}$ g) $\frac{7}{4}$ h) $\frac{9}{10}$ i) $\frac{4}{5}$ j) $\frac{24}{40}$

4. a) Change the fraction to a decimal using long division. Keep dividing until the remainder is 0.

   $\frac{1}{8} = 8\overline{)1.000} = ?$ $\frac{2}{8} = 8\overline{)2.000} = ?$ $\frac{3}{8} = 8\overline{)3.000} = ?$

   b) What is the pattern in the decimal equivalents in part a)?

   c) Extend the pattern from part a) to predict the decimals equivalent to $\frac{4}{8}, \frac{5}{8}, \frac{6}{8}, \frac{7}{8}$, and $\frac{8}{8}$.

5. Convert each fraction to a decimal fraction. Then change the fraction to a decimal. Check your answers using a calculator.

   a) $\frac{3}{40} = \frac{75}{1000} = 0.075$ b) $\frac{17}{20} = \frac{}{100}$ c) $\frac{19}{125} = \frac{}{1000}$

   Check: $3 \div 40 = 0.075$ Check: Check:

   d) $\frac{17}{25}$ e) $\frac{7}{20}$ f) $\frac{273}{500}$ g) $\frac{111}{250}$ BONUS ▶ $\frac{9}{16}$

NS8-63 Repeating Decimals

> A **repeating decimal** is a decimal with a digit or group of digits that repeats forever.
>
> The digit or sequence of digits that repeats can be shown by a bar. Example: $4.121212\ldots = 4.\overline{12}$.
>
> A **terminating decimal** is a decimal that does not go on forever. Examples: 5.68, 0.444
>
> Some decimals do not terminate or repeat. Example: $\pi = 3.14159\ldots$

1. Write each decimal to eight decimal places.

   a) $0.\overline{3} \approx 0.\underline{3}\ \underline{\ }\ \underline{\ }\ \underline{\ }\ \underline{\ }\ \underline{\ }\ \underline{\ }\ \underline{\ }$

   b) $0.0\overline{3} \approx 0.\underline{0}\ \underline{3}\ \underline{3}\ \underline{3}\ \underline{\ }\ \underline{\ }\ \underline{\ }\ \underline{\ }$

   c) $0.00\overline{3} \approx 0.\underline{\ }\ \underline{\ }\ \underline{\ }\ \underline{\ }\ \underline{\ }\ \underline{\ }\ \underline{\ }\ \underline{\ }$

   d) $0.\overline{52} \approx 0.\underline{\ }\ \underline{\ }\ \underline{\ }\ \underline{\ }\ \underline{\ }\ \underline{\ }\ \underline{\ }\ \underline{\ }$

   e) $0.\overline{817} \approx 0.\underline{\ }\ \underline{\ }\ \underline{\ }\ \underline{\ }\ \underline{\ }\ \underline{\ }\ \underline{\ }\ \underline{\ }$

   f) $0.8\overline{17} \approx 0.\underline{\ }\ \underline{\ }\ \underline{\ }\ \underline{\ }\ \underline{\ }\ \underline{\ }\ \underline{\ }\ \underline{\ }$

   g) $0.9\overline{26} \approx 0.\underline{\ }\ \underline{\ }\ \underline{\ }\ \underline{\ }\ \underline{\ }\ \underline{\ }\ \underline{\ }\ \underline{\ }$

   h) $0.2\overline{537} \approx 0.\underline{\ }\ \underline{\ }\ \underline{\ }\ \underline{\ }\ \underline{\ }\ \underline{\ }\ \underline{\ }\ \underline{\ }$

   i) $7.2\overline{3} \approx 7.\underline{\ }\ \underline{\ }\ \underline{\ }\ \underline{\ }\ \underline{\ }\ \underline{\ }\ \underline{\ }\ \underline{\ }$

   j) $8.2\overline{539} \approx 8.\underline{\ }\ \underline{\ }\ \underline{\ }\ \underline{\ }\ \underline{\ }\ \underline{\ }\ \underline{\ }\ \underline{\ }$

2. Circle the repeating decimals.

   0.123412312   0.77   0.222222222…   0.512512512…   0.123238…

3. Write each repeating decimal using bar notation.

   a) 0.555555… = _____

   b) 2.343434… = _____

   c) 5.237237… = _____

   d) 57.121212… = _____

   e) 8.162626… = _____

   f) 0.910591059105 = _____

4. Find the decimal value of each fraction to 3 decimal places. Then write the fraction as a repeating decimal.

   a) 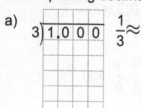 $\dfrac{1}{3} \approx$

   b) 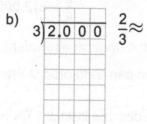 $\dfrac{2}{3} \approx$

5. Use long division to calculate the decimal equivalent of the fraction to 6 decimal places. Then write the decimal using bar notation.

   a) $\dfrac{1}{6}$ b) $\dfrac{4}{9}$ c) $\dfrac{1}{11}$ d) $\dfrac{5}{12}$

6. Match the fractions with their decimal equivalents. Use a calculator.

A $\frac{1}{3}$　　B $\frac{55}{99}$　　C $\frac{2}{3}$　　D $\frac{2}{9}$　　___ $0.\overline{6}$　　　___ $0.\overline{2}$　　　___ $0.\overline{3}$　　　___ $0.\overline{5}$

7. Round the repeating decimals to the nearest tenth, hundredth, and thousandth.

	nearest tenth	nearest hundredth	nearest thousandth
$\frac{2}{7} = 0.285714285714285714285714...$			
$\frac{5}{13} = 0.384615384615384615384615...$			

How to Compare Decimals

Step 1: Write out the first few digits of each decimal. (Add zeros at the end of terminating decimals.)

Step 2: Circle the first digits where the decimals differ.

Step 3: The decimal with the greater circled digit is greater.

Example:

$.678 \boxed{?} .\overline{67}$

$.6\ 7\ 8\ 0\ 0\ 0$

$.6\ 7\ 6\ 7\ 6\ 7$

$.678 \boxed{>} .\overline{67}$

8. Compare the decimals.

a) $.349 \boxed{} .3\overline{49}$

b) $.278 \boxed{} .\overline{27}$

c) $.\overline{613} \boxed{} .61\overline{3}$

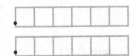

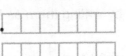

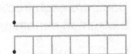

9. Write each group of numbers in order from least to greatest.

a) 0.4　　$0.4\overline{2}$　　$0.\overline{42}$　　0.42

b) 0.16　　$0.\overline{1}$　　$0.1\overline{6}$　　$0.\overline{16}$

c) 0.387　　$0.38\overline{7}$　　$0.3\overline{87}$　　$0.\overline{387}$

d) 0.546　　$0.54\overline{6}$　　$0.5\overline{46}$　　$0.\overline{546}$

e) 0.383　　$0.38\overline{3}$　　$0.3\overline{83}$　　$0.\overline{383}$

f) 0.786　　$0.78\overline{6}$　　$0.7\overline{86}$　　$0.\overline{786}$

10. a) Use long division to write the fractions as repeating decimals. Copy your answers below.

$\frac{1}{9} =$　　　　$\frac{2}{9} =$　　　　$\frac{3}{9} =$　　　　$\frac{4}{9} =$

b) Use the pattern you found in part a) to find...

$\frac{5}{9} =$　　　$\frac{6}{9} =$　　　$\frac{7}{9} =$　　　$\frac{8}{9} =$　　　$\frac{9}{9} =$

NS8-64 Using Decimals to Compare Fractions

1. Write each fraction as a decimal. Circle the decimal that is closest to the fraction.

a) $\frac{1}{4}$ __.25__

$\frac{1}{4}$ is closest to: 0.2   0.4   0.6

b) $\frac{3}{4}$ _____

$\frac{3}{4}$ is closest to: 0.5   0.7   0.9

c) $\frac{1}{5}$ _____

$\frac{1}{5}$ is closest to: 0.14   0.25   0.36

d) $\frac{2}{5}$ _____

$\frac{2}{5}$ is closest to: 0.25   0.42   0.52

2. Express each fraction as a decimal (round your answer to three decimal places). Circle the fraction that is closest to the decimal.

a) $\frac{4}{5}$ [.800] $\frac{7}{10}$ [   ] $\frac{2}{3}$ [   ]   0.65 is closest to: $\frac{4}{5}$ $\frac{7}{10}$ $\frac{2}{3}$

b) $\frac{1}{7}$ [   ] $\frac{1}{8}$ [   ] $\frac{1}{9}$ [   ]   0.125 is closest to: $\frac{1}{7}$ $\frac{1}{8}$ $\frac{1}{9}$

c) $3\frac{1}{2}$ [   ] $\frac{10}{3}$ [   ] $\frac{8}{3}$ [   ]   3.28 is closest to: $3\frac{1}{2}$ $\frac{10}{3}$ $\frac{8}{3}$

3. Use decimal equivalents to order these fractions from greatest to least: $\frac{5}{6}$, $\frac{13}{17}$, $\frac{56}{73}$, $\frac{4}{5}$.

4. a) Compare each fraction and decimal by writing them as fractions with a common denominator.

   i)   0.57 and $\frac{3}{5}$ ii)   0.83 and $\frac{4}{5}$ iii) $\frac{2}{3}$ and 0.37

   b) Compare each fraction and decimal from part a) by writing the fraction as a decimal.

   c) Do you prefer the method you used in part a) or part b)? Explain.

5. a) Which of $\frac{6}{11}$, $\frac{23}{45}$, and $\frac{11}{21}$ is closest to $\frac{1}{2}$?   b) Which of 0.285, $0.\overline{286}$, and $0.28\overline{5}$ is closest to $\frac{2}{7}$?

6. 0.24 is close to 0.25, so a fraction close to 0.24 is $\frac{1}{4}$. Write a fraction that is close to…

   a) 0.52   b) 0.32   c) 0.298   d) 0.38   e) 0.59   f) 0.12

7. a) Use a calculator to write each fraction as a decimal: $\frac{8}{13}$, $\frac{9}{11}$, $\frac{5}{36}$, $\frac{3}{17}$, $\frac{89}{121}$.

   b) Order the fractions in part a) from least to greatest.

NS8-65 Is the Fraction a Terminating or Repeating Decimal?

INVESTIGATION ▶ How can you tell from the fraction whether the equivalent decimal repeats or terminates?

A. Write three different fractions, one with each denominator: 10, 100, and 1 000. Will the decimal representations of these fractions terminate? Explain.

B. Why can a terminating decimal always be written as a decimal fraction?

Examples: $0.3 = \dfrac{3}{10}$, $0.17 = \dfrac{17}{100}$

C. Divide using a calculator. Does the decimal equivalent of the fraction terminate or repeat?

a) $\dfrac{5}{8}$ b) $\dfrac{7}{12}$ c) $\dfrac{6}{13}$ d) $\dfrac{7}{15}$ e) $\dfrac{3}{17}$ f) $\dfrac{13}{2000}$

Write the fractions with equivalent terminating decimals as decimal fractions.

D. 10 2 × 5. Write 100 and 1 000 as a product of 2s and 5s.

E. Write a fraction with a denominator that is a product of 2s, 5s, or a combination of 2s and 5s. Use a calculator to divide the numerator by the denominator. Does the equivalent decimal terminate?

F. Write $\dfrac{1}{6}, \dfrac{2}{6}, \dfrac{3}{6}, \dfrac{4}{6}$, and $\dfrac{5}{6}$ in simplest form. Why is $\dfrac{3}{6}$ the only one of the sixths that terminates?

How to Decide If a Fraction Is Equivalent to a Terminating Decimal or a Repeating Decimal

Step 1: Write the fraction in **lowest terms**.

Step 2: Look at the **denominator**.
If it can be written as a product of only 2s and/or 5s, the decimal terminates.
If it cannot be written as a product of only 2s and/or 5s, the decimal repeats.

---

1. a) Calculate the first few powers of 3 (3, 3 × 3, 3 × 3 × 3, ...).

b) Are the decimal equivalents for $\dfrac{1}{3}, \dfrac{1}{9}$, and $\dfrac{1}{27}$ repeating decimals? How can you

tell without calculating the decimal?

2. a) Write out the twelfths from $\dfrac{1}{12}$ to $\dfrac{11}{12}$. Write them all in lowest terms.

b) Predict which of the twelfths will terminate. Explain.
c) Use a calculator to calculate the decimal equivalents for all the twelfths.
d) Which of the twelfths terminate? Was your prediction in part b) correct?

3. The denominators of $\dfrac{3}{6}, \dfrac{3}{12}, \dfrac{6}{12}, \dfrac{3}{15}, \dfrac{6}{15}, \dfrac{9}{15}$ and $\dfrac{12}{15}$, all have 3 as a factor. But they

are all terminating decimals. Why?

NS8-66 Adding and Subtracting Repeating Decimals

1. Add or subtract the decimals by lining up the decimal places.

a) $.\overline{25} + .\overline{33} = .58\overline{25}$

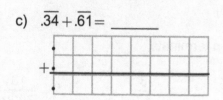

b) $.125 + .\overline{2} =$

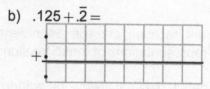

c) $.\overline{34} + .\overline{61} =$ _____

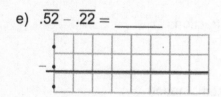

d) $.\overline{342} + .2\overline{51} =$ _____

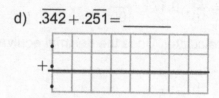

e) $.\overline{52} - .\overline{22} =$ _____

f) $.\overline{345} - .\overline{123} =$ _____

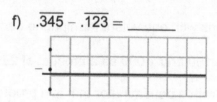

2. $\dfrac{1}{9} = 0.111...,$ $\dfrac{2}{9} = 0.222...,$ $\dfrac{3}{9} = 0.333...,$ and so on.

a) Add the repeating decimals by lining up the decimal places.

i) $0.\overline{1} + 0.\overline{2} =$ _____

ii) $0.\overline{2} + 0.\overline{5} =$ _____

iii) $0.\overline{4} + 0.\overline{4} =$ _____

b) Add the repeating decimals in part a) by changing them to fractions, adding the fractions, then writing the sum as a decimal.

c) Do you prefer the method you used in part a) or part b)? Explain.

3. a) Add by lining up the decimal places.

i) $0.3 + 0.7$

ii) $0.33 + 0.77$

iii) $0.333 + 0.777$

iv) $0.3333 + 0.7777$

b) Use the pattern in part a) to predict $0.\overline{3} + 0.\overline{7}$.

c) Why is it not possible to add $0.\overline{3} + 0.\overline{7}$ by lining up the decimal places?

d) Change the repeating decimals in part b) to fractions. (Hint: Use the pattern in Question 2.)

Add the fractions. Was your prediction in part b) correct?

4. Add or subtract by...

a) lining up the decimal places.

b) changing the decimals to fractions, adding or subtracting the fractions, then changing the fraction to a decimal by dividing.

i) $0.25 + 0.\overline{3}$

ii) $0.\overline{3} - 0.25$

iii) $0.5 + 0.\overline{4}$

iv) $0.5 - 0.\overline{4}$

NS8-67 Writing Repeating Decimals as Fractions

1. a) Use long division to write $\frac{1}{11}, \frac{2}{11}, \frac{3}{11}$, and $\frac{4}{11}$ as decimals.

b) Extend the pattern to find $\frac{5}{11}, \frac{6}{11}, \frac{7}{11}, \frac{8}{11}, \frac{9}{11}, \frac{10}{11}$, and $\frac{11}{11}$.

c) Use $\frac{9}{9} = \frac{11}{11} = 0.\overline{9}$ to show that $0.\overline{9} = 1$.

d) Calculate the first three products, then predict the fourth.

$$\begin{array}{r} 0.09 \\ \times 5 \\ \hline \end{array} \qquad \begin{array}{r} 0.0909 \\ \times 5 \\ \hline \end{array} \qquad \begin{array}{r} 0.090909 \\ \times 5 \\ \hline \end{array} \qquad \begin{array}{r} 0.\overline{09} \\ \times 5 \\ \hline \end{array}$$

e) Calculate $0.\overline{09}\ 5$ by changing the decimal to a fraction. Then change your answer back to a decimal. Was your prediction correct?

2. a) Use long division to show that $\frac{1}{99} = 0.\overline{01}$.

b) Calculate the first three products, then predict the fourth.

$$\begin{array}{r} 0.01 \\ \times 17 \\ \hline \end{array} \qquad \begin{array}{r} 0.0101 \\ \times 17 \\ \hline \end{array} \qquad \begin{array}{r} 0.010101 \\ \times 17 \\ \hline \end{array} \qquad \begin{array}{r} 0.\overline{01} \\ \times 17 \\ \hline \end{array}$$

c) Write $\frac{17}{99}$ as a repeating decimal. Explain your answer.

3. Write the fraction as a repeating decimal.

a) $\frac{25}{99}$ b) $\frac{38}{99}$ c) $\frac{97}{99}$ d) $\frac{86}{99}$ e) $\frac{7}{99}$ f) $\frac{4}{99}$

4. Change the fraction to an equivalent fraction with denominator 9 or 99. Then write the repeating decimal.

a) $\frac{13}{33}$ b) $\frac{2}{3}$ c) $\frac{4}{11}$ d) $\frac{34}{66}$ e) $\frac{10}{18}$ f) $\frac{30}{55}$

5. Change each repeating decimal to a fraction. Write your answer in lowest terms.

a) $0.\overline{46}$ b) $0.\overline{07}$ c) $0.\overline{15}$ d) $0.\overline{98}$ e) $0.\overline{6}$ f) $0.\overline{48}$

6. a) We know that $\frac{1}{9} = 0.\overline{1}$ and $\frac{1}{99} = 0.\overline{01}$.   Predict: $\frac{1}{999} = $ _____

Check your answer by long division.

b) Use your answer in part a) to calculate the equivalent decimal for…

i) $\frac{34}{999}$ ii) $\frac{8}{999}$ iii) $\frac{734}{999}$ iv) $\frac{46}{999}$ v) $\frac{25}{333}$ vi) $\frac{47}{111}$

NS8-68 Writing Repeating Decimals as Fractions (Advanced)

1. Write the repeating decimal as a fraction.

   a) $0.\overline{7} = \dfrac{}{9}$

   b) $0.\overline{23} = \dfrac{}{99}$

   c) $0.\overline{05} = \dfrac{}{99}$

   d) $0.\overline{441} = \dfrac{}{999}$

   e) $0.\overline{652} = \dfrac{}{999}$

   f) $0.\overline{98} =$

   g) $0.\overline{5} =$

   h) $0.\overline{461} =$

   i) $0.\overline{38} =$

   j) $0.\overline{061} =$

2. Multiply or divide by moving the decimal point the correct number of places, left or right.

   a) $25.44444\ldots \times 10$

   b) $2.66666\ldots \times 100$

   c) $24.919191\ldots \div 10$

   d) $0.3\overline{2} \times 100$

   e) $0.3\overline{2} \div 100$

   f) $54.\overline{361} \times 100$

   g) $0.3\overline{41} \div 10$

   h) $7.4\overline{32} \div 1000$

   i) $36.\overline{432} \times 10$

3. a) $\dfrac{1}{9} = \underline{\;0.111\ldots\;}$

   b) $\dfrac{4}{9} = \underline{\qquad}$

   c) $\dfrac{2}{3} = \underline{\qquad}$

   So $\dfrac{1}{90} = \underline{\;0.0111\ldots\;}$

   So $\dfrac{4}{900} = \underline{\qquad}$

   So $\dfrac{2}{3000} = \underline{\qquad}$

4. $\dfrac{137}{999} = 0.\overline{137}$. What is $\dfrac{137}{9990}$? $\underline{\qquad\qquad}$

5. a) $13 \times 0.01 = \underline{\qquad}$ $13 \times 0.011 = \underline{\qquad}$ $13 \times 0.0111 = \underline{\qquad}$

   b) Predict: $13 \times 0.0111\ldots = \underline{\qquad}$

   c) Why should $\dfrac{13}{90}$ be equal to your answer to part b)? Check using a calculator.

   d) Use $\dfrac{13}{9} = 1\dfrac{4}{9}$ to find $\dfrac{13}{90}$ in a different way.

6. Write each decimal as a fraction.

   a) $0.\overline{1} = \underline{\quad}$ $0.\overline{8} = \underline{\quad}$ $0.0\overline{8} = \underline{\quad}$

   $0.5\overline{8} = 0.5 + 0.0\overline{8} = \underline{\quad} + \underline{\quad} = \underline{\quad}$

   b) $0.\overline{01} = \underline{\quad}$ $0.\overline{27} = \underline{\quad}$ $0.0\overline{27} = \underline{\quad}$

   $0.4\overline{27} = 0.4 + 0.0\overline{27} = \underline{\quad} + \underline{\quad} = \underline{\quad}$

   c) $0.\overline{001} = \underline{\quad}$ $0.\overline{253} = \underline{\quad}$ $0.0\overline{253} = \underline{\quad}$

   $5.6\overline{253} = \underline{\quad} + \underline{\quad} = \underline{\quad} + \underline{\quad} = \underline{\quad}$

   d) $0.\overline{5} = \underline{\quad}$ so $4.\overline{5} = \underline{\quad}$

   $0.0\overline{5} = \underline{\quad}$ so $4.0\overline{5} = \underline{\quad}$

   e) $0.1\overline{5}$

   f) $1.\overline{7}$

   g) $2.\overline{35}$

   h) $0.24\overline{361}$

   i) $2.4\overline{361}$

No unauthorized copying

NS8-69 Percents

The words "per cent" mean "out of 100." A percent is a ratio that compares a number or amount to 100.

The symbol for a percent is %. Example: 45% 45 : 100 $\frac{45}{100}$

1. a) 40 out of 100 squares are shaded. The ratio of shaded squares

    to all squares is __40__ : 100.

    So, __90__ % of the grid is shaded.

    b) 49 out of 100 letters are Bs. The ratio of Bs to all letters

    in the set is __49__ : 100.

    So, __49__ % of the letters are Bs.

    BBBBCCBBAABBCABBBCCB
    AAABBBCCBBAABAAABBBC
    CBCABBBCCBBBCCBBAAAB
    BAAABBABCBBAABCCBBAB
    BCCBAABBAAAABBCCABAB

2. Write the ratio as a percent.

    a) 50 : 100 __50__ %   b) 72 : 100 __72__%   c) 7 : 100 __7__ %   d) 43 : 100 __42__%

3. Write the percent as a ratio.

    a) 70% __70__ : __100__   b) 13% __13__ : __100__   c) 38% __8__ : __100__   d) 8% __6__ : __100__

4. Write the ratio as a fraction and as a percent.

    a) 60 : 100 $\frac{60}{100}$ __60__ %   b)   10 : 100 $\frac{0}{100}$ __100__%

5. Write the fraction as a percent.

    a) $\frac{52}{100}$ __52__ %   b) $\frac{39}{100}$ __39__ %   c) $\frac{18}{100}$ __80__%   d) $\frac{2}{100}$ __2__   e) $\frac{6}{100}$ __1__

6. Write the percent as a fraction.

    a) 12% $\frac{21}{100}$ b) 7% $\frac{7}{100}$ c) 49% $\frac{49}{100}$ d) 3% $\frac{3}{100}$ e) 100% $\frac{100}{100}$

7. Complete the chart.

Drawing				
Fraction	$\frac{34}{100}$	$\frac{52}{100}$	$\frac{67}{100}$	$\frac{}{100}$
Percent	34%	52%	__67__ %	__18__ %

NS8-70 Adding and Subtracting Percents

1. There are 100 squares on the grid.

   Colour 10 out of 100 squares red. The red area is ____% of the grid.

   Colour 40 out of 100 squares blue. The blue area is ____% of the grid.

   There are now 10 + 40 = ____ coloured squares on the grid.

   So, ____% of the grid is coloured.

2. Write the percents as fractions. Add or subtract. Then write the sum or difference as a percent.

   a) $40\% + 30\% = \dfrac{\quad}{100} + \dfrac{\quad}{100} = \dfrac{\quad}{100} = $ ____%

   b) $60\% + 10\% = \dfrac{\quad}{100} + \dfrac{\quad}{100} = \dfrac{\quad}{100} = $ ____%

   c) $60\% - 35\% = \dfrac{\quad}{100} - \dfrac{\quad}{100} = \dfrac{\quad}{100} = $ ____%

   d) $80\% - 40\% = \dfrac{\quad}{100} - \dfrac{\quad}{100} = \dfrac{\quad}{100} = $ ____%

3. Calculate.

   a) $17\% + 30\% = $ ____%

   b) $22\% + 68\% = $ ____%

   c) $49\% - 16\% + 7\% = $ ____%

4. Determine the missing percent in the circle graph. The whole circle represents 100%.

   a) **Gases in Earth's Atmosphere**

   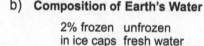

   oxygen: _____%

   b) **Composition of Earth's Water**

   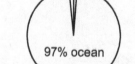

   unfrozen fresh water: _____%

   c) **Land Cover in North America**

   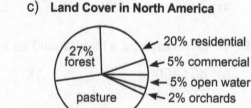

   pasture: _____%

5. a) The ratio of cents in a penny to cents in a dollar is 1 : 100, so a penny is ____% of a dollar.

      The ratio of cents in a dime to cents in a dollar is ____ : 100, so a dime is ____% of a dollar.

      A quarter is ____ cents out of 100, so a quarter is ____% of a dollar.

   b) What percent of a dollar is 35 cents? _____%

      What percent of a dollar is two pennies and two quarters? ____%

   c) You have a dollar and you spend 26¢. What percent of the dollar do you

      have left? ____%

NS8-71 Tenths, Decimals, and Percents

1. Shade the percent.

a) 60%

b) 40%

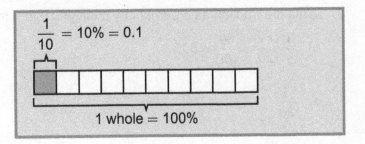

$\frac{1}{10} = 10\% = 0.1$

1 whole = 100%

2. ____% of the 10 dots are white.

____% of the 10 dots are grey.

3. a) Shade 70% of the 10 dots.

b) What percent of the dots are not shaded? _____

4. 10% of 100 marbles are blue. How many of the marbles are not blue? _____

5. Write the percent as a fraction and then as a decimal.

a) $80\% = \dfrac{}{100} = 0.\_\_ \_\_$ b) $75\% = \dfrac{}{100} = 0.\_\_ \_\_$ c) $21\% = \dfrac{}{100} = 0.\_\_ \_\_$ d) $9\% = \dfrac{}{100} = 0.\_\_ \_\_$

e) $15\% = \_\_\_ = \_\_\_$ f) $42\% = \_\_\_ = \_\_\_$ g) $7\% = \_\_\_ = \_\_\_$ h) $100\% = \_\_\_ = \_\_\_$

6. Write the percent as a decimal.

a) $25\% = 0.\_\_ \_\_$ b) $75\% = 0.\_\_ \_\_$ c) $13\% = \_\_\_$ d) $40\% = \_\_\_$

e) $7\% = \_\_\_$ f) $9\% = \_\_\_$ g) $70\% = \_\_\_$ h) $1\% = \_\_\_$

7. Write the decimal as a percent.

a) $0.2 = \dfrac{2}{10} = \dfrac{}{100} = \_\_\_\%$ b) $0.3 = \dfrac{}{10} = \dfrac{}{100} = \_\_\_\%$ c) $0.7 =$

d) $0.23 = \dfrac{}{100} = \_\_\_\%$ e) $0.57 =$ f) $0.08 =$

8. Write the decimal as a percent by moving the decimal point two places to the right.

a) $0.5 = \_\_\_\%$ b) $0.7 = \_\_\_\%$ c) $0.4 =$ d) $0.1 =$ e) $0.9 =$

f) $0.27 = \_\_\_\%$ g) $0.60 = \_\_\_\%$ h) $0.53 =$ i) $0.07 =$ j) $0.99 =$

9. Approximately what percent does the decimal represent? Example: $0.1234 \approx 0.12 = 12\%$.
Hint: Remember to round to two decimal places.

a) $0.382 \approx \_\_\_\%$ b) $0.925 \approx \_\_\_\%$ c) $0.3779 \approx$ d) $0.1036 \approx$

10. Ken bought 7 classical CDs and 3 jazz CDs. What fraction of the CDs are classical?
What percent are jazz?

NS8-72 Fractions and Percents

1. Write the fraction as a percent by changing it to a fraction over 100.

   a) $\dfrac{3 \times 20}{5 \times 20} = \dfrac{60}{100} = 60\%$

   b) $\dfrac{4}{5}$

   c) $\dfrac{3}{20}$

   d) $\dfrac{8}{25}$

2. Two out of five friends, or $\dfrac{2}{5}$, ordered pizza. What percent ordered pizza? ____

3. Change the fraction to a percent. Reduce the fraction to lowest terms if necessary.

   a) $\dfrac{9}{15} = \dfrac{3}{5} = \dfrac{60}{100} = 60\%$

   b) $\dfrac{3}{15} =$

   c) $\dfrac{9}{18} =$

   d) $\dfrac{6}{24} =$

   e) $\dfrac{2}{5}$ f) $\dfrac{7}{10}$ g) $\dfrac{3}{15}$ h) $\dfrac{17}{20}$ i) $\dfrac{12}{48}$

4. Divide to change the fraction to a decimal. Then write the decimal as a percent.

   a) $\dfrac{3}{4} = 3 \div 4 = 0.\underline{\quad}\ \underline{\quad} = \underline{\quad}\%$ b) $\dfrac{4}{5}$ c) $\dfrac{6}{15}$ d) $\dfrac{15}{25}$ e) $\dfrac{65}{500}$

5. Write the percent as a decimal, then as a fraction, then in lowest terms.

   a) 30%   b) 84%   c) 55%   d) 4%   e) 90%

6. Is the fraction closest to 10%, 25%, 50%, 75%, or 100%?

   a) $\dfrac{4}{5}$ b) $\dfrac{2}{10}$ c) $\dfrac{2}{5}$ d) $\dfrac{9}{10}$ e) $\dfrac{11}{20}$ f) $\dfrac{16}{20}$ g) $\dfrac{4}{25}$

7. Estimate what percent the fraction is. Say what fraction you used to make your estimate. Then divide to change the fraction to a decimal. Was your estimate close?

   a) $\dfrac{11}{40}$ b) $\dfrac{23}{49}$ c) $\dfrac{60}{84}$ d) $\dfrac{14}{24}$ e) $\dfrac{4}{42}$ f) $\dfrac{21}{31}$

8. Write the fraction as a decimal. Round to two decimal places. Write the approximate percent.

   a) $\dfrac{5}{12} = 5 \div 12 = 0.4\overline{16} \approx 0.42 \underline{\quad}\%$ b) $\dfrac{1}{3}$ c) $\dfrac{2}{3}$ d) $\dfrac{2}{9}$ e) $\dfrac{5}{6}$ f) $\dfrac{1}{7}$

NS8-73 Visual Representations of Percents

1. What percent of the figure is shaded?

   a)  ____%

   b) ____%

   c) ____%

   d) ____%

   e) ____%

   f) ____%

   g) ____%

2. Shade 50% of each figure.

   a)

   b)

3. Write different expressions for the shaded area.

   $$\frac{}{20} = \frac{}{100} = 0.\underline{\quad} = \underline{\quad}\%$$

4. Write the percents that are equivalent to the fractions.

   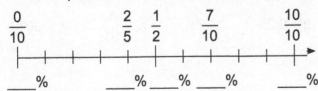

   $$\frac{0}{10} \qquad \frac{2}{5} \quad \frac{1}{2} \qquad \frac{7}{10} \qquad \frac{10}{10}$$

   ____% ____% ____% ____% ____%

5. Measure the line segment. Extend the segment to show 100%.

   a) ⊢ 50% ⊣

   b) ⊢20%⊣

   c) ⊢ 75% ⊣

6. Estimate the percent of the line segment to the left of the mark.

   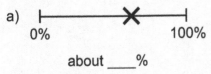

   a) 0% 100%

   about ____%

   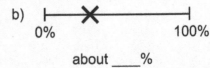

   b) 0% 100%

   about ____%

7. 25 out of 50 squares in a grid are shaded. What fraction and percent of the squares are shaded?

8. Alice must do 40 hours of community service. She has completed 10 hours. What fraction and percent of the hours has she completed? What percent of the hours must still be completed?

9. When would you use the measurement to describe the amount, and when would you use the percent (if ever)? Write a sentence using each expression.

   a) 3 h of the school day or 50% of the school day

   b) 12 kg of berries or 40% of the berries

NS8-74 Comparing Fractions, Decimals, and Percents

1. Complete the chart.

Fraction	$\frac{1}{4}$		$\frac{3}{20}$			$\frac{6}{15}$	$\frac{23}{25}$		
Decimal		0.35			0.60				0.55
Percent				40%				75%	

2. Write < or > or = between each pair of numbers. First change the numbers to a pair of decimal fractions with the same denominator.

a) $\frac{1}{2}$ 47%   b) $\frac{1}{2}$ 57%   c) $\frac{1}{5}$ 22 %   d) $\frac{3}{5}$ 80%

$\frac{1}{2\times 50}^{50}$ $\frac{47}{100}$

$\frac{50}{100}$ $\boxed{>}$ $\frac{47}{100}$ $\Box$ $\Box$ $\Box$

e) $\frac{3}{4}$ 67%   f) 0.26   42%   g) 0.05   7%   h) $\frac{3}{10}$ 30%

$\Box$ $\Box$ $\Box$ $\Box$

i) $\frac{21}{25}$ 18%   j) $\frac{39}{50}$ 76%   k) 0.8   15%   l) $\frac{16}{20}$ 32%

$\Box$ $\Box$ $\Box$ $\Box$

3. Change the numbers in each set to decimals. Then order the decimals from least to greatest.

a) $\frac{3}{5}$, 42%, 0.73   b) $\frac{1}{2}$, 0.73, 80%   c) $\frac{1}{4}$, 0.09, 15%

4. a) In Abeed's school, $\frac{3}{5}$ of students like gym and 65% like drama. Which class is more popular?

b) In Rachel's class, 0.45 of the students like pepperoni pizza best, 35% like cheese, and $\frac{1}{5}$ like vegetarian. Which type of pizza do the most students like best?

NS8-75 Finding Percents

If you use a thousands cube to represent 1 whole, you can see that taking $\frac{1}{10}$ of a number is the same as dividing by 10 (the decimal shifts one place left):

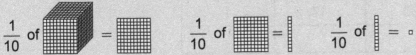

$\frac{1}{10}$ of 1 = 0.1 $\frac{1}{10}$ of 0.1 = 0.01 $\frac{1}{10}$ of 0.01 = 0.001

1. Find $\frac{1}{10}$ of each number by shifting the decimal. Write your answers in the boxes provided.

   a) 7   b) 10   c) 35   d) 210   e) 6.4   f) 50.6

2. 10% is short for $\frac{10}{100}$ or $\frac{1}{10}$. Find 10% of each number.

   a) 1   b) 3.9   c) 4.05   d) 6.74   e) 0.09   f) 60.08

How to Find Percents That Are Multiples of 10

Step 1: Find 10% of the number.

Step 2: Multiply the result by the number of tens in the percent.

Example: Find 30% of 21.

10% of 21 = $\boxed{2.1}$

There are 3 tens in 30 (30 = 3 × 10).

3 × $\boxed{2.1}$ = 6.3

So 30% of 21 = 6.3.

---

3. Find the percent using the method above.

   a) 30% of 15

      10% of _15_ = ☐

      3 × ☐ = ___

   b) 40% of 35

      10% of ___ = ☐

      ___ × ☐ = ___

   c) 20% of 2.7

      10% of ___ = ☐

      ___ × ☐ = ___

   d) 50% of 62

      10% of ___ = ☐

      ___ × ☐ = ___

   e) 80% of 17

      10% of ___ = ☐

      ___ × ☐ = ___

   f) 30% of 0.7

      10% of ___ = ☐

      ___ × ☐ = ___

NS8-75 Finding Percents *(continued)*

4. If you know 10% of a number *n*, then 5% of *n* is 10% divided by 2. Complete the chart.

5%	3			
10%	6	20	42	1
100%	60			

Use these steps to find 1% of a number:

Step 1: Change the percent to a decimal and replace "of" with "×."

Step 2: Multiply by 0.01 by shifting the decimal two places left.

---

5. Fill in the blanks.

    a) 1% of 300 = ___0.01___ × ___300___ = _____   b) 1% of 2000 = _____ × _____ = _____

    c) 1% of 15 = _____ × _____ = _____   d) 1% of 60 = _____ × _____ = _____

6. Find 1% of 200 and use your answer to calculate each percent.

    a) 2% of 200 = _____   b) 3% of 200 = _____   c) 12% of 200 = _____

7. Use the method of Question 6 to calculate...

    a) 4% of 800   b) 2% of 50   c) 11% of 60   d) 2% of 4   e) 7% of 45

8. Fill in the missing numbers. (Hint: 8% = 4% + 4%.)

2%	4%	8%	10%	20%	50%	25%	100%
	20						
	30						
					60		
			50				

9. a) If 45% is 9, what is 90%?   b) If 3% is 12, what is 1%?
     c) If 40% is 64, what is 100%?   d) If 20% is 13, what is 100%?

10. Arti wants to leave a 15% tip on a meal that cost $60. How much tip
should she leave? (Hint: 15% = 10% + 5%.)

11. a) A shirt that usually costs $40 is on sale for 25% off. What is 25% of $40?
      What is $40 − (25% of $40)? What is the sale price of the shirt?

    b) How would you estimate the price if a shirt that usually costs $32.99 is on sale
      for 25% off?

NS8-76 Further Percents

35% is short for $\frac{35}{100}$. To find 35% of 27, Sadie finds $\frac{35}{100}$ of 27.

Step 1: She multiplies 27 by 35.

$$\begin{array}{r} \overset{2}{} \overset{3}{} \\ 2\ 7 \\ \times\ 3\ 5 \\ \hline 1\ 3\ 5 \\ 8\ 1\ 0 \\ \hline 9\ 4\ 5 \end{array}$$

Step 2: She divides the result by 100.

$$945 \div 100 = 9.45$$

So 35% of 27 is 9.45.

1. Find the percent using Sadie's method.

   a) 23% of 34

   Step 1:

   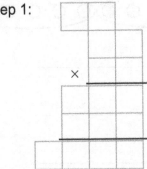

   Step 2: _____ ÷ 100 = _____

   So _____ of _____ is _____.

   b) 17% of 85

   Step 1:

   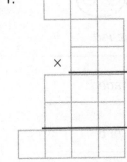

   Step 2: _____ ÷ 100 = _____

   So _____ of _____ is _____.

2. Find the percent using Sadie's method.

   a) 22% of 33   b) 14% of 48   c) 22% of 90   d) 69% of 44

   e) 83% of 75   f) 40% of 18   g) 31% of 52   h) 17% of 90

3. a) Find 35% of 40 in two ways. Do you get the same answer both ways?

   i) Use Sadie's method.

   ii) Use 35% = 25% + 10%.

   b) 35% is less than 50% = $\frac{1}{2}$. Is your answer to part a) less than half of 40?

   c) Is 35% closer to 0 or $\frac{1}{2}$? _____

   Was your answer to part a) closer to 0 or to half of 40? _____

   Is your answer to part a) reasonable? Explain.

4. Find 30% of 50 and 50% of 30. What do you notice? Why is this the case?

These are equivalent statements:

$\frac{6}{9}$ of the circles are shaded.

$\frac{2}{3}$ of the circles are shaded.

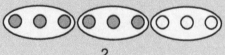

6 is $\frac{2}{3}$ of 9.

6 : 9 = 2 : 3

part   whole

1. Write four equivalent statements for each picture.

a)

$\frac{4}{6}$ are shaded

_____

$\frac{2}{3}$ are shaded

_____

4 is $\frac{2}{3}$ of 6

_____

4 : 6 = 2 : 3

b)

_____

_____

_____

_____

c)

_____

_____

_____

d)

_____

_____

_____

2. For each picture, write a pair of equivalent ratios.

a)

4 is $\frac{1}{2}$ of 8

$\frac{4}{\text{part}}$: $\frac{8}{\text{whole}}$ = $\frac{1}{}$: $\frac{2}{}$

b)

6 is $\frac{3}{5}$ of 10

$\frac{}{\text{part}}$: $\frac{}{\text{whole}}$ = ___ : ___

c)

2 is $\frac{1}{4}$ of 8

$\frac{}{\text{part}}$: $\frac{}{\text{whole}}$ = ___ : ___

3. For each statement, write a pair of equivalent ratios and equivalent fractions.

a) 15 is $\frac{3}{4}$ of 20 $\frac{}{\text{part}}$: $\frac{}{\text{whole}}$ = ___ : ___ $\frac{\text{part}}{\text{whole}}$ ___ = ___

b) 18 is $\frac{9}{10}$ of 20 $\frac{}{\text{part}}$: $\frac{}{\text{whole}}$ = ___ : ___ $\frac{\text{part}}{\text{whole}}$ ___ = ___

NS8-77 Writing Equivalent Statements for Proportions *(continued)*

4. Write a question mark where you are missing a piece of information.

a) 12 is $\frac{4}{5}$ of what number? $\quad \underset{\text{part}}{\underline{12}} : \underset{\text{whole}}{\underline{?}} = \underline{4} : \underline{5}$ $\quad \underset{\text{whole}}{\text{part}} \quad \dfrac{12}{?} = \dfrac{4}{5}$

b) 6 is how many quarters of 8? $\quad \underset{\text{part}}{\underline{6}} : \underset{\text{whole}}{\underline{8}} = \underline{?} : \underline{4}$ $\quad \underset{\text{whole}}{\text{part}} \quad \underline{} = \underline{}$

c) What is $\frac{3}{4}$ of 16? $\quad \underset{\text{part}}{\underline{}} : \underset{\text{whole}}{\underline{}} = \underline{} : \underline{}$ $\quad \underset{\text{whole}}{\text{part}} \quad \underline{} = \underline{}$

d) 20 is how many thirds of 30? $\quad \underset{\text{part}}{\underline{}} : \underset{\text{whole}}{\underline{}} = \underline{} : \underline{}$ $\quad \underset{\text{whole}}{\text{part}} \quad \underline{} = \underline{}$

5. For each statement, write a pair of equivalent ratios and a pair of equivalent fractions.

a) 15 is what percent of 20? $\quad \underset{\text{part}}{\underline{15}} : \underset{\text{whole}}{\underline{20}} = \underline{?} : \underline{100}$ $\quad \underset{\text{whole}}{\text{part}} \quad \dfrac{15}{20} = \dfrac{?}{100}$

b) What is 25% of 80? $\quad \underset{\text{part}}{\underline{}} : \underset{\text{whole}}{\underline{}} = \underline{} : \underline{}$ $\quad \underset{\text{whole}}{\text{part}} \quad \underline{} = \underline{}$

c) 9 is what percent of 12? $\quad \underset{\text{part}}{\underline{}} : \underset{\text{whole}}{\underline{}} = \underline{} : \underline{}$ $\quad \underset{\text{whole}}{\text{part}} \quad \underline{} = \underline{}$

d) 18 is 3% of what number? $\quad \underset{\text{part}}{\underline{}} : \underset{\text{whole}}{\underline{}} = \underline{} : \underline{}$ $\quad \underset{\text{whole}}{\text{part}} \quad \underline{} = \underline{}$

6. Write the two pieces of information you are given and what you need to find (?). Then write an equation for the problem.

a) What percent of 30 is 5? part $\underline{5}$ whole $\underline{30}$ percent $\underline{?}$ $\dfrac{5}{30} = \dfrac{?}{100}$

b) If 7 is 20%, what is 100%? part $\underline{}$ whole $\underline{?}$ percent $\underline{}$ $\dfrac{}{?} = \dfrac{}{100}$

c) What is 6% of 24? part $\underline{?}$ whole $\underline{}$ percent $\underline{}$ $\dfrac{?}{} = \dfrac{}{100}$

d) If 3 is 12%, what is 100%? part $\underline{}$ whole $\underline{}$ percent $\underline{}$ $\dfrac{}{} = \dfrac{}{100}$

e) What percent of 90 is 4? part $\underline{}$ whole $\underline{}$ percent $\underline{}$ $\dfrac{}{} = \dfrac{}{100}$

f) What is 52% of 18? part $\underline{}$ whole $\underline{}$ percent $\underline{}$ $\dfrac{}{} = \dfrac{}{100}$

g) 7 is what percent of 25? part $\underline{}$ whole $\underline{}$ percent $\underline{}$ $\dfrac{}{} = \dfrac{}{100}$

NS8-78 Using Proportions to Solve Percent Problems

> If 5 subway tickets cost \$4, how much do 20 tickets cost? Write the ratio of tickets to dollars as a fraction, then find an equivalent fraction by multiplying.

Step 1: $\dfrac{4}{5} = \dfrac{?}{20}$	Step 2: $\dfrac{4}{5} \overset{\times 4}{\underset{\times 4}{\rightrightarrows}} \dfrac{}{20}$	Step 3: $\dfrac{4}{5} \overset{\times 4}{\underset{\times 4}{\rightrightarrows}} \dfrac{16}{20}$

1. Solve the ratio. Draw arrows and show what you multiply by.

   a) $\dfrac{3}{4} = \dfrac{}{20}$ b) $\dfrac{1}{5} = \dfrac{}{15}$ c) $\dfrac{3}{5} = \dfrac{}{35}$ d) $\dfrac{4}{7} = \dfrac{}{49}$

   e) $\dfrac{3}{8} = \dfrac{}{24}$ f) $\dfrac{2}{3} = \dfrac{}{18}$ g) $\dfrac{13}{20} = \dfrac{}{100}$ h) $\dfrac{5}{9} = \dfrac{}{72}$

2. Solve the ratio as you did in Question 1. Note: The arrows will point from right to left.

   a) $\dfrac{15}{} = \dfrac{3}{4}$ b) $\dfrac{12}{} = \dfrac{2}{5}$ c) $\dfrac{15}{} = \dfrac{3}{7}$ d) $\dfrac{12}{18} = \dfrac{}{3}$

3. For each question, you will have to reduce the fraction given before you can find the equivalent fraction. The first one has been started for you.

   a) $\dfrac{8}{10} = \dfrac{4}{5} = \dfrac{}{15}$ b) $\dfrac{4}{6} = \dfrac{}{} = \dfrac{}{15}$ c) $\dfrac{40}{100} = \dfrac{}{} = \dfrac{}{45}$

   d) $\dfrac{15}{18} = \dfrac{}{} = \dfrac{}{30}$ e) $\dfrac{70}{100} = \dfrac{}{} = \dfrac{}{90}$ f) $\dfrac{50}{75} = \dfrac{}{} = \dfrac{}{36}$

4. Write a proportion to represent the percent problem. Solve the proportion.

   a) What percent of 20 is 4?   part ____   whole ____   percent ____ $\dfrac{}{} = \dfrac{}{100}$

   b) If 6 is 25%, what is 100%?   part ____   whole ____   percent ____ $\dfrac{}{} = \dfrac{}{100}$

   c) What is 17% of 10?   part ____   whole ____   percent ____ $\dfrac{}{} = \dfrac{}{100}$

   d) What is 17% of 50?   part ____   whole ____   percent ____ $\dfrac{}{} = \dfrac{}{100}$

   e) 4 is what percent of 5?

   f) 6 is 25% of what number?

   g) 24 is 80% of what number?

5. Explain why the proportion $\frac{3}{25} = \frac{x}{100}$ will be easy to solve.

6. Write a proportion $\frac{a}{b} = \frac{x}{100}$ to represent each problem. Solve by first writing $\frac{a}{b}$ in lowest terms.

a) What percent of 15 is 3?   b) What percent of 24 is 6?   c) What percent of 30 is 12?

7. Write a proportion to represent the percent problem. Find an equivalent ratio to rewrite the proportion.

a) If 6 is 40%, what is 100%?   part __6__   whole __?__   percent __40__ $\frac{6}{?} = \frac{40}{100}$ $\frac{6}{?} = \frac{2}{5}$

   Hint: Start by writing $\frac{40}{100}$ as an equivalent ratio with numerator 2.

b) What is 75% of 48?   part ____   whole ____   percent ____ $\frac{\quad}{\quad} = \frac{\quad}{100}$ $\frac{\quad}{\quad} = \frac{\quad}{\quad}$

   Hint: Start by writing 75% as an equivalent ratio with denominator 4.

c) What percent of 60 is 45?   part ____   whole ____   percent ____ $\frac{\quad}{\quad} = \frac{\quad}{100}$ $\frac{\quad}{\quad} = \frac{\quad}{\quad}$

   Hint: Start by writing $\frac{45}{60}$ as an equivalent ratio with denominator 20.

d) What is 64% of 15?   part ____   whole ____   percent ____ $\frac{\quad}{\quad} = \frac{\quad}{100}$ $\frac{\quad}{\quad} = \frac{\quad}{\quad}$

   Hint: Start by writing $\frac{64}{100}$ as an equivalent ratio with denominator 5.

8. Solve the proportions in Question 7. Explain why the proportions in Question 7 were more challenging to solve than those in Question 4.

9. Solve.

a) 8 is 40% of what number?   b) What is 60% of 30?

c) 15 is 75% of what number?   d) What percent of 240 is 60?

10. If 4 of 25 fish are blue, what percent of the fish are blue? What percent are not blue?

11. If 45% of 180 students voted for Kendra for student council, how many of the students voted for Kendra?

12. 12 students in a class (60% of the class) are fluent in French. How many students are in the class?

NS8-79 Solving Percent Problems — Advanced

$\dfrac{3}{4} = 0.75$ means the same thing as $3 \div 4 = 0.75$.

1. a) Write $\dfrac{a}{b} = c$ as a division statement. ____ ÷ _____ = _____

b) Use the information from part a) to write a as a product. $a =$ _____ × _____

2. Change the equation to a multiplication statement.

a) $\dfrac{9}{x} = 2$

_____9 = 2x_____

b) $7 = \dfrac{x}{5}$

_____$7 \times 5 = x$_____

c) $\dfrac{x}{3} = 11$

_____

d) $3 = \dfrac{21}{x}$

_____

e) $\dfrac{12}{x} = 11$

f) $\dfrac{x}{9} = 7$

g) $\dfrac{24}{x} = 8$

h) $6 = \dfrac{x}{7}$

3. Write the equation as a multiplication statement. Then solve for x.

a) $\dfrac{7}{x} = 3$

$7 = 3x$

$\dfrac{7}{3} = \dfrac{3x}{3}$

$\dfrac{7}{3} = x$

b) $8 = \dfrac{x}{5}$

c) $2 = \dfrac{5}{x}$

d) $\dfrac{x}{3} = 10$

e) $5 = \dfrac{20}{x}$

f) $9 = \dfrac{x}{8}$

g) $\dfrac{x}{5} = 11$

h) $\dfrac{36}{x} = 4$

$\dfrac{3}{4} = \dfrac{9}{12}$ so $3 \div 4 = 9 \div 12$

$12 \times 3 \div 4 = 12 \times 9 \div 12$ Multiply both sides by 12.

$12 \times 3 \div 4 = 9$ Rewrite the right side.

$12 \times 3 \div 4 \times 4 = 9 \times 4$ Multiply both sides by 4.

$12 \times 3 = 9 \times 4$ Rewrite the left side.

To rewrite $\dfrac{3}{4} = \dfrac{9}{12}$ as $12 \times 3 = 9 \times 4$ is called **cross-multiplying** because the products can be

obtained from an "X":

4. Check that cross-multiplying works for these equivalent fractions.

a) $\dfrac{2}{5} = \dfrac{6}{15}$

b) $\dfrac{3}{4} = \dfrac{6}{8}$

c) $\dfrac{1}{2} = \dfrac{5}{10}$

d) $\dfrac{2}{3} = \dfrac{8}{12}$

e) make your own

$2 \times 15 = 5 \times 6$

$30 = 30 \checkmark$

NS8-79 Solving Percent Problems — Advanced *(continued)*

5. Cross-multiply and write = (equal) or ≠ (not equal) in the box. Then decide if the fractions are equivalent.

a) $\frac{3}{4}$ and $\frac{10}{13}$

___3___ × ___13___ ☐ ___4___ × ___10___

Are $\frac{3}{4}$ and $\frac{10}{13}$ equivalent? _____

b) $\frac{2}{5}$ and $\frac{10}{25}$

_____ × _____ ☐ _____ × _____

Are $\frac{2}{5}$ and $\frac{10}{25}$ equivalent? _____

c) $\frac{9}{10}$ and $\frac{81}{100}$

_____ × _____ ☐ _____ × _____

Are $\frac{9}{10}$ and $\frac{81}{100}$ equivalent? _____

d) $\frac{5}{7}$ and $\frac{28}{35}$

_____ × _____ ☐ _____ × _____

Are $\frac{5}{7}$ and $\frac{28}{35}$ equivalent? _____

e) $\frac{3}{4}$ and $\frac{15}{20}$

f) $\frac{5}{6}$ and $\frac{35}{42}$

g) $\frac{91}{105}$ and $\frac{104}{120}$

h) $\frac{14}{21}$ and $\frac{30}{48}$

6. Cross-multiply to write an equation for x. (Do not solve.)

a) $\frac{7}{x} = \frac{3}{5}$

___7 × 5 = 3x___

b) $\frac{x}{9} = \frac{2}{5}$

___5x = 2 × 9___

c) $\frac{11}{x} = \frac{5}{2}$

_____

d) $\frac{4}{9} = \frac{x}{3}$

e) $\frac{5}{21} = \frac{3}{x}$

f) $\frac{x}{52} = \frac{4}{8}$

g) $\frac{20}{x} = \frac{12}{25}$

h) $\frac{12}{x} = \frac{3}{10}$

7. Solve for x.

a) $\frac{9}{6} = \frac{x}{3}$

b) $\frac{4}{x} = \frac{2}{3}$

c) $\frac{3}{4} = \frac{6}{x}$

d) $\frac{100}{7} = \frac{9}{x}$

e) $\frac{2}{x} = \frac{10}{4}$

You can solve percent problems by first writing a proportion and then cross-multiplying.

Example: What is 70% of 9? $\frac{x}{9} = \frac{70}{100}$ so $100x = 12 × 3$

$$100x = 630$$

$$\frac{100x}{100} = \frac{630}{100}$$

$$x = 6.3$$

---

8. Solve the problem by first writing a proportion.

a) What is 90% of 6?

b) 9 is 2% of what number?

c) 5 is what percent of 8?

Write an equation for each of the problems below and solve the equation. Use a calculator.

9. a) What percent of 32 is 8?   b) What percent of 125 is 5?
   c) What percent of 128 is 32?   d) What percent of 15 is 0.6?

10. Round the solution to the nearest one.

    a) 5 is about what percent of 24?   b) About what percent of 17 is 9?
    c) 4 is about what percent of 9?   d) About what percent of 7 560 is 3 000?
    e) 1.3 is about what percent of 27?

11. If Yvonne has read 54 of the 297 pages in her library book, about what percent of the book has she read so far?

12. Find the amounts. Include units in your answers.

    a) 26% of 130 g   b) 11% of 407 m
    c) 32% of 11 mL   d) 99% of 8 m²
    e) 40% of 2 222 min

13. About 3% of 592 students are vegans. About how many of the students are vegans?

14. A basketball team won 60% of the 25 games it played this year.

    a) What percent of the games played did the team lose?
    b) How many games did the team lose?

15. Find 100% if...

    a) 25% is 30   b) 15% is 30   c) 3% is 12

16. Round the solution to the nearest one.

    a) 10 is 7%. About what is 100%?   b) 74 is 32%. About what is 100%?
    c) 2 is 9%. About what is 100%?

17. In a Grade 8 class, 6 students, or about 27%, were on the honour roll. How many students were in the class?

18. Kai bought a new computer at a 15% discount. He paid $1 020.

    a) What percent of the original price did he pay?
    b) What was the original price?
    c) How many dollars did Kai save by buying the computer at a discount?

19. A computer costs $1 000 plus 15% tax. Which of these is the best deal?

    A: The store offers a 15% discount on the $1 000 purchase price, then adds the tax onto the sale price.

    B: The store will pay the tax.

    C: The store offers a 15% discount, calculated after the tax is added.

NS8-80 Percents Less Than 1%

1. $100\% = 1$, $10\% = \dfrac{1}{10}$, 1% is $\dfrac{1}{100}$. What fraction is equivalent to 0.1%? _____

2. Circle the two numbers in the set that are equal.

   a) 0.3%   0.03   0.003   b) $\dfrac{9}{10}$ 0.9% $\dfrac{9}{1000}$ c) 0.25   25%   0.25%

To write the decimal 0.235 as a percent, multiply by 100:

   If $0.235 = x\,\%$, then $0.235 = \dfrac{x}{100}$, so $x = 0.235 \times 100 = 23.5$

So $0.235 = 23.5\%$.

---

3. Write the decimal as a percent.

   a) $0.273 =$ _____.___% b) $0.848 =$ _____   c) $0.369 =$ _____   d) $0.405 =$ _____

   e) $0.005 =$ _____   f) $0.125 =$ _____   g) $0.077 =$ _____   h) $6.242 =$ _____

4. Each small rectangle on the grid is one thousandth of the whole grid.

   a) Shade 21.5% of the grid.   b) Shade 45.3% of the grid.

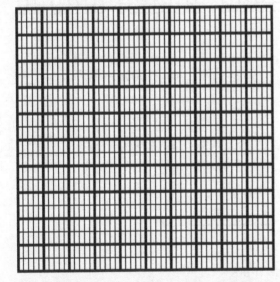   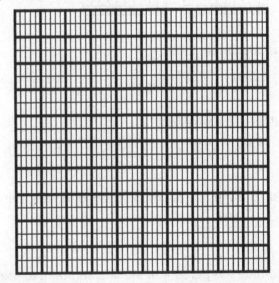

Grasslands make up $2\dfrac{1}{2}\%$ of the habitat of birds in North America. $2\dfrac{1}{2}\% = 2.5\% = \dfrac{2.5}{100}$.

To get a proper fraction, multiply the numerator and denominator by 10. $\dfrac{2.5 \times 10}{100 \times 10} = \dfrac{25}{1000} = \dfrac{1}{40}$

---

5. Express the percent as a proper fraction and rewrite the fraction in lowest terms.

   a) 17.5%   b) 0.7%   c) 6.4%   d) 0.04%

   e) $33\dfrac{1}{3}\%$ f) $12\dfrac{1}{2}\%$ g) $3\dfrac{1}{8}\%$ h) $66\dfrac{2}{3}\%$

NS8-81 Percents Greater Than 100%

1. Determine the total percent of the grids that is shaded as a fraction, decimal, and percent.

a)

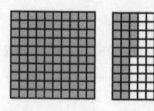

Fraction: $\dfrac{}{100} + \dfrac{}{100} = 1\dfrac{}{100}$

Decimal: _____ + 0._____ = _____

Percent: _____% + _____% = _____%

b)

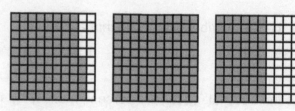

Fraction: _____ + _____ + _____ = _____

Decimal: _____ + _____ + _____ = _____

Percent: ____% + ____% + ____% = _____%

2. a) Shade the grids to represent 134%.

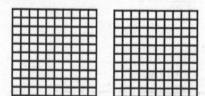

b) Shade the grids to represent 273%.

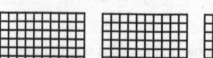

3. Add the percents.

a) 125% + 240% = _____%   b) 80% + 60% = _____%   c) 150% + 75% = _____%

4. Subtract the percents.

a) 117% − 17% = _____%   b) 125% − 40% = _____%   c) 675% − 50% = _____%

5. Measure the line segment. Extend the segment to show 150%.

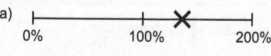

a) |———50%———|

b) |———75%———|

6. Estimate the percent of the line segment to the left of the mark.

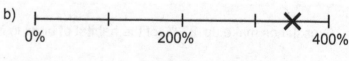

a)

0%   100%   200%

about _____%

b)

0%   200%   400%

about _____%

7. Write the ratio as an improper fraction and as a percent.

a) $110 : 100 = \dfrac{}{100} = $ ____%   b) $350 : 100 = \dfrac{}{100} = $ ____%   c) $261 : 100 = \dfrac{}{100} = $ ____%

8. Write the percent as a mixed number with the fractional part in lowest terms.

a) 130%   b) 275%   c) 308%   d) 1505%   e) 785%

NS8-81 Percents Greater Than 100% (continued)

9. Complete the chart. Hint: If a decimal with one decimal place is given, add a zero to make two decimal places.

Percent			190%	535%			
Mixed Number						$1\frac{76}{100}$	$1\frac{8}{100}$
Decimal	$9.2 = \underline{9.20}$	2.32			$3.4 = \underline{}$		

10. About what percent does the decimal represent? Example: $4.715 \approx 4.72 = 472\%$

a) $4.382 \approx \underline{}\%$ b) $5.925 \approx \underline{}\%$ c) $5.007 \approx$ d) $2.999 \approx$

11. Write the percent as a decimal, then as a mixed number, then in lowest terms.

a) 350% b) 540% c) 275% d) 360% e) 515%

12. Write the mixed number as a percent.

a) $2\frac{1}{2}$ b) $3\frac{3}{4}$ c) $8\frac{3}{10}$ d) $1\frac{1}{5}$ e) $20\frac{3}{20}$ f) $17\frac{9}{25}$

13. Write the mixed number as a decimal. Round the decimal to two places. Then write the approximate percent.

a) $3\frac{5}{12} = 3 + 0.41\overline{6} \approx 3.42 = \underline{}\%$ b) $3\frac{1}{3}$ c) $4\frac{2}{3}$ d) $1\frac{2}{9}$ e) $2\frac{1}{7}$

14. Change the numbers in each set to decimals. Then order the numbers from greatest to least.

a) $1\frac{1}{2}$ 1.73 180% b) $1\frac{6}{10}$ 157% 1.62 c) $6\frac{1}{4}$ 6.09 615%

15. Determine the amount mentally.

a) 300% of 20 = \underline{} b) 250% of 50 = \underline{} c) 110% of 6 = \underline{} d) 330% of 2 = \underline{}

16. If 30% = 150, what is 10%? \underline{} What is 100%? \underline{}

17. Determine 100% mentally.

a) If 40% = 200, then 100% = \underline{}. b) If 5% = 20, then 100% = \underline{}.

c) If 150% = 12, then 100% = \underline{}. d) If 300% = 18, then 100% = \underline{}.

18. Estimate the solution. Use a calculator to check your estimate. Was your estimate close?

a) What percent of 20 is 30? b) What percent of 45 is 87? c) What percent of 2 is 17?
d) What percent of 7 is 13? e) What percent of 1.5 is 4.4? f) What percent of 1.1 is 59.3?

NS8-82 Percent Problems

1. Calculate.

   a) 80% – 65% + 22% = _____   b) 41% + _____ = 100%   c) 96% – _____ = 25%

2. What is the sales tax where you live? _____

   Calculate the amount of tax you would pay on each price.

   a) $15 _____   b) $40 _____   c) $67.25 _____   d) $82.52 _____

3. In the school elections, $\frac{2}{5}$ of the students voted for Anne and 17% voted for Ravi.
   The rest voted for Yen. What percent voted for Yen?

4. A builder spent $400.00 on equipment. Complete the chart.

Item	Money spent		
	Fraction	Percent	$ Amount
Drywall			$220.00
Paint	$\frac{2}{5}$		
Wallpaper		30%	

5. A student hopes to raise $500 for his favourite charity. He has already raised $100
   by having a garage sale. What percent of the $500 does he still need to raise?

6. Complete the chart.

Item	Regular Price	Discount (percent)	Discount ($ amount)	Sale Price
Gloves	$36.00	10%	$3.60	$36.00 – $3.60 = $32.40
Shoes	$49.92	25%		
CD	$14.90	30%		

7. Clare bought a computer at a 40% discount. She paid $800. How many dollars did
   she save by buying the computer at a discount?

8. John spent $720 on furniture. He spent 25% on a chair, $327.60 on a table, and the
   rest on a sofa. What fraction and what percent of the $720 did he spend on each item?

9. Erik had 1 400 stamps? 20% of the stamps were Canadian. Recently he bought 300
   new Canadian stamps. How many Canadian stamps does he have now? What
   percent and what fraction of his stamps are Canadian?

NS8-83 Relating Fractions, Ratios, and Percents

1. Write the number of boys (**b**), girls (**g**), and children (**c**) in each class.

   a) There are 7 boys and 6 girls in a class.   **b** _____   **g** _____   **c** _____

   b) There are 5 boys and 9 girls in a class.   **b** _____   **g** _____   **c** _____

   c) There are 18 boys and 22 girls in a class.   **b** _____   **g** _____   **c** _____

   d) There are 15 girls in a class of 27 children.   **b** _____   **g** _____   **c** _____

2. Write the number of boys, girls, and children in each class. Then write the fraction of children who are boys and the fraction who are girls in the boxes provided.

   a) There are 6 boys and 9 girls in a class.   **b** ___ ☐   **g** ___ ☐   **c** ___

   b) There are 17 children in the class and 9 are boys.   **b** ___ ☐   **g** ___ ☐   **c** ___

3. Fill in the missing numbers for each classroom.

	Ratio of boys to girls	Fraction of boys	Fraction of girls	Percentage of boys	Percentage of girls
a)	$3 : 2$	$\dfrac{3}{5}$	$\dfrac{2}{5}$	$\dfrac{3}{5} = \dfrac{60}{100} = 60\%$	40%
b)	$1 : 5$				
c)		$\dfrac{11}{20}$			
d)				30%	
e)		$\dfrac{12}{25}$			
f)	$32 : 18$				
g)					
h)					45%
i)				19%	

4. Fill in the missing numbers for each classroom.

	Number of students	Fraction of boys	Fraction of girls	Number of boys	Number of girls
a)	20	$\frac{4}{5}$	$\frac{1}{5}$	$\frac{4}{5} \times 20 = 16$	4
b)	40	$\frac{1}{5}$			
c)	24		$\frac{1}{4}$		
d)	38	$\frac{5}{19}$			

5. Determine the number of girls and boys in each class.

   a) There are 20 children and $\frac{2}{5}$ are boys.

   b) There are 42 children and $\frac{3}{7}$ are girls.

   c) There are 15 children.
   The ratio of girls to boys is 3 : 2.

   d) There are 24 children.
   The ratio of girls to boys is 3 : 5.

   e) There are 25 children and 60% are girls.

   f) There are 28 children and 25% are boys.

6. For each question, say which classroom has more girls.

   a) In classroom A, there are 40 children and 60% are girls.
   In classroom B, there are 36 children. The ratio of boys to girls is 5 : 4.

   b) In classroom A, there are 28 children. The ratio of boys to girls is 5 : 2.

   In classroom B, there are 30 children and $\frac{3}{5}$ of the children are boys.

7. Ron and Ella shared $35 in the ratio 4 : 3. What fraction of the money did each person receive? What amount of money did each person receive?

8. Students in a class each chose one sport to participate in for a sports day. Complete the chart. How did you find the number of students who chose swimming?

Chosen sport	Fraction of the class that chose the sport	Percent	Decimal	Number of students who chose the sport
Soccer	$\frac{1}{5}$			4
Swimming		40%		
Baseball				
Gymnastics			.15	

NS8-84 Finding the Whole from the Part

$\frac{2}{3}$ of a number is 100. What is the number?

$\frac{2}{3} = \frac{100}{?}$ part whole

$\frac{2}{3} \overset{\times 50}{\underset{\times 50}{\rightrightarrows}} \frac{100}{?}$

$\frac{2}{3} = \frac{100}{150}$

The number is 150.

1. Find the number.

   a) $\frac{2}{5}$ of a number is 4.

   b) $\frac{3}{7}$ of a number is 9.

   c) $\frac{5}{11}$ of a number is 25.

2. A box holds red and blue beads. Find the total number of beads in the box.

   a) $\frac{3}{4}$ of the beads are red. Six beads are red.

   b) $\frac{3}{5}$ of the beads are blue. Twelve beads are blue.

   c) 60% of the beads are red. Fifteen beads are red.

   d) The ratio of red to blue beads is 4 : 5. There are 20 red beads.

3. Ron and Lisa share a sum of money. Ron receives $\frac{2}{5}$ of the money. Lisa receives $24.

   a) What fraction of the sum does Lisa receive?   b) How much money do Ron and Lisa share?

4. At Franklin Middle School, $\frac{3}{8}$ of the students take a bus to school, $\frac{3}{5}$ walk, and the rest bike. There are 20 students who bike to school. How many students are in the school?

5. In a fish tank, $\frac{2}{3}$ of the fish are red, $\frac{1}{4}$ are yellow, and the rest are green. There are 42 more red fish than green fish.

   a) What fraction of the fish are green?

   b) What fraction of the total number of fish does 42 represent? Hint: 42 is the difference between the number of red and green fish.

   c) How many fish are in the tank?

6. In Tina's stamp collection, 70% of the stamps are Canadian and the rest are international. Tina has 500 more Canadian stamps than international stamps. How many stamps does she have?

7. On a neon sign, $\frac{1}{5}$ of the lights are yellow and the rest are blue and red. There are twice as many blue lights as yellow lights, and there are 200 red lights on the sign. How many lights of all colours are on the sign?

No unauthorized copying

NS8-85 Introduction to Powers

Multiplication is a short form for repeated addition. Example: $5 \times 3 = 3 + 3 + 3 + 3 + 3$

Add five 3s

A **power** is a short form for repeated multiplication. Example: $3^5 = 3 \times 3 \times 3 \times 3 \times 3$

Multiply five 3s

The **exponent** in a power tells you how many times to write the **base** in the product.

base → $\mathbf{3^5}$ ← exponent

1. Write the exponent and base for the power.

   a) 2^3

   base: _2_ exponent: _3_

   b) 3^2

   base: ____ exponent: ____

   c) 7^4

   base: ____ exponent: ____

2. Write the power as a product.

   a) $9^2 = 9 \times 9$

   b) $7^3 =$

   c) $8^4 =$

3. Write the product as a power.

   a) $3 \times 3 \times 3 =$

   b) $4 \times 4 \times 4 \times 4 =$

   c) $9 \times 9 =$

   d) $8 \times 8 \times 8 \times 8 =$

4. Evaluate the power.

   a) $2^3 = 2 \times 2 \times 2$

   $=$ _____

   b) $3^4 = 3 \times 3 \times 3 \times 3$

   $=$ _____

   c) $4^2 = 4 \times 4$

   $=$ _____

   d) $5^2 = 5 \times 5$

   $=$ _____

   e) $2^4 = 2 \times 2 \times 2 \times 2$

   $=$ _____

   f) $5^3 = 5 \times 5 \times 5$

   $=$ _____

5. Circle two powers from Question 4 that have the same answer.

INVESTIGATION ▶

In a product, changing the order of the numbers does not affect the answer.
(Example: $2 \times 4 = 4 \times 2$)

In a power, does changing the order of the numbers affect the answer?
(Example: $2^4 = 4^2$ but does $2^3 = 3^2$?)

A. Calculate the powers.

   i) $2^3 = 2 \times 2 \times 2 =$ _____ and $3^2 = 3 \times 3 =$ _____

   ii) $3^5 = 3 \times 3 \times 3 \times 3 \times 3 =$ _____ and $5^3 = 5 \times 5 \times 5 =$ _____

   iii) $10^2 = 10 \times 10 =$ _____ and $2^{10} = 2 \times 2 \times 2 \times 2 \times 2 \times 2 \times 2 \times 2 \times 2 \times 2 =$ _____

B. Does changing the order of the numbers change the answer in a power? _____

NS8-85 Introduction to Powers *(continued)*

6. Evaluate the power.

a) $3^1 =$ _____   b) $5^1 =$ _____   c) $8^1 =$ _____   d) $13^1 =$ _____   e) $2057^1 =$ _____

$3^1 = 3$ is the **first power** of 3.

$3^2 = 3 \times 3$ is the **second power** of 3.

$3^3 = 3 \times 3 \times 3$ is the **third power** of 3.

7. Write the power as a product. Example: The fourth power of 2 is $2 \times 2 \times 2 \times 2$.

a) the fourth power of 3   b) the fifth power of 3   c) the sixth power of 3

e) the fourth power of 5   e) the fifth power of 4   f) the seventh power of 8

8. Write the power as a product and evaluate.

a) the second power of 8   b) the third power of 3   c) the fifth power of 2

9. Write the product as a power of 1.

a) $1 \times 1 =$ _____   b) $1 \times 1 \times 1 =$ _____   c) $1 \times 1 \times 1 \times 1 =$ _____   d) $1 \times 1 \times 1 \times 1 \times 1 =$ _____

10. Evaluate the power of 1.

a) $1^1 =$ _____   b) $1^2 =$ _____   c) $1^3 =$ _____   d) $1^4 =$ _____   e) $1^{523} =$ _____

11. The table shows the buttons you should press on a calculator to calculate a power.

a) How many times would you press the $\boxed{=}$ button to calculate the power?

  i) 2^7 _____ times   ii) 5^3 _____ times

  iii) 8^5 _____ times   iv) 3^{15} _____ times

		Press
2^2	2×2	$\boxed{2}\;\boxed{\times}\;\boxed{=}$
2^3	$2 \times 2 \times 2$	$\boxed{2}\;\boxed{\times}\;\boxed{=}\;\boxed{=}$
2^4	$2 \times 2 \times 2 \times 2$	$\boxed{2}\;\boxed{\times}\;\boxed{=}\;\boxed{=}\;\boxed{=}$

b) Write the power as a product and then use a calculator to find the answer.

  i) $6^3 =$ ii) $4^5 =$ iii) $7^4 =$

12. Evaluate the powers, then multiply, divide, add, or subtract. Show your work.

a) 5×2^2 b) 3×2^3 c) $4^2 \div 2$ d) 2×5^2 e) $2^2 \times 3^2$

  $= 5 \times 4$

  $= 20$

f) $3^2 \times 2^3$ g) $10^2 \div 5^2$ h) $2^2 + 3^2$ i) $7^2 + 6^2$ j) $8^2 - 2^2$

Glossary

algebraic expression a combination of one or more variables that may include numbers and operation signs

array an arrangement of things (for example, objects, symbols, or numbers) in rows and columns

base (in a power) the number that is being multiplied by itself repeatedly

billion 1 000 000 000

cancel to eliminate parts of an expression when their sum is equal to zero

centimetre (cm) a unit of measurement used to describe length, height, or thickness

circumference the distance around a circle

coefficient a number that is multiplied by a variable in an expression

common multiple a multiple of two or more numbers

composite number a number that has more than two factors

consecutive numbers numbers that occur one after the other on a number line

constant term a number that is not multiplied by a variable in an expression

decimal fraction a fraction in which the denominator is a power of ten

decimal place one place value to the right of the decimal point

decimetre (dm) a unit of measurement used to describe length, height, or thickness; equal to 10 cm

decreasing sequence a sequence where each number is less than the one before it

denominator the number in the bottom portion of a fraction

diagonal things (for example, objects, symbols, or numbers) that are in a line from one corner to another corner

diameter the distance across a circle, measured through its centre

distributive law a law that shows how multiplication is combined with addition or subtraction

dividend in a division problem, the number that is being divided or shared

divisible by containing a number a specific number of times without having a remainder (for example, 15 is divisible by 5 and 3)

divisor in a division problem, the number that is divided into another number

equation a mathematical statement that two expressions are equal

equivalent fractions fractions that represent the same amount but have different denominators (for example, $\frac{2}{3} = \frac{4}{6}$)

equivalent ratios two ratios that represent the same ratio

Eratosthenes' sieve a method of obtaining prime numbers by discarding multiples

exponent (in a power) the number that tells how many times the base is repeated

factor rainbow a diagram that shows the pairs of factors of a number

factors whole numbers that are multiplied to give a product

factor tree a diagram that uses branches (lines) to show prime factorization

Fibonacci sequence the sequence 1, 1, 2, 3, 5, 8, . . ., where each term is the sum of the previous two terms

greatest common factor (GCF) the greatest number that is a factor of two or more given numbers

hexagon a polygon with six sides

improper fraction a fraction that has a numerator that is larger than the denominator; this represents more than a whole

increasing sequence a sequence where each number is greater than the one before it

integer a whole number that is either positive, negative, or zero

kilometre (km) a unit of measurement for length; equal to 1 000 cm

litre (L) a unit of measurement to describe capacity; equal to 1 000 mL

lowest common multiple (LCM) the least nonzero number that is a multiple of two or more given numbers

lowest terms terms that have a GCF of 1

metre (m) a unit of measurement used to describe length, height, or thickness; equal to 100 cm

millilitre (mL) a unit of measurement used to describe capacity

millimetre (mm) a unit of measurement used to describe length, height, or thickness; equal to 0.1 cm

mixed fraction or number a mixture of a whole number and a fraction

model a physical representation (for example, using base-10 materials to represent a number)

multiple of a number that is the result of multiplying one number by another specific number (for example, the multiples of 5 are 0, 5, 10, 15, and so on)

numerator the number in the top portion of a fraction

numeric expression a combination of numbers, operation signs, and sometimes brackets, that represents a quantity

part-to-part ratio a ratio of one part to another part of a whole

part-to-whole ratio a ratio of one part to the whole

pentagon a polygon with five sides

percent a ratio that compares a number to 100

perfect square the product of a positive whole number with itself

perimeter the distance around the outside of a shape

place values the values of ones, tens, hundreds, and so on, that are represented by the placement of digits in a number

polygon a figure containing three or more vertices joined by line segments

prime factorization a number written as a product of prime numbers

prime number a number that has only two factors: itself and 1

proportion an equation between two equivalent ratios

quadrilateral a polygon with four sides

radius the distance from any point on a circle to its centre

rate a comparison of two quantities measured in different units

ratio a comparison indicating the relative size of two or more numbers, e.g. 2 : 3 or "2 to 3"

reciprocal 1 divided by a number

remainder the number left over after dividing or subtracting (for example, 10 ÷ 3 = 3 R1)

repeating decimal a decimal with a group of one or more digits that repeats forever

rhombus a parallelogram with all four sides equal

sequence an ordered set of terms: 1st term, 2nd term, 3rd term, . . .

set a group of like objects

solve for a variable to find the value(s) of a variable for which an equation is true

square centimetre (cm²) a unit of measurement used to describe area

square root a number that may be multiplied by itself to produce a given number

substitute to replace a variable in an expression with a number

term a number in a sequence

term number the position of a term in a sequence

terminating decimal a decimal that does not repeat forever

unit fraction a fraction with numerator 1

unit rate a comparison of two quantities where one quantity is equal to 1

variable a letter or symbol that represents a number

About the Authors

JOHN MIGHTON is a mathematician, author, and playwright. He completed a Ph.D. in mathematics at the University of Toronto and is currently a fellow of the Fields Institute for Mathematical Research. The founder of JUMP Math (www.jumpmath.org), Mighton also gives lectures to student teachers at York University and the Ontario Institute for Studies in Education, and invited talks and training sessions for parents and educators. He is the author of the *JUMP at Home* workbooks and the national bestsellers *The Myth of Ability* and *The End of Ignorance*. He has won the Governor General's Literary Award and the Siminovitch Prize for his plays.

DR. ANNA KLEBANOV received her B.Sc., M.Sc., Ph.D., and teaching certificate from the Technion – Israel Institute of Technology. She is the recipient of three teaching awards for excellence. She began her career at JUMP Math as a curriculum writer in 2007, working with Dr. John Mighton and Dr. Sindi Sabourin on JUMP Math's broad range of publications.

DR. SINDI SABOURIN received her Ph.D. in mathematics from Queen's University, specializing in commutative algebra. She is the recipient of the Governor General's Gold Medal Award from Queen's University and a National Sciences and Research Council Postdoctoral Fellowship. Her career with JUMP Math began in 2003 as a volunteer doing in-class tutoring and one-on-one tutoring, as well as working on answer keys. In 2006, she became a curriculum writer working on JUMP Math's broad range of publications.